PRAISE FOR *WE LOVE LOVE*

'Britt and Laura are the best friends that are brave enough to say what everyone else is thinking! The stories they share are what you would only spill to your closest girlfriends – the difference is, they share them with the entire nation. It's absolutely brilliant.'

Samantha Wills, author of *Of Gold and Dust*

'This book is like a comforting hug from your big sister. Britt and Laura will make you laugh until you cry and cry until you laugh, with their refreshing honesty, wit, humour and relatable life experience. A must read for those who love love.'

Emma Carey, author of *The Girl Who Fell From The Sky*

ABOUT THE AUTHORS

Brittany Hockley has become one of *The Bachelor* franchise's most recognisable faces. She didn't find the happy ever after there, but she's now carving out one of her own! Known for her laugh and her tendency to operate at one hundred miles an hour and rarely sit still, the former emergency radiographer juggles hosting the wildly popular podcast *Life Uncut* with her work as an actor and writer. Britt is currently working on her own TV series.

(O) @brittany_hockley

Laura Byrne rose to fame in 2017 when she fell in love with Matty J on *The Bachelor*. An Australian *Bachelor* success story, Laura and Matt are the proud parents of two wild toddlers, Marlie-Mae and Lola. Laura is the founder and creative director of one of Australia's leading bohemian jewellery brands, ToniMay, 2019 *Cosmopolitan* Fashion Designer of the Year and host of *Life Uncut*.

(O) @ladyandacat

Together, Britt and Laura have a weekly radio show on KIIS and *Life Uncut*, twice winner of the People's Choice Award at the Australian Podcast Awards, has more than 30 million downloads.

lifeuncutpodcast.com.au

(O) @lifeuncutpodcast

AN UNFILTERED A TO Z
OF MODERN ROMANCE
AND SELF-LOVE

We
LOVE
Love

LAURA BYRNE
BRITTANY HOCKLEY

All Accidentally Unfiltereds have been sent in voluntarily, anonymously and for the purpose of making you laugh and feeling a little less alone. We've contacted as many of you as we could, but we haven't been able to reach every person. If your Accidentally Unfiltered story has been included here and you want to get in touch with us about it, please reach out.

EBURY PRESS

UK | USA | Canada | Ireland | Australia
India | New Zealand | South Africa | China

Ebury Press is part of the Penguin Random House group of companies whose addresses can be found at global.penguinrandomhouse.com

Penguin
Random House
Australia

First published by Ebury Press in 2022

Cover and internal design by Andy Warren Design
© Penguin Random House Australia Pty Ltd
Author photo by Mel Cartmer

Typeset in 12/17.5 pt Adobe Garamond Pro by Midland Typesetters, Australia

Printed and bound in Australia by Griffin Press, an accredited ISO AS/NZS 14001 Environmental Management Systems printer

A catalogue record for this book is available from the National Library of Australia

ISBN 978 1 76104 496 0

penguin.com.au

We at Penguin Random House Australia acknowledge that Aboriginal and Torres Strait Islander peoples are the Traditional Custodians and the first storytellers of the lands on which we live and work. We honour Aboriginal and Torres Strait Islander peoples' continuous connection to Country, waters, skies and communities. We celebrate Aboriginal and Torres Strait Islander stories, traditions and living cultures; and we pay our respects to Elders past and present.

Dedicated to our wonderful Lifers who have ridden the lollercoaster with us, and to those who are about to join the ride. Thank you.

CONTENTS

INTRODUCTION

*Tell your mum, tell your dad, tell your dog, tell
your friends and share the love, because . . .*
WE LOVE LOVE

Would you believe it?!

Who would have thought, back in 2019 when we sat in Laura's bedroom late one evening and pressed 'record' on the podcast machine for the very first time, that over the next three years more than 300 episodes of *Life Uncut* would fly by? Not us! And if you listened to the recording quality of that very first episode – well, you certainly wouldn't have predicted it either.

But here we are: 33 million podcast downloads later, with an incredible community of Lifers from all over the world, and finally – after many months of typing away, countless emails and a whole lot of gentle deadline reminders by our editors – a book! Written to answer some of your deepest, darkest, burning questions.

So, why embark on the slightly mad project of writing a book? Well, we really wanted to create a home for the most precious conversations that we've had over these magical few years, for the lessons that have changed our lives and for the stories that you're yet to hear. A home for the wisdom gained from our own experiences, from those so generously shared with us by our guests and from the hilarious anecdotes we've received from our Lifers in our much-loved 'Accidentally Unfiltered' segment. These conversations have helped us navigate life (so far) in all its chaotic, confusing, embarrassing, hilarious, tumultuous wonder.

We Love Love is an A to Z of life, a heartfelt and hope-filled guide that covers the light stuff and the hard stuff that life slings at us all, from navigating heartbreak to learning to set boundaries, from society's ridiculous timelines to unsolicited dick pics. Because, yep . . . we've all been there. The book has been lovingly designed so that you can read it in whatever order you see fit: from front to back, or pick a chapter that tickles your fancy and handcuffs you to the bed (such as Kinks . . .). Go for it!

Now, we do not propose to have all the answers for every person (and we're conscious that we have plenty of personal biases and privileges at play), so we say 'guide' in pretty loose terms. In fact, as you will discover within these pages, our lives have been a messy shit show at times too – but whose hasn't?!

We have written this book for anyone who has found themselves singing 'WE LOVE LOVE!' as the outro music started to play. We hope that these alphabetical essays about romance and self-love may help you feel a tiny bit seen or less alone in your struggles. As the last thing any of us are is alone in our struggles.

We wanted to create a space for people to connect, to improve their relationships, to strengthen their sense of self and to ask the tricky questions with no fear of shame or judgement. We never could have imagined the family and the sisterhood that would follow.

To our Lifers, but also to anyone muddling their way through life: this book is for you.

With love, because we *love* love,
Britt and Laura xx

ADVENTURE

Let the adventure begin!

BRITT AND LAURA

SEE ALSO: MANIFESTING, SOLITUDE, TIMELINES

BRITT: When I hear the word 'adventure' the first thing that comes to mind is travel. The moment I finished school, while all my friends were partying it up at schoolies, I bought a plane ticket with no set return date to Italy. I found myself a random nannying job, packed my bags and, four weeks later, off I went. The only international trip I had been on prior to this was a family vacay to Fiji. I didn't know a soul in Italy, I couldn't speak the language and I was leaving behind everything and everyone I called home, including my boyfriend of three years. I had no itinerary, and no idea how long I would go for. There was a whole world out there waiting to be seen and it had been calling me. Even so, I got on the plane and cried the whole way over, feeling petrified. What was I doing? Where was I going? How was I going to get around? Was I crazy?

What felt like an eternity later, I landed in Italy, equal parts nervous and excited for what was to come. I remember standing next to the carousel waiting for my bags to come through, thinking about how I would spend my first day in this foreign country. I waited as, slowly, everyone else's bags arrived and the crowd started to disperse. Still I waited . . . until I was the last person left. I saw an attendant walking nearby, so I tried to ask her where my luggage could be, and if there was any chance it was still coming. This was lost in communication, so she took me to speak with someone else who informed me that my bag had indeed gone missing. They didn't know where it was and when or even *if* it would be found. Cute. Love that for me.

There I was, fresh out of school, alone on the other side of the world with no direction and no one to call for help. I couldn't speak the language besides the essentials I had learned on the plane – like how to order a gelato and a wine, and how to ask the time (purely so I could ensure it was an appropriate time to start with the gelato and wine). Armed with only the clothes on my back (and wishing I hadn't worn *such* a daggy old tracksuit for the flight in the name of comfort), my handbag and my little language book, I tentatively exited the airport and started my first big adventure.

After a year of travelling around Italy I came down with a serious case of the travel bug. I couldn't believe how big the world was, how different it was to what I knew back in Australia but mostly how the time I spent travelling shaped me as a person. It was a formative year that I am so grateful for. Learning to be on my own, facing challenges head-on and dealing with the speed bumps life threw at me set me up for what was to come.

Fast forward a few years, and my sister Sheri and I found ourselves working long hours together in an emergency department as emergency diagnostic radiographers. One evening, after a very stressful shift, we said to each other, *Work can't be it in life. We need to have more fun.* So, we quit our jobs the next day and bought one-way tickets to Brazil. It was impulsive, but it felt right and over the next three weeks, I sold my house and nearly everything I owned, and before I knew it, we were on a plane. We had no real plan other than to explore the world and see where life took us.

What ensued were without doubt the greatest moments of my life. We travelled to more than fifty countries together over a three-year period. We trekked into the Amazon jungle and camped alongside crocodiles, caught and ate piranhas, and swam in the Amazon River with pink dolphins and anacondas. We went diving in Belize and we saw the northern lights in the Arctic Circle. We camped in minus-30-degree weather and learned how to dog sled. We went bungee jumping and cliff diving. We sailed among the most magical islands in Greece and Turkey, hot-air-ballooned through Cappadocia and explored remote isles off the coast of Scotland. We snowboarded through breathtaking snow-capped scenery, won an axe-throwing competition in Canada, settled for a few months in London's Notting Hill (because I love me some rom-coms), surfed the coast of England and toured waaaay too many wineries throughout Europe. We hiked alongside elephants in Thailand, spent a month with a Buddhist monk, and dived headfirst into freezing waters in Iceland. It was a glorious and life-changing time – and that's only the half of it.

I hate to say it, but mine is the classic story of a girl who went travelling and found herself. Travelling helped me grow into who I was meant to be. Who I wanted to be. It healed wounds that I couldn't heal on my own. I feel so lucky to have been in this position, but before anyone asks how I could have travelled for so long, we worked along the way and I had saved for many years to be able to do this. I will always be grateful that I took the leap and pushed myself to jump into the unknown, both alone and with my sister. Sheri and I now have a bond that I think is very rare. We have experienced so much together, memories that we will hold onto until the day we die – which I hope is a very, very long, adventure-filled time away.

Laura, did you have a 'travelled-the-world-and-found-myself moment', too?

LAURA: All right, all right, we're both walking clichés of #travel #blessed. It's funny how when we think of 'adventure' the first thing that pops into mind is jumping on a plane (or off a cliff for you, Britt).

Ah, travel, how I miss you now that I have two kids and a whole lot of responsibilities. And I'm not talking about the cushy holiday with massages, room service and a kids' club (although I'd take that in a heartbeat). I'm talking about the gritty sort of travel that teaches you skills to problem-solve and serves you up life lessons with a side of chaos, like crossing the border between India and Nepal on foot and alone with only $400 in your bank account.

Britt, I think so many of us can relate to the feeling you described, of just wanting to throw it all in – the life plans, the timelines, the responsibilities – and book a one-way ticket. When I was twenty-four, I thought life was exactly where I wanted it to be. I had a boyfriend, we lived together, we owned a cat (that's where the Instagram handle @ladyandacat came from, for anyone curious) but still, something was missing. I didn't realise then that I had a lot of personal baggage that I needed to work through; my relationship was safe and comfortable but ultimately unfulfilling. After some deep soul-searching, I broke up with my boyfriend, got a big stupid tattoo of a Hamsa hand down the side of my ribs (not all decisions were good decisions) and booked a flight to Nepal in my very own *Eat, Pray, Love* moment – like I said, a walking cliché.

I'd taken holidays in the past, but this was the first time I had ever travelled by myself without an itinerary, or a return flight. I touched down in Kathmandu and unlike you, Britt, I distinctly remember my backpack being the very first one to come off the baggage carousel. I hailed a taxi to the hotel that I had booked on my phone as I waited at the departure gate back in Sydney. It was the start of travelling between Nepal, India, Sri Lanka and Indonesia, crossing countries by foot, bus, plane, train and taxi – some of it with my best friend, Kiah, and the rest of it alone.

For me, those adventures were a transformative time. Travelling solo and without a rigid plan can put you so far outside your comfort zone that you feel more at ease with chaos. I learned that if you can handle things going wrong when you're far away from all your creature comforts, then it sets you up to be better equipped to problem-solve on the home front as well.

But when I think about what adventure means to me, some of my biggest life moments have nothing at all to do with foreign countries, or long-haul flights, and everything to do with mindset. For me, the biggest adventures in life have come from saying yes to new opportunities. From shaking off the belief that you need to have everything figured out before you take the first step towards change, and from taking risks and living life not bound by society's timelines or expectations.

B: So true! Adventures come in all shapes and sizes. They can be big and life altering, or they can be peppered throughout the day-to-day. Starting a new job, moving cities, even just getting out there dating again can be one hell of an adventure – trust me . . . it's wild out there. For me, signing up for *The Bachelor* comes straight to mind; it was an adventure that changed the course of my life even if I didn't end up with the guy in the end.

L: I mean, could *The Bachelor* pass as travel? We packed 30 kilograms worth of luggage, spent three months away from our homes, slept in bunk beds akin to those in a budget hostel, and everyone was making out with the same guy – kind of like a Contiki tour!

I wholeheartedly agree, though. *The Bachelor* was one of the craziest adventures I have ever thrown myself into – however, it almost didn't happen for me. It might come as a surprise to some to know that I got cold feet just before *The Bachelor* started filming and momentarily pulled out of the show.

Each girl from my season was given a secret time and location, which was their discreet collection point for the day that they entered the experiment. A driver was to come and collect each contestant and take them to another undisclosed location, where the first lot of filming would take place before we all entered the mansion. Everything was meticulously scheduled by the production team in order to throw off the paparazzi and I had received instructions that a driver would be waiting for me at 3.15 pm sharp in a park in the Sydney suburb of Alexandria.

But, come 3.15 pm when I was meant to be at the pick-up location, I was at home with not even a suitcase packed. I had monumentally freaked out about doing the show and ghosted the driver.

The confused producers called me later that afternoon, and I told them that I'd had a change of mind. I remember getting off the phone feeling resolved in my decision. Half an hour later I received a text from someone at Warner Brothers, and it said if I changed my mind that I needed to be at the Ultimo Hotel by 10 am the next day. It was the very last chance I would have to enter the mansion.

The truth is, I wanted to go, but I kept going over all the things that could have gone wrong. What if I ruined my reputation or had my heart broken? Was I completely insane for thinking I might meet someone on a TV show?!

That evening I ate dinner with my housemates, watched Netflix and went to bed, but at about 2 am I woke up feeling frantic. I can't explain what came over me in my sleep, but I had this searing conviction that I had made the wrong choice and I had to take a chance and go on *The Bachelor* – that something big and life-changing was waiting for me. So, I packed my bags, called my sister to drive me to the hotel, and there began the biggest adventure of my life.

Never in my wildest dreams could I have imagined that saying yes to a reality TV show would lead me to the love of my life and so much more. I met you, Britt, we started the *Life Uncut* podcast, and I've become a mum. It's funny how saying yes to one thing can truly change everything.

B: Do you ever think where your life would be had you not woken up and changed your mind?

L: Yes! All the time! I'd probably have more stupid tattoos. I almost said no to the best thing that has ever happened to me because I was scared shitless that it might go poorly.

B: Sometimes we can be reluctant to take big risks in life because we're held back by fear – worried things won't go in our favour – but what about when they do?! When taking a risk exceeds our wildest expectations? Okay, so maybe my *Bachelor* experience wasn't as successful on paper as yours, Laura, but in a lot of ways it was! My worst fear was getting to the end of *The Bachelor*, and not having Nick choose me, and then it happened. But what I learned from that experience is that even when things go wrong and we feel like a complete failure, that's where we do our greatest growth. It's in those moments that we see how strong and resilient we really are.

That's the thing about living life with an adventurous spirit – it's not always going to be smooth sailing and often there will be setbacks. But it's about being adaptable and trusting that sometimes when things don't go to plan there are even better things in store just beyond the horizon.

ATTACHMENT THEORY

*Some call it daddy issues, but maybe
it's your attachment style*

LAURA

SEE ALSO: GHOSTING, JEALOUSY, LOVE LANGUAGES, WORTHINESS

I first stumbled across the theory of attachment styles a few years back. I was freshly thirty, going through a raw and painful break-up and had leaped head-first down the rabbit hole of self-help literature. My ex was a serial cheater, yet I had taken him back every time. Unsurprisingly, my self-worth was shot to shit. Even though I wanted better for myself, I was considering giving him another chance because I loved him, and the fear of being on my own was just too great.

By this point I had dated a string of guys who struggled with commitment but, paradoxically, I was wildly co-dependent. And on the off-chance I did ever find a great catch . . . well, you could bet your cotton socks I'd sabotage it anyway.

It took me a long time to come to the sobering realisation that I was the common denominator in my shitty dating choices. I had barely been single in more than a decade, jumping from one relationship to the next. And yet I had spent a great chunk of that time in relationships where I felt insecure and unstable, worried that my partner would walk out the door any minute.

Learning about attachment styles allowed me to look back on

my childhood and my relationship with my parents in order to help me unpack a lot of the junk I was carrying around. We have spent a lot of time on the podcast advocating for survivors of domestic violence, and it is a cause I hold very close to my heart. I haven't shared much about my childhood on the podcast; it's the one thing I still struggle to put into words. Even so, when it came to writing this book, I tried to sort back through the filing cabinet of childhood memories that I have locked away to give you an understanding of that time in my life.

My dad was an army major and was away a lot when I was a kid. I barely remember my parents' divorce, which happened when I was three. I remember a lot of yelling, a lot of crying and waking up to the streetlights coming in the car window outside my nana and papa's house, where Mum and us kids would live for the next eighteen years. This was a really hard time in my mum's life.

It wasn't long after my parents' separation that my mum started dating again, and soon she met the man who would become my stepdad: Alex. Alex was a landscaper. Tattooed, tall and sinewy, with long dark hair, he smoked Winfield Blues and grew marijuana in our back shed.

I was terrified of Alex.

It wasn't until I was much older and Alex was just a memory that I came to understand that he was a heroin addict.

On one Christmas Eve, my mum was curled up, crying, in an armchair in the sunroom. She had been waiting hours for Alex to come home. She finally bundled my older sister, our younger stepsister and me into the car and we drove to a sketchy pub just outside of Wollongong. We pulled into the gravel driveway to find Alex in the carpark with another woman straddled around him, kissing against the tray of his truck. I was only eight years old, but I understood the magnitude of what was happening.

Mum and Alex's fights were explosive, and he was violent. He would rip the phone line out of the wall so that my mum couldn't call for help, and he plummeted our family into crippling debt. Alex's cruelty was also directed at us kids, and he carried it out behind closed doors, without Mum's knowledge. He would say, 'If you tell anyone, I will kill you.' I spent my childhood believing that he would.

My mum left Alex when I was eleven, and in 2014 he died from cancer. I remember getting the phone call that he was dead and the only emotion I felt was relief.

Despite the difficult parts of that time in my life, I still have a lot of really wonderful memories from my childhood – memories of swimming carnivals with Papa, catching tadpoles in Nana's creek, picking mulberries with Dad, and Mum spending countless hours patiently helping me with my schoolwork.

As I grew up and started bumbling my way through the dating world, I rarely thought about my childhood, and had never even considered how the adults around me had modelled healthy relationships. I was hellbent that I would not be defined by that period of my life and was certain that my past played no role in my decision-making as an adult. I certainly didn't think it was impacting my dating ... but I hadn't yet discovered the theory of attachment.

How do you behave when you're in a relationship? Are you clingy, jealous, aloof, fearful of commitment or scared of abandonment? Are you always attracted to people who aren't very good for you, and therefore have the same dysfunctional relationships on repeat? Well, it could be because of your attachment style. Unpacking your relationships with your primary caregivers (usually your parents) might help explain how you're showing up in your adult relationships – especially romantic ones.

Attachment theory was pioneered by a couple of psychiatrists, John Bowlby and Mary Ainsworth, beginning in the 1960s. In a nutshell, it suggests that the quality of care, bonding, consistency and love you experienced during your first ever relationship – the one with your parents – has a profound impact on the way you relate to others and respond to intimacy throughout life. For the most part we learn a lot of relationship skills from our parents, who modelled them in our childhoods. Thanks to the work of Bowlby and Ainsworth, and other psychology experts since then, we now understand that our parents set the blueprint for how we create healthy attachments in our adult life – familial, platonic and romantic.

Now, I want to make it clear that this doesn't mean your parents are to blame for any shitty dating choices you may have made – just like my parents aren't responsible for me sticking with a guy who cheated on me over and over. Yep ... that was on me. However, understanding my attachment style and how my parents and stepdad modelled some toxic and unhealthy attachment styles in my childhood helped me to better comprehend why I stayed in that relationship for so long, and where my co-dependent tendencies came from.

By identifying your attachment style, you can start to learn more about how you tick, challenge your insecurities and develop a more securely attached way of relating to others. Ultimately this could lead to stronger, healthier and more fulfilling relationships long term – and we love a bit of conscious self-development here at *Life Uncut*!

THE FOUR ATTACHMENT STYLES

There are four different attachment styles and of these, one is considered secure and three are insecure. If (like me) you identify with an insecure attachment style, *you are not broken*. These are very common. Instead, have some compassion for yourself by recognising that learning your attachment style and understanding the 'why' behind it is the first step in working towards a secure one.

Secure attachment means that you're able to form loving, stable, well-balanced relationships. Now this is the sweet spot! To be securely attached means you feel confident, loved, at ease and understood in romantic relationships. You aren't struck by the urge to flick through your partner's phone when they pop off to the loo, you aren't scared they are going to dump you if you do or say the wrong thing, you aren't anxiously waiting by the phone counting the minutes until they text you back. (And if you do feel any of those things, you're less likely to stay in a relationship where someone is compromising your self-worth.)

There is a high level of mutual respect in a secure relationship: you're happy when you're together but you also have your own individual identities when you're apart, and you're okay with some separation from each other to do your own things. A securely attached person isn't afraid of intimacy, but they also don't freak out when their partner needs space.

To link this style of attachment back to our relationship with our primary caregivers, if you're secure it's probable that you had your needs met as a child, were loved and cared for, and had parents who were consistent, trustworthy and set a good example for healthy relationships. This absolutely does not mean that you had to have been raised surrounded by a white picket fence with perfect parents, though. Secure attachment can come from all different households with all different relationship dynamics. It just means that your basic needs for love, shelter, care and protection were sufficiently fulfilled.

About 56 per cent of adults have a secure attachment type. Now for the rest of us ...

Anxious attachment (fear of abandonment)

Anxious attachment is one of the three forms of insecure attachment. Almost all behaviours and characteristics that form this attachment style stem from a deep-rooted fear of being abandoned. Looking back, this was me in my late twenties.

If you're anxiously attached, then your chief fear, if you're in a relationship, is that your partner will leave you. This insecurity manifests in needing a significant amount of validation. Paradoxically, someone who is anxiously attached may stay in a relationship with someone who is cheating on them and betraying their trust because they feel undeserving of anything better, and fear being on their own.

Anxious attachment is associated with co-dependency and clingy behaviour. It could indicate that the love you were shown by your primary caregiver was inconsistent: you often felt loved, but you also often felt scared, abandoned and confused. It's the inconsistency and unreliability of the source of connection and love that creates the issues here.

Some 19 per cent of adults have an anxious attachment style.

Avoidant attachment

Avoidant attachment is the second form of insecure attachment. We can call this one the commitment-phobe. It is characterised by an intense fear of intimacy and reluctance to commit. This goes beyond your regular dude with Peter Pan syndrome – you know him, the guy who 'never wants to settle down'. Avoidants pride themselves on being independent and self-reliant, and as such, they tend to keep their partners at a distance, both emotionally and mentally, as their fear of intimacy means that any steps in this direction make them feel trapped.

Avoidant attachment tends to occur in children who don't experience sensitive responses to their needs or distress, and so they develop their own armour of sorts, in the form of being very independent, both physically and emotionally.

Around 25 per cent of adults have an avoidant attachment style.

Anxious–avoidant attachment

This is the rarest and also the most confusing form of attachment style. Anxious–avoidant combines traits of both the anxious and avoidant attachment styles. People with anxious–avoidant attachment are both desperate for affection and desperate to avoid it. This can make for tumultuous and rocky terrain. Anxious–avoidant attachment is usually attributed to those who grew up in households where their parents were not a safe harbour for them, but a source of fear. Their childhoods were often marked in some way by trauma and possibly abuse.

A relationship with someone who is anxious–avoidant will often feel volatile, with the sorts of extreme highs and lows that will give you a severe case of emotional whiplash. It's an attachment style characterised by fear, mistrust and inner conflict. As adults, these people tend to backflip on what they want. They may make big commitments and grandiose statements of love and adoration, then turn around the following week and say they've changed their mind. It's common for them to cling to their partner when they feel rejected, then feel trapped when they are close.

Curious to find out what your attachment style is? Check out the Resources on page 322 for the online quizzes you can take to find out.

Now, we don't have enough pages here to fully dive into the nuances of attachment theory – there are many, and it's a totally fascinating topic. However, it's important to know a few things:

♥ Attachment styles are not black and white, so no one is 100 per cent securely attached or 100 per cent insecurely attached. There is a spectrum. You could be mostly secure yet struggle from time to time with some anxious attachment and feelings of co-dependency. Or different relationships may inflame insecure attachments, whereas others may bring out your more secure side.

♥ They are not static, either. This means that, no matter your current style, it doesn't mean it will stay that way forever. There are ways to heal, and it's important that you do so for yourself, your relationships and to break the cycle of insecure attachment, which can be passed down to our children.

1. **It is not your fault. Have compassion for yourself.**
   Understand that if you have an insecure attachment style, you're not broken, you're not deficient and you're not unlovable.

2. **Find a partner who has a secure attachment style.**
   If you have an insecure attachment style, partnering with someone who is secure will give you the best chance of healing your own insecurities and shortcomings. However, that won't solve all your problems.

3. **Vulnerability, openness and communication are key.**
   Practise self-regulation and open communication with your partner. Talking about all the unique experiences that make you the way you are brings insight and closeness. It also allows your partner to better understand why you may act in a certain way, and make them more understanding and available to your needs.

4. Work on emotional regulation.

At the end of the day, your attachment style is not your fault – but it IS your responsibility. No one is going to do the hard work for you, and when you know better, you do better. We hope the pages of this book will be a road map in the right direction. You can do hard things, and you're deserving of a relationship that is loving, peaceful and harmonious.

The most valuable take-home that I have learned from attachment theory is that it's not what happened to you as a child that matters most – it is how you deal with it as an adult. The influences in your life will have shaped your attachment style, but you can break the cycle.

BOUNDARIES

How to set and stick to them, to show
yourself respect and love

LAURA

SEE ALSO: EMOTIONAL CHEATING, THE ICK, JEALOUSY, KINKS, MONEY,
NUDES, OVERWHELM, UNCONDITIONAL LOVE, WORTHINESS

'Personal boundaries' is one of those buzzy terms that pops up all through the self-improvement and wellbeing space. We're told over and over again, 'You've got to set boundaries', that doing so 'is an act of self-love and respect'.

But WTF actually *are* boundaries when we're not talking about the perimeter of your property? And how do you decide what sorts of boundaries you need to have in place, let alone how to build them?

It can seem daunting, especially if you're a people-pleaser who doesn't like to rock the boat, and while there's no instruction manual per se, I've pulled together some general principles that might just help you with the building and maintenance. Grab a hard hat and let's go.

FIRST UP, WHAT ARE BOUNDARIES AND WHY ARE THEY IMPORTANT?

Simply put, boundaries create rules for how you allow other people to treat you, and they define what you will and won't accept in your relationships. Have you put up with some monumentally cruddy behaviour in your relationships? Do you let other people's needs and wants overwhelm your own? Well, there's a good chance you have some poor boundaries in place.

Personal boundaries come in all shapes and sizes. There are little boundaries, like: I won't answer my work emails after 6.30 pm, and there are big boundaries, like: I won't stay in a relationship where there has been infidelity. Everyone's boundaries are unique to their own values, and will vary depending on the person that you're dealing with and the situation you're in. They can be (and often are) psychological or they can take the form of a physical action, such as blocking the number of your ass-hat of an ex who keeps calling you.

Here are some situations where personal boundaries are lacking:

♥ You are the emotional dumping ground for your friend, who is constantly involved in drama. You offer advice over and over again that they don't seem to take on board, and the relationship feels like a non-reciprocal venting space for them.
♥ You allow your partner to dictate what you can and can't do with your own time and energy. You do things like cancel plans with your friends as you'd rather avoid the guilt trip at home.
♥ You reply to your boss at 8.30 pm on a Saturday night when you work a Monday-to-Friday, nine-to-five job.
♥ You put up with your mum making comments about your weight.
♥ You overextend yourself with responsibilities because you don't want to let anyone down, and it's 'easier' to just do it yourself.

Now these are just a few examples, but when your boundaries have been compromised, it can leave you feeling burned out, overwhelmed, hurt and frustrated. On the other hand, having healthy boundaries and sticking to them can help you cultivate confidence and respect for yourself. Boundaries are also associated with having a strong sense of self-worth and a low level of co-dependency. Plus they're sexy – because knowing your worth is hot!

TIME FOR A BOUNDARY INSPECTION: HOW ARE YOURS LOOKING?

All this requires a fair amount of self-awareness. So, let's run through a bit of a checklist to see where your current level of boundaries lies:

- ☐ Do you ever feel as though you are saying yes to everything, even at the risk of depleting your own energy?
- ☐ Do you ever feel as if people take advantage of you and your easygoing nature?
- ☐ Are you the 'fixer' or the 'saver' in difficult situations?
- ☐ Do you struggle to say no to things that you don't necessarily want to do, or feel guilty when you do say no?
- ☐ Do you seem to be involved in drama or conflict even though you may not be the instigator of it?
- ☐ Do you find that you can become invested in romantic relationships too quickly, regardless of how much time you've spent together?
- ☐ Do you feel the desire to be there for people when they aren't deserving of that loyalty?
- ☐ Do you hang on to relationships that no longer have a positive impact on your life for longer than you should?
- ☐ Does it feel as if your romantic relationship is either terrible or spectacular, with no happy medium? Are you constantly breaking up and getting back together?

If you have put a tick next to anything from a few of these to almost all of them, then it's boundary bootcamp for you, baby!

Mark Manson, the author of *The Subtle Art of Not Giving a F*ck*, says there is no one-size-fits-all when it comes to setting boundaries in your life, and those that you have for one person can be infinitely harder to maintain for another, depending on the closeness of that relationship. As Mark puts it, 'The difficulty level of setting boundaries largely depends on your relationship with the person. If it's a stranger, it's usually quite easy: just tell them to fuck off. If it's a friend, it can be a bit harder. If it's family, it's really hard. And if it's you who's being the shit person, then it's literally impossible.'[1]

I feel that Mark Manson quote in my soul. For me, setting boundaries, particularly in my romantic life, was something that I always struggled with. My late twenties were a murky period in my love life, and my self-esteem took a real beating. At that time, I sought a lot of personal validation from being in relationships and from my romantic partners. The problem was, in a lot of cases, the relationship I was in was not just lacking in boundaries, but the boundaries had been totally eroded by infidelity and lying. I had become used to the cycle of extreme highs and lows that comes with poor boundaries: roaring fights, wild make-up sex, two weeks of bliss, followed by a week in hell. Rinse, repeat.

I was so focused on not wanting to lose the relationship and being the 'fixer' that I allowed my boundaries to be decimated, and my self-esteem and self-worth went with them. I remember thinking, *Why is he doing this to me?* But then there came a point where I had to ask myself another question: *Why am I allowing myself to be treated this way?*

Co-dependency and boundaries

These two go hand in hand: co-dependent relationships often contain many of the hallmarks of poor personal boundaries. In its simplest terms, a co-dependent relationship is when there is an imbalance of power where one partner needs the other partner, who in turn, needs to be needed. This dynamic creates what experts refer to as the 'cycle' of co-dependency.

When we take part in these needy or co-dependent relationships, and we constantly prioritise another person's needs and wants over our own, it's like jumping on an emotional roller-coaster. We can become so desperate for validation, love or attention from our partner that we lose sight of who we are and what we actually want.

WHAT DO HEALTHY BOUNDARIES LOOK LIKE AND HOW DO WE SET THEM?

A person with good boundaries takes responsibility for the way that they react to a situation. They have a clear understanding of how they will allow other people to treat them and they are not scared of losing relationships or upsetting someone if that person refuses to respect their boundaries. Boundaries don't push people away (at least not the people who love and respect you) – what they do instead is form the framework for healthy, loving connections.

If you're the type of person who tends to struggle with boundaries, then it might be worth writing a list of certain aspects of your life that you think you need to change and outlining what you are willing and not willing to tolerate. To help with this, think about scenarios that have made you feel upset or taken advantage of – these emotions are clues that an important line was crossed for you.

Having a clear idea of this gives you an understanding of where your boundaries lie. For example, say you have a work friend who is constantly showing up late and asking you to cover for them. Draw your line in the sand by explaining to them, 'I am not willing to lie to cover up your lateness to the boss. I won't go out of my way to make it known, but if I am questioned about it, I will tell the truth.' Sure, they might not be happy about the situation, because setting boundaries, especially initially, can be hard, but the more you flex that muscle, the less you'll get walked all over.

Another example: maybe you feel run down and want to establish a boundary to protect your need for time by yourself to recharge. That may look like replying to a friend's suggestion to hang out with, 'I love you but I'm feeling a bit mentally exhausted and need to stay at home to recharge my batteries. How about we catch up next week?'

The key to both of these examples is clear communication. You cannot assume that someone knows your limits – it's up to you to verbalise your boundaries, people are not mind-readers. Don't expect other people to automatically know where you have drawn the line on something; you have a responsibility to tell them about it so they have a genuine chance to adhere to it. So, make your boundaries known to the important people in your life. There may be some who fall into a bit of a grey area, such as your boss, and you're going to have to handle those situations on a case-by-case basis. But for your partner, close friends and family, if you take the time to explain your boundaries and why they're important to you, it's likely to pay dividends in those relationships.

So what happens when somebody oversteps your boundaries? Sure, there will be exceptions to the rules, but you need to think about how you are going to respond if someone fails to respect a boundary you have communicated to them. It's probably going to happen at some point, particularly if setting boundaries is new to you, because the people around you have likely become used to treating you a certain way.

It can be very hard to uphold boundaries in the heat of the moment, with tears and apologies flying around, which is why you need to be clear on where you stand *before* things go wrong. Remember: boundaries without consequences are just fluff.

At the very core of personal boundaries is a deep sense of compassion for yourself. You cannot pour from an empty cup. You can't endlessly give without being left empty. Aim to be gentle with yourself, but firm with what makes you uncomfortable. Although you may feel uneasy at first communicating where your boundaries lie, much like anything else in life, the more you practise it, the more confident you become and the more your sense of self-worth, self-respect and worthiness grows. Do not settle for less than your worth.

BROKEN HEARTS

*How to survive one and come back
more resilient than ever*

BRITT

SEE ALSO: DATING, EMOTIONAL CHEATING, QUITTING,
SITUATIONSHIPS, WORTHINESS, YESTERDAY

I wish it weren't so, but I truly believe we will all at some stage die of a broken heart. Okay, slight exaggeration . . . we may not actually *die*, but at some stage we will all FEEL like we are going to die of a broken heart. If you are reading this and haven't yet experienced this all-consuming pain – that deep, dull ache; that heaviness that weighs you down so you can't even get out of bed – well, to you I say, bask in this ignorance! Run free and love fiercely! But if you know these feelings all too well, you are not alone.

I remember my first real heartbreak. I had been in what I thought was the most amazing relationship I would ever have. It was a year of intense love, laughter and making plans for the future. We were together almost every day. I thought I had found my soulmate and couldn't believe how lucky I was.

Then one day, completely out of nowhere and for no apparent reason, he broke up with me. My heart was smashed into a thousand pieces. Oh, the pain! The wailing! The despair! The tears that wouldn't stop falling! I locked myself in my room and refused to speak to anyone, certain I would never recover.

It was my mum who finally got through to me. One day she

came into my room, sat on the edge of my bed and said, 'Britt, I know you think you will never meet anyone again, but you're fifteen and I promise you that you will. This is probably the first of many heartbreaks and many loves, and it will also probably hurt the most.'

Cat Stevens was right: the first cut is by far the deepest. Yes, I was only fifteen when I was sure my life was over – and yes, I did love again, and yes, I had my heart broken again. Such is life.

The thing is, each new heartbreak hurts in its own way. Every heartbreak is painful, but I think as we grow older we learn to sit in the pain. We have more life experience and are more equipped to deal with it. We understand more about love, relationships and how the world works – which also unfortunately means we have to lose some of our innocence along the way. Now, this isn't to say the pain isn't still all-consuming, because it is. We just learn how to live with it better.

THE MILLION-DOLLAR QUESTION: CAN YOU ACTUALLY DIE OF A BROKEN HEART?

The surprising thing about the saying 'they died of a broken heart' is that you actually can! Broken heart syndrome is a real thing. Go figure. Here's what you need to know about it:[2]

♥ 'Stress-induced cardiomyopathy' or 'Takotsubo cardiomyopathy' are the medical terms for broken heart syndrome. Basically, it's severe chest pain caused by a huge surge of stress hormones in a highly emotional situation.

♥ Women are more likely to experience it than men. (Why am I not even slightly surprised by that?)

♥ Broken heart syndrome occurs when a part of the heart temporarily grows bigger and doesn't pump blood around the body properly, while the rest of the heart behaves normally, or even pumps blood around more energetically than usual.

♥ It can often be misdiagnosed as a heart attack, but the main difference is that there aren't any issues with your arteries when you have broken heart syndrome.

So there you go! Although, just because it's real, it doesn't mean we have to add worrying about experiencing literal broken heart syndrome to the list of potential consequences of a break-up. According to Harvard Medical School, it's a temporary condition, it's relatively rare to experience and even rarer to actually die from it.[3] So at least there's that.

HOW TO GET OVER A BROKEN HEART

Thoughts affect feelings, and feelings affect actions. This is something to remember when we are grieving the end of a relationship. Our thoughts directly affect the way we show up to the world, and if we tell ourselves negative things, we will start to believe them. And what's more, we will take this negativity to the people around us – to our work environment, to our relationships, and to our family and friends. That cycle of negativity can be hard to break. But it starts with our thoughts.

There are so many layers and feelings in a break-up; it is like peeling an onion. Who broke up with whom? Was it you, or are you the one left wondering why? If you are the breakerupperer (yep, a totally legit word), you may feel like you're leaving someone in a painful place. Chances are you will be filled with sadness, guilt and confusion. If you're the one who's been broken up with, you may be in a state of shock. You might go through different stages of grief such as anger, confusion, pleading, despair, numbness, depression and anxiety. We know this because medical professionals have spent years studying bereavement and grief, and the emotions that go hand in hand with it. Loss can come in many forms: the death of a loved one, a break-up, an illness or diagnosis, job loss, or even the ending of a friendship. At the end of the day, there is no right or wrong reason for grief and no right or wrong way to grieve. What's important is how you feel.

One of the experts who dedicated a lot of her time to the cause was a Swiss-American psychiatrist named Elisabeth Kübler-Ross. She created the Kübler-Ross Model, a theory that outlines five stages of grief. These five stages can be broken down into the following dominant emotions or states:

1. Denial

For many, denial is the first stage. This is the part where we lie to ourselves. We pretend the loss didn't happen. We pretend it doesn't bother us. You've probably gone through something like this if a significant other has broken up with you out of the blue. They tell you in clear terms that they don't love you anymore and don't want to be with you, but still you spend the next month saying to yourself, and those closest to you, 'They will come around any day now. They will realise they have made a mistake. They just need time to miss me, then they'll be back.' When the truth is they've probably already moved on.

We tell ourselves we are fine! Everything is fine! The floor is lava but everything is fine! This is because we're in a state of shock. Denial is a powerful thing, and it's not uncommon to feel completely numb when you're in the thick of it. I know I have been there before, in a place where I felt absolutely nothing. There is no better way to describe it. It is almost like your body shuts down. I didn't feel happy but I didn't feel sad either. I was just existing, walking around like a zombie. But there's a reason for this: denial and numbness are coping mechanisms that allow us to survive the initial shock and make it to the next stage.

There is something sort of beautiful about denial in this way. It is a way for the body to say, 'Hey, I know there is a lot going on right now and it's too much for you to handle all at once. So, we are going to pace these feelings out. I'll drip-feed them to you and once you can cope, I'll allow you to feel a little bit more.' As you start to accept the situation, your body will allow you to edge forward in the slow acceptance process. And when the denial fades, it's time to face the music.

2. Anger

Anger, frustration, anxiety, fury, rage or impatience are all things you may feel during this next stage. You may be angry at yourself, angry at the world or angry at the person who left you and made you feel this way. It can also be infuriating and a little soul-destroying to see people around you happy and in love while you are feeling so miserable. Rationally you may know that ending your relationship was for the best, or that the person didn't mean to cause you pain, but emotionally ... well, to put it bluntly, you don't give a fuck. You're mad at them for making you feel this way.

It's important to acknowledge these feelings, no matter how tricky they are. The longer we suppress the anger, the longer it stays with us, so ride out that wave, baby. For example, when I was in this stage I started going to boxing. I had so much energy and frustration I needed to get out of my body and boxing felt so good!

Accidentally Unfiltered

Okay, so I have a confession, which might be one of the pettiest things I've ever done. My ex and I went on holidays to Bali together, but I had to go home early to start a new job. Anyway, long story short, he cheated on me two days after I left. He'd left his email logged in on my computer, and as we had booked separately, I had access to all his return flight details. I initially changed his flights to a day earlier, turned off notifications and deleted all the confirmation emails, but then got cold feet about leaving him stranded overseas, so I changed his flight back to the correct day, but six hours later, so that he would arrive at the airport way too early with all his luggage (he had a surfboard so couldn't really go anywhere with it) and on a red-eye flight. I also selected a middle seat for him and changed his $15 in-flight voucher to a cup of tea and a muffin. I have never laughed so hard as I did after I heard from a mutual friend about how confused, angry and uncomfortable he was for the whole trip home.

3. Bargaining

Bargaining is a way to hold on to hope in intense and overwhelming situations. It's a method of trying to reason your way back to the sense of equilibrium you had before the loss. You might tell yourself that you're willing to do or give up anything for your life to be restored to its previous state. You might start to ruminate over pressure points in your old relationship – maybe your partner wanted to move somewhere that you didn't, or maybe you had conflicting views about marriage and kids – and wonder if you might be able to salvage the relationship if you conceded those points. Anything to appease your (ex) partner; anything to win them back and restore things to the way they were before your heart was ripped out and stomped on.

4. Depression

Ah, this ugly old thing. The phase during which you start to face reality. The sadness hits you like a tonne of bricks and settles in deep. You are on your way to acceptance but still have some hurdles to jump first, in the form of fatigue, confusion, not wanting to get out of bed, loss of motivation, lack of energy and reduced appetite (although that last one has never happened to me. There aren't many things in this world that keep me away from food, let me tell ya!).

According to David Kessler, co-author of multiple books dedicated to grief, in this instance depression is a natural response to a loss. As I write this chapter, I am deep in these feelings. I am experiencing a break-up, going through the process of losing someone I thought was my forever, and while it has been a horrendous few months, I know for sure that I am in stage four.

Many days I wake up sad and I go to sleep sad. There are some days I don't even want to get out of bed. Some days I burst into tears for no reason. My heart is physically hurting more than it ever has. A real, visceral pain that is all-consuming. I want to curl up into a ball and speak to no one. As I write these words, tears are running down my face, because writing it means it is real. I have a lump in my throat that feels so big, but I think it is because I am trying not to break down completely. I am sick of crying, to be honest. But it is just about riding the wave and moving on from that time with Jordan. Trying to look forward instead of backwards, which is easier said than done.

Just today, while with my radio family – Laura, Mitch and Keeshia – we were chatting life. They suggested it might be time to return to online dating and I immediately started crying. The thought of it made me anxious, and from that reaction, I knew that I wasn't ready. So, I'll listen to my body, and for now I will just keep focusing on me until the thought doesn't make me feel sick.

5. Acceptance

Acceptance refers not just to acceptance of what happened to you, but acceptance of the new reality you find yourself in. It means looking to the future, thinking about how you can rebuild your life in the wake of experiencing your loss. You're finally able to step forward without wanting to dive back under the covers. That doesn't mean that from here on in you're only going to experience peace, calm and confidence, though. None of these stages are completely linear, so you might feel accepting of your reality one day and ready to throw it all out the window the next. But, bit by bit, you'll adjust. When you're in the throes of pretty much any of these other stages of grief, it might not feel like you will ever reach this stage, but, trust me, eventually it happens. I'm not quite there yet myself, but I know I'm close. And that's enough to keep me moving forward.

Now that we have explored the stages we will go through after a heartbreak or loss, let's look at things we can do to heal and get back on track to living a happy and healthy life. You will heal and you will feel happiness and love again. Based on research and lived experience, I have compiled a list of things you can do to get back on the happiness horse:

♥ Embrace your feelings. Really feel them. Cry your eyes out. Scream. Punch your pillow. Lie in bed. Sleep. Just feel.

♥ Next up, are you still talking to your ex? WHY?! I know I don't know you, but I can tell you that there is a 99.95 per cent chance it is too soon. This is a pretty universal rule in a break-up. Sure, you can still have contact with them at some much later stage, but not until you are well and truly in the green zone. Do yourself a favour and stop communicating. If you have no self-control, delete their number and block them on the 'gram for a while. Until you are in a place where seeing them and thinking about them no longer feels like you're being stabbed directly through the heart with a chopstick.

♥ Write down what sucked. Remember why it sucked. It is very easy to forget the bad and live in a fantasy world where you only remember how great things were. Sometimes it is helpful to revisit this list when you're thinking about turning up on their doorstep.

♥ Exercise! I can't stress this enough. Go work up a sweat and flood your body with endorphins! Exercise will make you feel better, release stress and anger, fill in time and, if all else fails, it will help you sleep better.

♥ Create new routines. If you two used to go to the same coffee shop every weekend, STOP GOING THERE! That is just unnecessary pain you don't need right now. Find a different local and start making fresh memories.

♥ Develop a new hobby or interest, something to get your mind off your situation and your ex. Try something you've never done before – it could be totally random, or maybe something you've been curious about for a while. I have tried multiple new things! I enrolled in a language school, went back to study, started jujitsu, went to acting school . . . I pretty much decided to pursue anything I had ever had an interest in!

♥ Practise some serious self-love. You need to fit your own oxygen mask first. Take some time each week to do one thing purely for yourself. (Each day is preferable, but hey, life can get crazy. So, at a minimum, I want you to be doing something nice every week.) Maybe it's a massage or a facial, a yoga class or treating yourself to a nice dinner (and dessert, let's be real). One thing that you know is going to make you feel better and is just for you. For example, I get a massage every week. I love it and it is the only time I ever truly feel relaxed and at ease.

♥ Surround yourself with a great support system – even if it is just one friend or family member you can download on and trust. I hope you already have this support system in place, but if you don't, now is the time to reach out for help. Friends, family, anyone you can rely on.

♥ Accept that closure is something you may need to achieve on your own. Despite what you might think, you don't always need closure to come from or be validated by other people. We can be in charge of that, and that's a great thing.

♥ Write down the reasons you broke up, followed by some positive things that will come from this next phase of your life, such as more time to explore new goals or hobbies, more time with your friends. You'll soon start to focus on all the fun parts of your life!

♥ Don't be scared to date again. But, with that said, don't force yourself into dating if you're not quite ready – and being ready will feel different for everyone. At the time of writing it's been about four months since my most recent break-up and I am yet to go on a date. I can't even think about it yet, to be honest, but I know I am getting closer! Be guided by how you feel – and when you're ready, don't be afraid. It doesn't have to be serious right away, just focus on having fun and meeting new people. Check out the Dating chapter for all our best tips on getting back out there!

I once read somewhere that it takes half the time of a relationship's duration to get over that person (okay, fine, it's from *Sex and the City*). Acceptance and healing *will* come, but it's a long road.

Having survived several broken hearts now – some worse than others, and recently my worst one yet – my number-one piece of advice would be to avoid bringing your past into your future. We only have this one short life, so it's important to not let whatever disappointments or heartbreaks you've experienced in previous relationships prevent you from loving openly and with your whole being. Everything we go through in life shapes who we are. Right now, in this moment, you are who you are because of every single thing you have been through. It is important to talk about things that have affected us, but share it as part of your story, rather than letting it define you.

Love is a beautiful and constantly evolving thing. We must run towards it, not away from it, because it is what makes the world go 'round.

CONFLICT RESOLUTION

Why arguments are healthy – and how
to get better at them

BRITT

SEE ALSO: GHOSTING, LOVE LANGUAGES, PENGUINS, RED FLAGS

Fighting. Disagreements. Arguments. Some of us thrive off them, some of us are indifferent to them and the rest of us would rather eat dog poop from our shoe than engage in any sort of conflict. But one thing we all have in common is that it is inevitably a part of any relationship because we're all human. Friction will happen and it's probably going to be uncomfortable, but relax! We are here to arm you with the knowledge needed to help you through it.

Conflict is not necessarily a sign or cause of trouble – in fact it's an inevitable, normal and even healthy part of any relationship. I can't think of a single relationship among my family and friends that hasn't featured arguments at some point or another. Sometimes they are silly and trivial ones, such as when one person hasn't been cleaning up after themselves, and other times they are more serious, caused by lying or infidelity. Either way, it's how you deal with conflict that can be the difference between a positive or negative resolution (unless you're dealing with infidelity, in which case there's rarely a positive way to resolve the situation). And let's be real, we all want positivity!

Let's suss out the main conflict styles and what they involve so you can go off and work out what your and your partner's styles are, to hopefully bring about a better understanding of each other, and a more effective approach to conflict. And do our best to dull those screaming matches, people!

THE FIVE TYPES OF CONFLICT RESOLUTION

First, a quick bit of background. In the 1970s, two professors of management, Kenneth Thomas and Ralph Kilmann, did a bunch of studies and worked out that there are five main styles of dealing with conflict, all of which vary in their levels of cooperativeness and assertiveness. Thomas and Kilmann found that individuals typically have a 'go-to' conflict resolution style, the one they automatically default to. This can be a result of many things but can be heavily impacted by your upbringing and people that are influential in your life. But it was also noted that different styles were more useful in different situations and it's therefore possible to swap styles to improve the outcome. Conflict styles can change, and, for me, they have changed over time and during different relationships. They have also shifted for me as I have grown up, and were definitely different back when I was in a toxic relationship compared to when I was in a healthy and loving relationship.

Okay, let's have a look at the five styles!

1. Accommodating

This is where you put others first and place their needs and concerns above your own. The accommodating style usually takes place when you've either simply had enough and want the situation to end, so you choose to give in; or you have been persuaded to give in, even when it is not warranted. This style is not assertive but is highly cooperative, with elements of people-pleasing.

When to use: This is a good conflict resolution style to use if you are not as invested in the issue as the other person, you're not sacrificing a great deal, you don't have the energy for the argument or you want to keep the peace. It might also come into play if you feel as though you *are* probably in the wrong, when the other person makes some excellent points, or if you feel like you won't make any progress until you acknowledge the other person's point of view.

Pros: Arguments are 'resolved' quickly and make the other person happy.

Cons: Are you giving up on something that you truly believe in? Something that is important to you? Are you ignoring your moral compass to appease someone else? Often in this case you will achieve peace in the immediate term, but the original issue will only rear its ugly head again down the track.

2. Avoiding

Thomas and Kilmann characterise the 'avoiding' style as being low in assertiveness and cooperativeness. This style completely evades the conflict – the individual will walk, run, skip, jump, scurry, roll or slither away from the discomfort of the situation and would rather pretend that it isn't happening.

When to use: You may find yourself adopting this style if the conflict you're facing seems silly, minor or trivial. Maybe you need more time to think about and process the situation, so the avoidance is only temporary; or maybe you feel helpless and don't want to acknowledge the fact that there is no way you will ever win.

Pros: Avoidance helps you achieve the short-term goal of reducing stress and worry. It is especially useful if the issue is minor.

Cons: You won't actually resolve any issue with avoidance. It's highly likely it will present itself again and again until dealt with.

They say ignorance is bliss, and while conflict-avoidant couples can be happy and independent, too much conflict avoidance may lead to resentment and attention-seeking behaviour. This is because no one likes to be ignored, which can be a by-product of avoidance. It's important for individuals who rely on avoidance to become more comfortable communicating openly about their feelings so they can truly resolve any problems.

3. Compromising

Compromising is an attempt to find middle ground; a solution that will give everyone some of what they want, but not everything. This style of conflict resolution can sometimes leave people feeling dissatisfied, or like the matter has not been fully resolved.

When to use: It's a good idea to opt for a compromise in situations where it's more important to reach a solution than for the solution to be exactly what everyone wants. It is useful when the cost of conflict is higher than the cost of agreeing and moving on – for example, maybe a deadline is looming or you need a temporary solution.

Pros: Compromising comes from a place of understanding and respect. It allows both parties to be heard, and relationships are maintained as conflicts are resolved. Both people should be relatively happy as they have received at least part of what they wanted.

Cons: Compromising may create a less-than-ideal outcome and, deep down, one or both parties might be resentful because they didn't get everything they wanted from the situation.

4. Collaborating

A collaborating approach to conflict resolution is one that seeks to satisfy everyone. It rejects compromising, or seeking a middle-ground solution, in favour of working together to come up with something that uniquely and totally works for everyone. Sometimes this involves shifting or reassessing expectations to get to a new and satisfying end result. Happy days!

When to use: Collaborating could be the right approach when it's important that multiple perspectives are addressed; when the final outcome is too important for anyone to be unhappy; or when it is important to make sure the beliefs and needs of all involved are acknowledged and catered for.

Pros: This style helps to build trust and develop respect, and also offers a chance for both or all people to learn from each other. It demonstrates a commitment to the relationship.

Cons: This style can require more time, energy and skill.

5. Competing

A competing style involves a refusal to budge or to acknowledge the perspectives of anyone else. Someone using this style may keep pushing their view onto others or rejecting alternative ideas until they get their way. Those who compete are assertive, uncooperative and willing to stop at nothing to get their own way, often at the expense of others' needs or wishes.

When to use: You might adopt this style if you feel like you have to stand up for something you truly believe in. It could perhaps also be used if you need to resolve a conflict quickly. Personally, I think this should be a last-resort conflict style to be used in a relationship, as relationships shouldn't be about competing in an unhealthy manner. It only takes a few clicks around the internet to see that experts caution against using this style too often.

Pros: My advice here is don't use this style when it comes to personal relationships. Just don't.

Cons: A competing style can be hostile and uncooperative. However, the biggest drawback of a competing style is that it can cause harm to relationships – sometimes beyond repair. For example, in a workplace environment, managers using this style will be viewed as unreasonable and authoritarian. Handling conflict by not allowing anyone else to express an opinion will not result in happy, productive employees, nor will it lead to finding the most effective result.

> *Wondering what your conflict resolution style is? Check out the Resources on page 322 for the online quizzes you can take to find out.*

Historically speaking, I have tended to adopt an avoiding conflict resolution style. (And yep, I took the quiz to confirm this!) Everyone who knows me knows I would rather sell everything I own and move to Siberia than have a showdown with, well, anyone. What I mean by that is that I'm happy to let the small stuff slide in order to keep the peace. For example, maybe I don't like the restaurant someone has chosen for dinner, but it won't kill me to just go there even though I would much prefer somewhere else. But don't get me wrong, when the time comes, I will stand up for what I believe in, I will hold my own and fiercely defend those I care about, even if I am dying on the inside.

The older I get, though, the more I find I'm leaning into the collaborating style. When I'm in a relationship, I want to work together with my partner to deal with any issues and I am learning that avoidance won't get me very far. Also, if I am being honest, I just don't have the energy to argue in any other way. Every year older is another more placid year for me!

♥

So that's a brief overview of the five conflict resolution styles. I recommend that you do a bit more reading on them in order to find out which styles you tend to favour, and which styles your partner is drawn to. Being aware of conflict resolution styles means being aware of how your disagreements will take shape, and learning how to have discussions in a sincere and productive way. And you can't underestimate the importance of that!

THE FOUR HORSEMEN OF THE APOCALYPSE

Okay, so now that you're familiar with various conflict resolution styles, it's time to broaden things out a little and look at communication styles, particularly during moments of friction or discord in your relationship. There are certain methods of communication during conflict that are so toxic they serve as harbingers of a failed relationship. Internationally renowned relationship expert and bestselling author John Gottman calls these communication styles 'The Four Horsemen of the Apocalypse'. They are Criticism, Contempt, Defensiveness and Stonewalling. Let's find out a little more.

Criticism

We all know what criticism is, and have probably at some point been on the giving or receiving end of it. And not all criticism is bad, of course. But in this context, criticism means that, if your partner does something that annoys or upsets you, you blame and/or give negative feedback about their entire personality or character rather than addressing the behaviour itself. Essentially, you're implying that their transgression, however big or small, represents a fundamental defect within them. Is that what you really mean? Probably not. Does that mean you should not tell your partner if their behaviour is upsetting you? Absolutely not. Honesty and open expression are part of any healthy relationship. It's all about framing, people.

Criticism vs complaint

Next time your partner does something that upsets you and you find yourself poised to unleash your wrath, try instead to spin it into a complaint. What's the difference? A complaint addresses the specific action and/or targets particular behaviours. It keeps the focus super tight and concentrates on concrete actions that can be changed.

Here is an example. You have discovered a pile of dirty dishes in the living room.

Criticism: 'The dishes don't belong in the living room. Why are you so lazy? Are you that incapable of cleaning up after yourself that you can't even carry them into the kitchen?'

Complaint: 'The dishes don't belong in the living room. Please remember to put them in the kitchen from now on.'

We remember and hold on to forms of negativity, and criticism can accumulate quickly. This is why it is so important to take care with your words and the manner in which you deliver them. They are more powerful than you think.

Contempt

Next up we have contempt. This is pretty much any action (verbal or non-verbal) that aims to belittle or insult your partner or attack their self-worth, such as sarcasm, eye-rolling, name-calling, sneering or hostile humour. Reading through these behaviours makes it clear that this is a terrible way to treat anyone, especially your partner. The aim should always be to communicate in a clear and respectful way, with the goal of finding a way to move forward. So, be respectful even when you are angry, let go of any unhelpful or cruel behaviours and make sure you tell your partner you appreciate them.

Defensiveness

Of course we want to protect ourselves. Of course we don't want to be in the wrong (and often aren't). And it's totally normal to feel defensive when under attack – in fact, it's a lot of people's default stance when arguing with a partner. However, defensiveness is rarely helpful – whether in the form of making excuses, complaining or 'yes-butting' – because it's just another form of deflection and blame.

Listening to and recognising your own role in your partner's complaints, no matter how small, is a cure for defensiveness. Acknowledging your partner's feelings is a way of saying to them, 'I hear you. Your opinion matters.' Think how nice it feels when someone actually *hears* you.

The other important thing about listening is that it means you're not speaking. Sometimes, it's better to pause and reflect before thoughtfully responding, rather than jumping in immediately with a spicy reaction. That never ends well! I always say never text, email or call when angry. Sit on it for a while and you'll be sure to respond differently after you've calmed down. This goes for arguments or heated conversations.

Stonewalling

One-word answers, silence, resisting eye contact, turning away and changing the subject are all examples of stonewalling. Where criticism, contempt and defensiveness are (unhelpful) forms of communicating unhappiness, stonewalling is actually a reluctance to directly communicate your thoughts or feelings at all. Maybe it is too painful to express or think about. Maybe you don't even understand what you're feeling. No matter the question, stonewalling is never the answer.

Some people use stonewalling in order to pacify themselves or the situation (as opposed to jumping headfirst into a heated argument), but that can actually exacerbate the conflict, because your partner might assume you just don't care enough about the issue to even acknowledge it. They might interpret your silence as a lack of respect or care, and may become more upset.

This is why it is important to communicate openly with your partner. Even if you don't quite know how to respond yet, telling them that is better than saying nothing at all. Saying something such as, 'I hear what you are saying and I just need some time to gather my thoughts,' is a great way to make your partner feel heard, but also understand that you need some space and time to process things. As mentioned above, save the spiciness for your Mexican food, not the important conversations with your partner.

Like it or not, conflict is going to rear its not-so-pretty little head in almost all relationships at one point or another. And, as I have mentioned, effective and honest communication is going to be the thing that will get you through it. I hope this chapter has introduced you to a few concepts and tools that will help you next time you encounter tension in any of your personal (or professional!) relationships. Remember, conflict is normal. Conflict is healthy. It's how you handle it that counts. And *that*, my friends, is the foundation of a strong relationship.

DATING

*A hot take on the big, wide, sexy, scary,
all-consuming world of dating*

BRITT

SEE ALSO: BROKEN HEARTS, GHOSTING, THE ICK, KINKS,
MANIFESTING, PENGUINS, SITUATIONSHIPS

The dating landscape has undergone some wild changes over the last few years, not least the Great Dating Disaster of the early 2020s that was one of many shitty side effects of COVID-19 coming in and tearing up our lives. But although it definitely wasn't ideal, I don't think the pandemic ended up being *all* bad in regards to dating. I for one had trouble finding a relationship in the eight to ten years DBC (Dating Before COVID), but mid-pandemic I found a beautiful love that I could have only dreamed of. I think the pandemic forced us all to take a step back and reassess what it was we really wanted and how we really felt once all the superficial aspects of our lives were taken away. Gone were the days of going out to a bar for some drinks with friends and meeting people organically. One-night stands? You're dreaming.

Luckily, app dating was still available throughout our locked-down lives – and boy, did we get busy. In March 2020, Tinder recorded 3 billion swipes in one day: its highest number ever. Meanwhile, from March to May 2020, OkCupid saw a 700 per cent increase in matches, and over on Bumble, video calls increased by

70 per cent. Bonkers. Shows you that people will stop at nothing to find love and connection.

Having unintentionally conducted some serious field research and case studies of my own, I am about to impart to you a plethora of knowledge (and some opinions) that I have accumulated firsthand during a decade of dating around the world, both pre-, mid- and post-COVID. It's also fair to say that on the podcast we dish out dating advice left, right and centre, so here I am, laying out a collection of our very best dating advice for your reading pleasure (and hopefully to help you!).

APP DATING LIKE A BOSS

Like it or not, app dating is here to stay. When done well (i.e. when you follow my advice!) app dating doesn't have to be a stress-filled needle-in-a-haystack swipefest. Read on for some firsthand advice about app dating like a boss:

♥ Be an active participant. Swipe away and don't be shy.

♥ Put effort into your profile. No one wants to date a wet cardboard box! Show your personality with a variety of photos that provide an insight into your life. Start with a photo of just yourself (so no one has to try to work out which one you are when confronted with group shot after group shot – the days of playing 'Where's Wally?' are in the past), include a full-length photo at least once and then include any other pics you think show off your hobbies and interests. No heavy filters or old photos! And don't forget to get creative when writing your 'About You' section or filling in the prompts. It is a way to show who you are AND serve them up an opening line on a platter. If you know you'd rather search the world for the best eateries as opposed to travel the world traversing mountains and hiking at sunrise, then do yourself a favour and say that, because let me tell you, no one's got time for that!

♥ Be honest about what you're looking for. Don't say you are looking for a one-night stand if you are looking for a relationship. The truth will come out sooner or later anyway. And just tell someone if you are no longer into them after one date or a few. Do not ghost them – we all know how shitty that feels.

♥ Make the first move when possible. Grab the bull by the horns and start the conversation! No one wants to waste time – plus, there is nothing worse than waiting around to see if someone is going to write to you.

♥ Say something – *anything* – more than 'Hey' to start a conversation. For me, that's an almost immediate turn-off and, honestly, it's lazy. Especially if you have put effort into your profile with great photos and conversation-starters – which you should have, because I literally just told you to, so you would expect more than just a 'Hey', am I right?! So go the extra mile and reference something in their bio so they know you have actually read it. Personalise it and make it really unique, which will help get their attention, too.

♥ Use their name the first time you write to them and comment on something they have posted about. This helps them to feel seen and separates you from the rest of the pack. I always notice when someone uses my name. Otherwise, who knows whether it's the old 'copy, paste and send out to the masses' trick?

♥ Try to move the conversation to a call, video chat or in-person meeting after a few days of talking (three is my rule of thumb). Most apps now have a video-call feature so you don't need to give your number out if you don't want to. Too much time can be wasted texting without ever really getting a true feel for who someone is or what the chemistry is actually like. I was caught out with this one too many times!

♥ Don't jump straight to a dinner date for the first date, especially if you have any hesitations. Organise a walk, or a drink, or even a lunch date, which I feel generally end up being more casual and relaxed than dinner dates are. I think a drink is a great go-to because if it's going well you can throw it out that you could find dinner somewhere and continue the date, but if you're not feeling it you don't have to be stuck there through a three-course meal. (Been there, gahhh.)

Why I ruled out dinner dates

I had been talking to a guy online for around two weeks. The banter was great! He was cute, quick-witted, messaged back straight away and didn't seem like he had anyone locked in his basement. When he asked me to dinner for our first date I thought, *Why not?* I was sure the chemistry we had online would make it a very easy and enjoyable dinner indeed.

I. Was. So. Wrong.

Within ten minutes of arriving I knew it was going to be a disaster. First, he sat right beside me instead of opposite me, just that *bit* too close for my liking, especially because he was sweating profusely. Next, he refused to talk.

Imagine my relief when the waitress finally came over and asked what we would like to drink. 'Thank god! About time! Where have you been?! I will take a bottle of your most expensive vodka and a funnel ASAP!' That was my internal monologue. In reality I just ordered a vodka. Then he ordered . . . nothing to drink. I ordered the chicken schnitzel with chips. He ordered . . . nothing to eat.

'You're not eating?' I asked. 'But you literally asked me out for dinner and a drink!'

'It's okay,' he replied. 'I'll just watch you.'

That was the point when I should have run.

Instead I was fixed to my chair, absolutely gobsmacked and uncomfortable with the whole situation. When my food came, he looked at it and told me that I would 'never eat all that'. So of course I saw that as a challenge and almost made myself sick finishing it. He stared at me the whole time, his sweaty bald head half a foot from mine, and watched me shovel into my mouth the biggest schnitzel you've ever seen. I was trying to carry the conversation entirely on my own while simultaneously stuffing my face as quickly as I could. The indigestion was worth it.

I think I was still chewing when I paid the bill (since I was the only one who'd consumed anything) and after I'd declined his offer to walk me home, he told me how much of an 'amazing connection' we had and launched himself at me for a kiss! As I ran home, I swore to myself I would *never* do dinner on a first date again.

I've only made one exception to this rule since, and that was my first date with Jordan. Which goes to show, you CAN still go with your gut and break your own rules sometimes!

DATING ETIQUETTE: WHAT TO DO AND WHAT NOT TO DO (THAT IS THE QUESTION!)

Okay, so you've made it off the apps and you're on a real-life date. Maybe you've had previous trouble getting past the first date, or feel like you've been doing something wrong but aren't sure what? Here are a few things to keep in mind:

♥ Be yourself. Because why wouldn't you? Catfishing never ends well for anyone. There is no point pretending to be anything you're not.

♥ Don't talk too much. Of course it's okay to speak a lot if it is in a give-and-take manner, just don't speak *at* your date. It is important to ask questions and listen intently because people like to feel seen and heard. So if you realise you have been talking too much about yourself, ask them a question and change the dynamic for a while.

♥ Don't be rude to staff (not that I expect you ever would be, of course!). Beyond being a bad way to treat whoever is hosting you, it will unsurprisingly give your date a bad impression of you. For me, if a date was rude to staff I would probably end the date then and there. Speaks volumes.

♥ Avoid discussing exes or anything too serious on the first date. This prospective new partner probably doesn't want to be imagining you with your ex and sure, you might be hoping to get married and raise 2.5 kids in the suburbs, but that isn't for Date Number One. Save the rest for later, once you know you're heading in the right direction in terms of what you're both looking for. Your first date should be fun, and all about getting a feel for each other's personalities!

♥ It's important to stick to your standards, but it's also important to have an open mind. Don't be too quick to judge your date if they show up wearing something you don't like or have a keen interest in something you don't.

♥ PUT YOUR PHONE AWAY. Unless you are waiting for your sister to give birth, your phone doesn't need to be in your hand. You can check it periodically (when they're in the bathroom is a good time), but be sure to give your date your full attention.

♥ Do not fight over the bill. If your date offers to pay, you can always offer to split it, but if they insist, leave it at that and thank them. It's not nice to cause a scene or end an otherwise pleasant evening with an argument. Hey, maybe you can get the second date, or even an ice cream or drink after?

♥ What about kissing and sex on the first date? We get this question all the time and honestly, there really are no rules! Do whatever feels natural and right. But what I will say here, and some people may not like it, is that I believe that if you want something more serious and long-term, it's probably not a good idea to sleep with them on the first date. Now, I can hear people saying 'I will do what I want!' and yes you should! Have sex when you want. With whomever you want. Live your best life. You shouldn't worry about the judgement of anyone else. But I think sex means more when there is a connection of sorts. And if you are looking for more than just sex, try to build a connection beforehand.

I also did my due diligence on this one. I asked a bunch of males from all age groups, walks of life and occupations for their thoughts on sleeping with someone on a first date and if and how that affects their feelings. The results are unfortunately very unfair, but I am going to share them with you anyway. Okay, so, around 75 per cent said that *of course* they would want to sleep with someone on a first date! They wouldn't say no and chances are they would try. But they were ashamed to admit that often their feelings change if they do. They said they knew it wasn't right and that it shouldn't be like that, but they couldn't help feeling like that. For them, some of the magic and the chase and excitement was taken away too soon. Some even went on to say that waiting until even just the second date would make a difference. This sucks, right?!

Do with this information what you will. Having said that, a bunch of men told me it wouldn't bother them at all and made no difference. Extremely frustrating, I know, but at the end of the day, do what feels right for you in the moment.

Relationship expert Matthew Hussey says, 'Have sex when you want. You absolutely shouldn't fear the judgement of somebody else and people shouldn't be judging you for how quickly you have sex. But be self-aware. Do you want it to mean something? If you do want it to mean something give it a minute because the experience will be greater for the moments you've shared together prior to that happening.'[4]

♥ If you enjoyed the date, I think it is always nice to send a text once you have got home. Some suggestions for you:

→ 'Hey, just got home. Thank you for tonight, I had a really great time. Hopefully we can do it again soon!'

→ 'I had a lot of fun tonight, thank you. Next time it's on me though!'

→ 'Hi, I had a great time last night. Hope you got some sleep! Have a great day today.'

If the date didn't go so well, don't worry, I have your back, too. If they haven't messaged you, I don't believe you need to message them. But chances are one of you enjoyed the date, meaning someone will be sending a text! If they text you asking to see you again but you just weren't vibing it, you can copy and paste this bad boy, which I have used many times: 'Hi, thank you so much for tonight, it was fun. You seem really great but if I am being honest I didn't really feel a connection. Take care and hey, I may see you around somewhere!'

I think it is important to start with a thank you (especially if they paid for the date) then to give them some sort of comment about how the night wasn't a total disaster. This is because they may feel embarrassed when you reject them, so this softens the blow. It's not the worst thing to finish with a casual line such as, 'Maybe see you around somewhere!' mainly because it is highly likely the people you are dating live in the same area as you, so this takes away any awkwardness if you run into them. I really am against ghosting and think people in the dating world deserve respect. Therefore, much like you would want someone to respond to you, you should respond to them.

Accidentally Unfiltered

So I went on a date with this guy in Brisbane. I'm English and this was the first Aussie guy I'd ever dated. The date was good and afterwards we went back to his place to watch a movie. After watching the ENTIRE movie (wtf!) he finally made a move and we went to his room. We were getting down to business and I asked, 'Wait, do you have a condom?' He said, 'Yeah, um . . . somewhere in the room . . .' and I said, 'Oh, it's okay, I have one in my bag. Here, I'll grab it.' So I grabbed one and passed it to him. He ripped it open and was like, 'WHAT is this?' I said, 'What? It's a condom?!' He said, 'No, it's a fucking teabag!' Hahaha, it was one of those Twinings teabags that comes in a little packet. We were dying. He was like, 'This is the most English thing that could have happened.' I still had that lemon and ginger tea for breakfast!

DEALING WITH DATING FATIGUE

Looking for a significant other is time-consuming and it can be tiring. Exhausting. Soul-crushing. I've been there! Eventually you want to give up because you just *cannot* anymore. This is normal – and there are some tricks for getting past this dating slump:

♥ Take a break. The world is not going to come crashing down if you put your swiping on hold for a little while – in fact, your thumbs will probably thank you for it! (RSI is real, people.) Try not to think about dating for a bit and just enjoy your life. Be with family and friends, have fun and don't put so much pressure on yourself.

♥ Be more selective about who you are dating. Start to limit your dating pool to people you actually think you have a connection with instead of lining up someone different every night and hoping one of them works out. And maybe take your radius down from 100 million kilometres to your local area to help ease the overwhelm.

♥ Don't take it personally! They aren't all going to be The One. Remember that someone else's behaviour has very little to do with you as a person but who *they* are as a person.

♥ Try to be positive about your dates, even the bad ones. At a minimum, they teach us about what we do and don't want, and give us stories to tell our friends.

♥ Don't travel far for your first date or you'll be over it before you get there.

♥ Don't overthink things and don't play games. Who has the time and energy for that? If you want to send a text, send it! If you don't want to see someone again, don't pretend to. Just be honest.

DATING IN A LONG-TERM RELATIONSHIP

So, you've made it past the early unknown days of dating and you're now in a committed long-term relationship. Guess what? You still need to date! You should never stop trying to woo your partner and keep the love alive. It is so easy to fall into a nightly routine of PJs and Netflix rather than getting dressed up and going out, but putting in effort and showing you care is a huge part of maintaining healthy and loving relationships. My tips for you:

♥ Check in with each other every day. You might talk a lot throughout the day, but take the time to sit down together and really ask how each other is doing. It shows you care and helps to continue to develop a deeper connection. You could turn this check-in into a daily routine (over breakfast, while walking the dog after work, etc.) or you can keep things a little looser – just as long as you do it regularly!

♥ Plan a date night, maybe once a week or once a fortnight, where you do something fun together. You could try a new activity or restaurant – something for the two of you to enjoy so you can continue to make memories.

♥ Be spontaneous! Maybe that is a surprise sexy date at home or a night away. Spontaneity helps keep the spark alive.

♥ Try something different in the bedroom. There are plenty of books to give you inspiration, as well as apps full of great sex ideas that you can use with your partner too!

Whew! That's a lot of information, but I hope by now you're feeling ready to handle the magical and sometimes maddening world of dating. And, best of all, I have saved my most important tip for last: HAVE FUN!

Dating can open up your world and lead to all sorts of new opportunities, perspectives and connections – romantic or otherwise. And, armed with all the pearls of wisdom in this chapter, you're in a prime position to get out there and go for it. So what are you waiting for?

Accidentally Unfiltered

My night was going so well. I had a Cinderella moment and met this gorgeous guy at a ball and decided to take him back to my place. Things were going smoothly and we took ourselves to the bedroom. I had some pretty hectic Spanx on under my dress, so left him sitting on my bed while I went to the bathroom to take them off. I came back to see him staring across at my desk. It was at this moment that I realised that my new strategy to get organised had been a little too effective – glaring back at him on the opposite wall in bright, highlighted colours was an A3-sized schedule detailing the bowel prep I had to do for an upcoming colonoscopy with the multiple boxes of laxatives stacked underneath it on my desk.

The shocked face said it all. Needless to say, I did not get laid that night.

EMOTIONAL CHEATING

It can be just as destructive as physical cheating, but harder to define

BRITT AND LAURA

SEE ALSO: BOUNDARIES, BROKEN HEARTS, GASLIGHTING, JEALOUSY, RED FLAGS, WORTHINESS

LAURA: Ahhh, the age-old question – what's worse, physical cheating or emotional cheating? I've always struggled to answer this question, because when it comes to infidelity it's hard to pick a 'worse' option. It's kind of like asking someone to choose between a poo burrito or a poo pie: no matter how you serve it up, they're both shit. Whenever someone cheats, the circumstances are unique, however the hurt and pain that is caused by infidelity – of any kind – is cutting and universal.

Physical cheating is usually easier to spot, but emotional cheating is typically when a partner gives another person outside the relationship their heart, their intimate thoughts, their deepest darkest secrets, their affection, attention, appreciation and time. They may even fantasise about that person sexually, but the thing about emotional cheating is that they don't cross the line into the physical – the desire is certainly there, but it is not acted upon.

What constitutes emotional cheating will be different in every relationship – and it's important to note that it isn't limited to monogamous relationships.

BRITT: I remember when we interviewed comedian Bianka Ismailovski about her open relationship we touched on emotional cheating, and she told us it was something that she has to consider in her polyamorous relationship. It can totally occur in non-monogamous relationships if you keep the intimacy you're developing with someone else a secret from your partner, or if you cross other boundaries that you've agreed on.

L: I know I said I don't really like the question, but for the sake of unpacking the unique betrayal that comes with emotional cheating . . . Britt, which do *you* think is worse?

B: In short – and this is just my opinion as someone who has been cheated on in every capacity possible – for me, emotional cheating is worse. It cuts deep. It leaves a trail of trust issues so profound they'll have you obsessing over your partner's phone, emails, why they were half an hour late getting home from work, to the point where you're consumed by thoughts such as, *Why have they been in the bathroom so long? Surely they aren't still pooping? Are they in there texting someone else?!*

Discovering that my partner had a deep connection with someone else, that he was giving them his thoughts and fantasies, imagining a life with them, imagining sex with them, thinking about them while he was with me, and sharing his secrets, worries, stresses, hopes and dreams with them – fuck, that shit hurts. I would genuinely rather he'd slipped up once physically with someone that he couldn't care less about and regretted it.

I'm not saying that cheating in any capacity is okay, because it isn't, and if it is happening there is something fundamentally wrong. But if I HAD to choose between the two, I think I would choose the one-night stand. I know I am not alone here!

L: Nope, you're not alone – even science backs you up! There have been studies done on this that show that men and women see different types of infidelity differently. Women tend to categorise emotional cheating as more serious, while men tend to be more upset by sexual infidelity.

A recent study in the *Sexual and Relationship Therapy* journal claims that this is because emotional infidelity can 'signal that a mate will either abandon the relationship or divert resources to a rival'.[5] Emotional fidelity basically equates to security and survival of our offspring.

So, if you asked the question, 'Would you rather your partner fall in love with another person but not sleep with them, or sleep with another person but not fall in love with them?' it's likely that most women would choose the second option. That's because we value emotional connections so highly.

B: I feel better knowing that checks out on a scientific level! It's good to know I'm not alone.

Talking of how we perceive things differently, I think one of the hardest things about emotional cheating is that it's subjective – what might constitute emotional cheating to one person can look quite different from what it means to someone else. For example, if my partner was frequently texting another woman, it would make me uncomfortable (unless of course it was someone such as a child-hood best friend, or someone else he'd been friends with for ages). For someone else, that might not really be an issue. Where do we draw that line? I think it's an individual thing.

Ultimately, if your partner is hiding something from you (and it's not secret plans for a proposal or another kind of special surprise) something is up. If either of you feels the need to conceal your conversations with someone outside the relationship, you need to ask why.

What's your position on that, Laura? When does a friendship cross the line into emotional cheating?

L: I am a staunch believer that men and women can be grown freaking adults and have wonderful, fulfilling platonic friendships, even when they are in committed monogamous relationships. One of my besties is a guy – we have travelled overseas together, got wildly drunk together and had movie marathons together, and it has never crossed my mind to be intimate with him. Having friends of the opposite sex does not automatically mean that you're going to end up developing feelings for them.

However, if your friend is someone you're sexually attracted to or have intense chemistry with, well ... that's a different story (as I know from my own experience, you're kidding yourself if you think you aren't playing with fire).

Generally, emotional cheating can happen without premeditation, and usually starts when there are poor boundaries in place. It is when people start to blur the line of emotional intimacy – sharing information that should only be discussed with their partner, for example – that trouble begins.

When there is chemistry bubbling away and then emotional boundaries are crossed, emotional cheating can start to occur. Two friends may start sharing more and more personal and intimate details with each other, and before one of them knows it, a deeper attraction has developed. It's not surprising that often emotional cheating turns into physical cheating, because as the closeness develops, so does the temptation. IT'S A GATEWAY DRUG! Jokes ... but also, seriously!

B: I remember many moons ago I had a partner who struck up an online 'friendship' with a girl he met on Facebook. I stumbled across their messages when he had left his account logged in on my computer. I will never forget the feeling of seeing that conversation on the screen: the laughing, the flirting, the connection. The way they seemed so familiar with each other. I felt so sick.

When I confronted him, he was a little sheepish, but he also didn't think he had done anything especially wrong. He said he had never met and never planned on meeting her, their chats were just something to pass the time. He enjoyed talking to her.

I asked him why he was spending so much time talking to a stranger and he told me it was because he felt neglected by me. I was always too busy with work, he said, and didn't give him enough attention. He said it in a way that didn't blame me; it was more just honesty. And while I don't think that excused what he did, I'll admit he was right – I hadn't been giving him much of my attention. We had a very candid chat following that: he understood he should have come to me and been open about his feelings instead of turning elsewhere, and I recognised I should have put more energy into my relationship. But I will never forget the sick feeling in the pit of my stomach when I realised that he'd turned to someone else with his feelings.

My next relationship was an absolute shit fight, filled with cheating left, right and centre. Emotionally, physically, mentally, spiritually . . . ways I didn't even think were possible. It was painful to find out the person I loved was a narcissistic, cheating, toxic stranger with a double life. It took me a long time to get over that.

But, interestingly, when I found out about the sheer number of women he had physically cheated on me with, it sort of hurt less. It was such an absurdly large amount that it was instantly clear to me that the issue was with him – and not a reflection of me. In a way it didn't even touch the sides in comparison to the pain I'd felt from my previous loving partner who had struck up this one long-distance emotional connection. They both hurt, but in very different ways. And I think that ties back in to what I was saying before about the different ways that emotional versus physical cheating can affect you.

L: Britt, I am in no way attempting to defend your ex – he's really in a league of his own in terms of bad behaviour – but I am going to put my hand up and say I've been on both sides of the cheating coin: I've been cheated on and I've been the cheater. Now, before y'all run out and grab your pitchforks, I've grown as a person and I understand the hurt I inflicted. I will obviously never do it again. But at the time I felt unloved and insecure in my relationship. Not a hall pass for bad behaviour, I know, but I was in my early twenties and was as reckless with other people's hearts as they were with mine.

Shortly after I had moved to a new city to be with my then boyfriend, things turned rocky. I hadn't really made any friends in the town and he was always too busy studying or playing music to spend time with me. I felt like a burden to him.

So when I started a new job in the local bar and became really close with a guy my age, I thought it was a good thing I had someone to spend time with. We hit it off and became the best of mates, always cracking jokes and staying back late to have a drink. As the weeks went on and we became closer, I started to develop feelings for him. There had always been chemistry there, but I was in absolute denial and didn't want to acknowledge that the friendship was anything deeper. I would confide in him that my relationship wasn't in a good place and he would listen, telling me I deserved better.

Looking back now, it's comical how it unfolded in such a clichéd way, but I started to form real feelings and so did he. Eventually, things progressed to a point where I genuinely thought I was in love with two people: my boyfriend, who was suspicious AF of my new friend; and my friend, who by this stage had confessed his love for me. It was a monumental train wreck.

The thing is, once you're in a love triangle that's been marred by emotional cheating there is no clean way to exit the situation. Someone always ends up hurt and broken, and often it's all three of you. I eventually cut ties with my 'friend' and tried to repair my relationship, but we never recovered from it. I broke my partner's trust, and in some messed-up way I had justified the whole thing because a) it was never physical and b) I felt unappreciated at home.

The real red flag early on that things were going down a slippery slope of emotional cheating was how I was using my phone. We all know that the way someone deals with their phone can be a telltale sign of fishy behaviour, especially when their phone habits change unexpectedly. Maybe they've all of a sudden started taking their phone everywhere they go and never leave it unattended, or they always put it face-down at dinner, or won't answer certain calls around you. I knew things had started to shift in my friendship with the other guy when I would tilt my phone away from my boyfriend so he couldn't see who I was texting. At that point I should have pumped the brakes – the signs were there! – but instead I learned the lessons the hard way.

Here's a test:

Would you feel comfortable with your partner reading over a conversation you had with a friend? (With your permission, of course! They shouldn't be doing it on the sly.)

If you can confidently answer 'Yes', then things are cool beans.

If the thought of your partner reading your conversation makes you feel a bit anxious, or like you need to quickly flick through and delete a few things ... you might want to take a closer look at that friendship.

B: OMG, yes, phones! And not just texting and calls – there are other, more subtle ways that emotional cheating can start to manifest, like something we've covered in the podcast called micro-cheating.

It's not as severe as full-blown emotional cheating but it's the name given to the grey area of small acts that add up to be problematic, such as liking the same girl's bikini photos on Instagram. Things that don't seem like a big deal as a one-off, but when they add up they demonstrate a pattern of behaviour that is . . . not quite right.

Social media makes it so insanely easy to flirt and show interest: to like a photo, drop a few flame emojis, see who is viewing your stories, send Snapchats . . . the list goes on. It also offers the opportunity to look up and rekindle 'missed connections' – an ex, a college crush, a casual fling. These things are now within such close reach that it's only fidelity, willpower or lack of curiosity that holds someone back from fulfilling that urge. As a result, social media can add a new dimension to emotional cheating because the contact is so accessible and seamless, and cheating can happen entirely online, like it did with my ex on Facebook.

L: In that case, Britt, what's your position on whether or not people should stay connected to their exes on social media?

B: I think it depends on the situation and the relationship you have. There have been some exes who I have blocked and deleted immediately. Then there have been others I still follow on socials and am still in contact with, and I would help them out if they ever needed anything.

Of course, there needs to be a level of respect when you start dating someone new. And if you've been keeping an ex-flame on the bench, then you need to add some distance. I don't believe you can stay best friends with an ex and have no feelings attached at all, and it can be hard to move forward in life and love when you're still holding onto what is behind you.

L: I used to think that I could be friends with my exes, but when I look back on the relationships where we were supposedly just 'friends' –

I was kidding myself. There was always a deeper level of attachment than that of a platonic friend, so I fully agree, Britt. That isn't to say that it's the same for everyone – there are loads of people who have great friendships with their exes. But I'm no longer close to any of my exes and life is a lot more carefree and drama-free because of it.

Let's get into what to do if you find out you've been cheated on – because it fucking sucks. The first phase of discovering that your partner has cheated on you emotionally (or physically) is total chaos. Feelings of betrayal and hurt flood in thick and fast and it's a full-on, angry overload. There is often rage and disbelief that the person you love could ever do this to you, but also confusion and sadness that your world isn't what you perceived it to be.

Once the burning fury and hurt dull slightly, it creates space to analyse not just the impact of the hurt, but also the motive. The why. Sometimes there is no reason, and people just do shitty things in relationships, but in other instances there can be vulnerabilities that weren't uncovered. Maybe there was a disconnect, a feeling of rejection, a lack of sex or physicality. Not that any of this excuses the betrayal, but seeking perspective around the why can be deeply healing if you decide you want to work through emotional cheating. As psychotherapist Terri Cole mentioned when we had her on the podcast, we love to think of the cheater as a terrible villain:

'We see things as black and white, that if there was cheating in a relationship it must mean that there was no love there at all – but that's just not the truth. Relationships are messy, and often people step out of their relationships because there is a need that is not being met.'[6]

This is certainly not to say that the person who has been cheated on is to blame, or that they should harbour any of the guilt – ultimately, the person who cheated broke that bond and betrayed the trust of the relationship – but it's important to look at it from a 360-degree perspective if you want to come back from it. For some people, cheating is a cold, hard deal-breaker, yet other couples can come back stronger than ever. But it takes work.

B: I'm a big believer that cheating doesn't always have to mean a break-up. For couples whose relationship is already dying, it's a way of gaining an exit; however, in some instances, affairs can remake a relationship. It sounds crazy, but couples can – as you said, Laura – emerge stronger and more deeply connected from this kind of thing. But ultimately, something has to change. Did you uncover the reason why there was cheating? Did you go to therapy? Did you fix your intimacy issues? What work did you do on the relationship so that history doesn't repeat itself? Promises can be broken – but actions and behaviour can show real change.

Gaslighting can be a common theme when emotional cheating takes place, especially because 'nothing physical even happened!'.

Be aware of this, know your boundaries and know your worth.

L: Yes, I totally agree. Infidelity, whether emotional or physical, can be a catalyst for you to really examine your relationship – the wrongdoings, the disconnect. Who do we want to be? What haven't we talked about? What other needs haven't been met? What other secrets have we been carrying? What do we do with our sexual stalemate? What do we do about our lack of connection? All these things can redefine the relationship. Although it can be possible, it is not easy to come back from infidelity, and for a lot of people the betrayal and the lack of trust it can bring into a relationship is too great to overcome – and that is okay. No one should ever stay in a relationship where they feel insecure, on high alert or anxious because cheating has ripped away the foundation of trust in that relationship. Having the resolve to walk away from a relationship takes a lot of resolve and self-love. Ultimately, only you know what you can and can't come back from.

FERTILITY

A short story about self-empowerment

BRITT

SEE ALSO: PREGNANCY LOSS, TIMELINES

When I was a little girl, I couldn't wait to grow up. I often thought about the future with excitement. I would imagine how my life would look: where I would be, who I would be with, what my children would look like. I knew I would travel as soon as I finished school; the burning desire to see the world was always inside me. Then I was supposed to get married to the man of my dreams, who would obviously be tall, dark, handsome and ridiculously funny. He would love me fiercely and together we'd have a house by the beach, great jobs, a bunch of beautiful, overachieving kids and a multitude of dogs.

What I didn't imagine was being thirty-three, childless and possibly the most single person in Australia after being very publicly dumped on *The Bachelor*, despite my best efforts to reach happily ever after as the last woman standing. Oh, and did I mention I had been flying solo for the best part of a decade by this stage?

So there I was: fast approaching my mid-thirties with not a husband, house, dog or child in sight. What a rude shock! Everyone around me was getting engaged and married, falling pregnant, buying houses and having babies, and I was just trying to work out what I would have for dinner. I'd always been one for running my own race, to be honest: while my friends were booking wedding venues I was booking a one-way ticket to Brazil, and while others were taking career breaks to have babies I was completely changing my career after ten years in healthcare to enrol in acting school and jump into the entertainment industry. I've always been somewhat unconventional.

As a single woman in my thirties, I was constantly asked 'Have you met anyone yet?' and 'When are you going to settle down?' These questions might have been well-intentioned, but as someone who's been on the receiving end of them for many, *many* years I can tell you: the pressure behind those questions is real, and it sucks. And it's particularly bad for women because we are constantly reminded that we have a body clock that is 'ticking away'.

It took a lot of soul-searching but I finally accepted the fact that my life just didn't look like the lives of a lot of other women I knew, or like what society expected of me. 'Settling down', whatever that means, was probably not going to happen in the near future, which meant it was time to make some big decisions.

I was not in a position to have a child. I was single, deep in my career and I knew that I didn't want to go down the track of having a baby alone. It's a personal thing but I just didn't have the desire to do that. I've never really felt that strong pull to have a baby like many women do; I love kids, and I think I see them in my future, but I don't know how or when. I believe I will just know when the time is right, but at this point in my life, I love my own space and time, my work and travel (or the post-COVID promise of it) too much to start a family.

But what I did want to be sure of was that when the time came I'd have the choice, that my biological clock wouldn't have taken that away from me. I wanted my future self to be empowered and have the option to create the life she wanted on her own timeline – not the one prescribed by society.

And that, dear reader, was how I decided that I needed to take control of my future and put my eggs on ice.

But how the hell do you go about actually doing that? And did I even have any left to freeze?

♥

Once I had decided to freeze my future babies, I needed to find out how many – if any – of my viable eggs were available to put in the deep freeze, so I took myself to my GP to have some tests. I started with an AMH blood test, which gave me an idea of my ovarian reserve, as well as an ultrasound, to have a general stickybeak around the old reproductive system to see if anything had gone rogue (i.e. they checked for endometriosis, polycystic ovarian syndrome or anything that wasn't supposed to be there). They also got up close and personal with my follicles, and I mean UP CLOSE and PERSONAL, to count them and get a really good look at those bad boys.

When I was booking the appointment for the ultrasound on the phone, they asked me, 'Who are you bringing as your support person? A partner or a friend?'

Support person?! What is this mythical person you speak of? I replied that I would be coming alone and that that was A-OK.

But then the universe interfered and my car broke down the night before my appointment. Of course it did! And bless my friend Renae, who asked me if I needed a lift anywhere while my car was being fixed. I hadn't told her – or anyone, really – about my appointment but when I did, she offered to drive me and also come in with me. She sat there as the probe was waaay up inside me, giggling about how the sonographer caught a glimpse of our matching screensavers on our phones, which was a picture of the two of us in front of a sunset, and 'gave us a moment' at the end. She thought Renae and I were a couple! We laughed at the misunderstanding and I realised how grateful I was that she was there with me.

I had a pretty big revelation while going through this initial testing experience. It was far more emotional than I could have imagined, for a reason I hadn't expected. To get an accurate fertility reading, ideally you should be off the contraceptive pill. Though you can have bloodwork taken while on the Pill, there is a chance you could get a false negative fertility reading because the Pill can suppress your count. So I guess what I am saying is, don't necessarily be too put off by your test results if they were lower than you had hoped and you were on the Pill, because maybe you will receive a different result once you are off the Pill!

Armed with this knowledge, and having temporarily given up on dating, I decided to stop taking the Pill, have my blood tests and let my body prepare for the big freeze.

At this point I had been on the Pill for eighteen years, which was more than half my life. I had been doing my own thing for a decade; travelling, moving cities, starting businesses and living alone. I was fiercely independent and hadn't 'needed' anyone for as long as I could remember. Nothing bothered me. Nothing really made me that upset. To be honest, I didn't really *feel* a whole lot. Someone on the *Bachelor* production team had even called me 'emotionally void' – apparently I wasn't great for the show because I didn't show enough emotion or break down enough. How lovely.

About two weeks after coming off the Pill, I was walking down the street with my sister Sheri when she started telling me about this great movie she had just watched about a dog. She pulled up the trailer on her phone for me to watch and it was there, in the middle of Bondi, that I burst into tears over a one-minute trailer and realised that in fact I wasn't an emotionally void sociopath! Hooray!

The tears didn't stop there. I wept every day for the next month while my hormones tried to get back on track. When you think about it, my hormones had been locked up in isolation for eighteen years, so it makes sense that once they were released back into the wild they didn't know which way was up! I cried from being happy, from being sad, from patting a cute dog at the beach and for no reason at all. Then, once I got those wild emotions somewhat under control, my hair started to fall out. I lost quite a bit – but it was temporary, and my friends who had also come off the Pill had warned me about that part, so at least I was armed and ready with a hair extension appointment.

This was all part of the process of coming off the Pill. I know everyone will experience that process differently, and for me it wasn't as hard to navigate as it can be for others, but I was relieved to discover it does pass and you do regulate again and go back to normal.

HOW MANY EGGS WOULD YOU LIKE TODAY, MA'AM?

Laura and I did an extensive amount of research on fertility clinics before releasing our egg-freezing episode on the podcast,[7] and Genea was the clinic we decided to feature because we were really impressed by their team, equipment and technology. Dr Cheryl Phua is an amazing doctor and I trusted her wholeheartedly, to the point where, after our podcast interview with her, I decided egg freezing was for me. So I set the wheels in motion.

When I found myself sitting alone in front of Dr Phua I wasn't feeling overly worried. I have lived a very healthy life: I've exercised daily since I was a child, I've never smoked or taken drugs, I eat well, have no other health problems and, let's be real, I was only thirty-three. Plenty of fuel left in the tank!

So I was stunned when Dr Phua informed me that basically from next year on, any pregnancy I might have would be classified as geriatric, and in terms of even getting to that point, things were not exactly looking great for me. Let's just say I wouldn't be leaving the local farmers' market with a dozen eggs.

She told me that, with my test results combined with my age, I had around a 15 to 20 per cent chance of falling pregnant naturally. If I was lucky I might get eight eggs, of which a few usually aren't viable, and not all of *those* would necessarily make the journey of being frozen and thawed.

Mind. Blown.

This was not how I'd imagined this conversation going. Even though Dr Phua was very encouraging and supportive, all I heard was '15 per cent'. I left feeling completely deflated and I cried all the way home. I had already felt unlovable after years of failed dates and relationships, plus the whole being-dumped-on-national-television thing and now, as I sat in the Uber, feeling more alone than ever, I had this overwhelming thought that it looked like love and kids were simply not for me. Even though I took the Pill for years, that was a hard pill to swallow.

Looking back on that moment through the wonderful lens of hindsight, I can see that it was an unreasonable train of thought. As humans, we tend to hold on to even the smallest trace of negativity and dwell on that – for example, all I heard was 'You ONLY have a 15 per cent chance' instead of, 'You HAVE around a 15 to 20 per cent chance'. It is about perception, isn't it? But at the time, I believed I would be alone forever. I felt as if the universe didn't want this for me, as if maybe at one point in my life I had done the wrong thing and this was my punishment. There are lots of people who don't have any chance at all. Fertility is unfortunately not a given, as some people know all too well. It is something we shouldn't take for granted and my heart goes out to those that may be going through this as we speak, preparing to go down that road, and those that have gone through it in the past. For me there actually were a lot of options; I just couldn't see through the cloud of disappointment or shake the feeling that I had somehow failed. I can only imagine how many women feel that sense of failure – but it is not you; you have not failed. Some things are beyond our comprehension and control.

HARVEST TIME

Around four months passed between my initial testing and actually starting the process. By that time I had met and fallen in love with Jordan and, as he only had about ten weeks before leaving to travel the world to play tennis, I wanted to make the most of that precious time with him. It was early days and we just wanted to enjoy each other before he left. Dr Phua assured me it would not be an issue for me to wait a few more weeks.

So we savoured those weeks, then Jordan set off to America, and the time came to flood my body with the copious amounts of hormones that would give me the best possible chance of putting my eggs safely on ice. I don't think I really understood beforehand how time-specific the whole thing was going to be – they prepped me for it during my consultation, of course, but I was still surprised at how demanding the process proved to be. For a period of about two weeks it's like you belong to your eggs and your hormones because you have to inject your specified level of hormones every day at the same time, in the same place on your body. After three days of giving myself only one injection, my specialists advised me to up that to two in order to effectively introduce the hormones into my body.

Now, this is where it could have got tricky. I live alone so I didn't have anyone to rely on to inject me. I am lucky that I worked in a hospital for more than ten years and cannulating other people was part of the job, so for me, this was probably the easiest part – I just grabbed the fatty part of my lower tummy and threw it straight in there! But for others I know this is not as easy, which is why I think it is important to make sure someone is available to inject you every day if you can't make yourself do it.

It started out fine enough. Besides an excruciating hormonal headache on day two, the first four days were great. In fact, up until about the halfway point on day seven, I actually asked the clinic if I was injecting correctly because I just wasn't feeling anything and I was starting to worry. I didn't feel the bloat or the pain, and my hormones felt okay. But then the second week came and I started to swell and cry. A formidable combination indeed!

Those surging hormones were what I found the hardest. If I had to describe how it felt, I would say it is like having your period, but when it's really pissed off, and then add in some steroids and an IBS reaction and you're sorta in the ballpark. Jordan really copped it over those three weeks. We already had the long-distance stress without the extra hormones that seemed to be totally taking over my body.

If a dog walked past the window I would cry. If a sad ad played on TV I would cry. If a series ended I would cry. If I couldn't speak to Jordan I would cry. If I ate too much ice cream I would cry. As someone who'd historically buried their feelings, it was probably a good thing!

Every two days, sometimes every day, I had to go in to the clinic for blood tests and internal ultrasounds. This is super import-ant to monitor the hormone levels and follicle growth. The tears and excessive ice cream consumption suggested that my hormone levels were probably where they needed to be but my silly little folli-cles weren't responding that well – some not at all. I had to increase my injections again for a few days at the end to give them a little boost and by the day of collection I could barely walk. Honestly, every step was so painful. The car ride to the clinic was horribly uncomfortable; every bump or corner was agony. I slowly waddled into the clinic, bent over and holding my belly carefully as if I was protecting those little eggs until the last moment, giving them every chance I could to survive!

Mercifully, the collection itself was very quick and easy. I was put under and it took about half an hour, apparently. I woke up, still high on the anaesthetic and hoping beyond hope that eight of my little mini-mes had been put on ice. I was ecstatic to hear that in fact fifteen were! That was beyond what I could have hoped for! Obviously this gives me more options when and if the time comes. And it means, for me, that very fortunately I won't have to do that process again.

THE MAGIC OF OPTIONS

It took a few weeks of commitment to my body and my future but it meant that I had secured the option of having kids in the future. A weight was immediately lifted off my shoulders and I didn't feel the same level of stress and pressure that I felt before. The anxiety around not knowing how fertile I was, of not knowing if I would meet anyone, of worrying about what I should do . . . I don't think I really noticed how much I'd been ruminating on those things until I no longer felt them as intensely.

More than anything, I was thankful to be in a position in life where I could afford to do it, which I know is a huge privilege. It was a choice I thought long and hard about; a considered decision.

I know that freezing my eggs is not a guarantee or a bulletproof insurance policy, because pregnancy from egg freezing isn't guaranteed to work, but now I have options, and a better chance if and when the time comes to try for kids. And for that, I am grateful.

G

GASLIGHTING

Am I fucking crazy? Or am I being gaslighted?

BRITT

SEE ALSO: EMOTIONAL CHEATING, JEALOUSY, NARCISSISM, RED FLAGS

Has anyone ever told you, 'You're overreacting' or 'You're insane'? And, in response, have you ever thought to yourself, *Am I going crazy? Am I imagining this?* It could be that you were being gaslighted.

You've probably heard the term 'gaslighting' before, as it has become widely used over the past few years. It describes a type of narcissistic behaviour that has been happening for a long time but just never had a dedicated name until relatively recently.

So, what is gaslighting and where did it come from? Gaslighting is the act of manipulating a person by making them question their thoughts, memories and the events occurring around them. The concept and the name were first coined in 1938 in a play called *Gas Light* written by British playwright Patrick Hamilton, which was adapted into critically acclaimed movies in the UK and US several years later. The *Guardian* describes it as 'the play that defined toxic masculinity' and it still appears on stages around the world today, as a result of its ongoing cultural relevance.

The premise of the play is that the oppressive husband, Jack, manipulates his anxious wife, Bella, into thinking she is going crazy by acting in ways to make her question and doubt her reality. Most notably, he causes the gaslights in their house to dim and insists that she is imagining it – that the gaslights are as bright as they have ever been – in an effort to slowly drive her insane. He does this so that he can steal from her.

If you have ever experienced behaviour like this – deliberate attempts to undermine your perception of reality – you will know how bad it feels and how confusing and upsetting it can be. I was on the receiving end of it for years and it was horrible, belittling and, frankly, fucked.

But perhaps one of the worst parts about gaslighting is that when the perpetrator is really good at it, we on the receiving end don't know it's being done at all. If a gaslighter is ever questioned or called out for their behaviour, they are scarily good at deflecting blame. They might dismiss concerns with tender or compassionate words such as, 'I would never say anything to hurt you. You know that, right? I love you so much.' This might be exactly the type of reassurance you're looking for, but it isn't genuine – especially if the same behaviour goes on to be repeated.

HOW DO YOU KNOW YOU ARE BEING GASLIGHTED?

According to Healthline.com, here are some signs to look out for:

- ♥ You are constantly second-guessing yourself or asking yourself 'Am I crazy?'
- ♥ You're always apologising, even when you aren't in the wrong.
- ♥ You may be arguing a lot with your partner over not much at all.
- ♥ You notice that your partner's actions, or those of their family members, do not match their words.
- ♥ Your friends always seem to be telling you they don't trust your partner, or that what your partner is saying doesn't sound right.

♥ You often make excuses for your partner's behaviour, almost like you're embarrassed about it.

♥ You start to withhold information from friends and family in order to avoid making those same excuses for your partner – again – because you know that something isn't right and you know they will have a go at you. Worse, you start outright lying to the people you love.

♥ You find yourself giving in, compromising and doing things you don't want to do.

♥ You are incredibly sad and know that you ought to feel happier than you do.

♥ You used to feel like a different person but now you feel like a lesser, unhappier version of yourself.

♥ You always feel as though nothing you do is right.[8]

Now, if you are experiencing some of these, it does not necessarily mean you are being gaslighted – maybe you are unhappy for other reasons or maybe you have other stresses going on in your life. But in case you are being victimised in this way, it is important to be aware of the signs.

Common techniques used by gaslighters include:

♥ **Countering:** Questioning your memory by denying that events occurred in the way that you remember them. They will also lie about what actually happened. 'I have no idea what you are talking about. I have literally never said that in my life.'

♥ **Trivialising:** Telling you that you're overreacting to upsetting behaviour. This can make you believe your emotions are misplaced or overwrought. 'You're being so ridiculous and you are always so emotional. No one else I know is this emotional. Everyone says the same thing about you, too.'

- ♥ **Withholding:** Refusing to acknowledge or understand concerns. 'You're not making any sense and I don't have time to listen to this shit anyway.'
- ♥ **Blocking/diversion:** Changing the subject to draw your attention away from what you were trying to say. 'You've been talking to your sister again, haven't you? She's always putting stupid ideas in your head.'
- ♥ **Flattery:** After an argument, they may praise or compliment you. This is to leave you thinking, 'Well, maybe they aren't so bad . . . Maybe I *am* overreacting.'[9]

If you are unsure, re-read the lists above and put a tick next to the signs and techniques you think are true to you and your relationship. Sometimes it is easier to see things when they are down on paper and staring you in the face.

I remember I once found women's clothing at my ex-boyfriend's house – not hiding anywhere, or thrown under the bed or anything, but blatantly hanging up in a cupboard, in plain sight. I immediately asked him who the hell it belonged to. He very calmly told me it was his ex-girlfriend's (spoiler alert: she wasn't an ex). When I said that was ridiculous and I had never seen the clothes hanging there before, he told me I was crazy. 'Brittany, it has literally always been there. I need to send it back to her but I just can't be bothered and I'm too nice to throw it away.' What a fucking lolcano that was.

But he ended up convincing me that he was right and I was just super unobservant. It seems crazy now when I write it down, but at the time there were so many little moments like that where he would just chip away at me. Eventually, convincing me of these ridiculous tales became really easy.

There were other red flags that should have jumped out at me, too – like how my friends and family, specifically my sister Sheri, were always saying things like 'That doesn't seem right, Britt' or 'That doesn't make sense' or 'That is not normal behaviour'. But I would always make excuses for him. Eventually I just started lying or omitting the truth. I didn't want to face the truth. I didn't want people in my life to hate him and I was tired of having the same conversations about him. To be honest, the whole thing from every angle was exhausting.

WHAT TO DO IF YOU BELIEVE YOU'RE BEING GASLIGHTED

Above all, you need to trust yourself. That means believing in yourself, your feelings, your memories and what you know to be true. Own your perception – what you remember, what you felt, what you experienced. Use phrases such as 'Don't tell me I'm lying, I know what I saw' or 'Don't put words in my mouth' or 'Don't tell me how to feel; this is how I feel'.

If you feel like you are being gaslighted, leave the conversation. You can come back to it if need be, but it is important to remove yourself early on. The aim of the gaslighter is to convince you that your perception and memory isn't real, so exit the situation before that can happen.

Write things down. Keep a diary. If you feel like the undermining and manipulation is starting to become a trend, get in the habit of jotting your feelings down, even if it isn't in extreme detail. This way you always have something to refer back to so you can confirm the chain of events, what was said and how you felt at the time. This way there can be no discrepancy.

Consider leaving the relationship entirely. It's never an easy option, but is certainly important to think about. It's also so important to seek help and/or advice from a professional. We've listed a few resources at the back of the book, which could be a good place to start.

Avoid blaming yourself – this is not about you, and you don't deserve to be treated in this way. And while it's not super common, you are not the only person to experience it – you are not alone.

Finally, make sure you have a great support system around you. You need people to lean on and talk to about it, to reassure you that you aren't in fact crazy. Part of gaslighting is breaking down your connection with others and decreasing your world outside your relationship, because you are easier to control and manipulate this way. So don't let these other important relationships suffer. You will need them sometime very soon.

GHOSTING

They're not busy, you're just being ghosted

LAURA

SEE ALSO: ATTACHMENT THEORY,
CONFLICT RESOLUTION, DATING, SITUATIONSHIPS

One dating term that we're all too familiar with – whether you've been on the receiving end or played a bit of Casper yourself (guilty!) – is ghosting. You know: making the statement that you no longer want to be with someone by saying nothing at all, cutting off all communication and leaving the poor bugger reeling from what the hell just happened. *Did I get dumped? Are they just busy? Or are they lying in a ditch somewhere?*

The concept of ghosting is not a new phenomenon. I remember my nana telling me a story about one of her friends, Olga, who was married to a man named Richard. They had three kids and led a happy life together. One morning, Richard made love to Olga, ate breakfast, kissed the kids goodbye, backed the car down the driveway and Olga never heard from him again. Turns out, dirty Rich drove all the way to Perth with his assistant to start a new family.

This is a pretty extreme example of ghosting, but all the same, I used to remind myself of this story whenever a guy I was mildly interested in stopped replying. And with the rising popularity of dating apps and so many of our connections being formed through social media, it has become a modern dating epidemic.

With communication being easier than ever before, you might think that ghosting wouldn't be so prolific. However, as we all know, it's the opposite, because online dating makes it easy to meet new potential partners who exist outside our established social connections. This means there is zero accountability if someone we meet online decides they want to go cold. It's not like the days of old, when everyone in the village would hear about their shitty behaviour.

So, anecdotally, we all know ghosting is very much A Thing, but Britt and I were curious to get some actual numbers behind this theory. We conducted a poll of *Life Uncut* listeners and 86 per cent of the 8000 voters said that they have been ghosted. I was pretty shocked to hear it was that high, even if I have ghosted a few people in the past myself . . . squeak! Have we become so conflict-avoidant that we'd rather stick our heads in the sand than have those uncomfortable yet necessary conversations? Have other people become so disposable that we can't even afford them the decency of an 'I'm not really feeling this anymore' text?

In most instances ghosting tends to happen in the early stages of a relationship, when you're in that weird dating purgatory between 'I really like this person' and 'Are we official?' But, as we heard with poor Olga and dirty Rich, that's not always the case. One *Life Uncut* listener wrote in to tell us how, after a disagreement, her boyfriend of two years unfollowed her on Instagram, unfriended her on Facebook and updated his relationship status to single. It wasn't until her best friend called her to see if she was okay that she even discovered she had been dumped. Fucking brutal!

Being ghosted can leave you at best confused and at worst heartbroken, diving headfirst into your own list of insecurities. When a relationship ends without explanation it is human nature to search for closure, and in the absence of any details from the other person, it's pretty common to turn inwards. *Maybe I was not interesting enough, or not pretty enough, or not funny enough, or 'too much' in general. Maybe he liked someone else more than me. Maybe I'll be single forever.*

Often, ghosting can happen right after a new relationship turns physical. Things seemed to be going great, you do the deed and then it's almost as if the engine runs out of steam. Their text messages become more and more infrequent, something in their tone shifts – and that's when you realise what they had really been in it for.

The truth is, the psychology behind ghosting says a lot more about the ghost than it does about the one left living. Ghosts aren't necessarily inherently bad people, or completely lacking in emotional empathy. Yes, there is an innate level of selfishness in the action – I don't deny that. However, as much as it hurts to be ghosted, I'm sure there are a lot of people reading this who have been both the victim and the perp in this narrative. As I said, I have ghosted in the past, but, looking back, I can see that it was during a time where I was critically conflict-avoidant and riddled with anxiety.

Some research suggests that ghosting can be closely linked with an avoidant attachment style (see Attachment Theory) because it can stem from fear of conflict and is essentially, well, avoidance.[10] Ghosting is a cowardly way to end a relationship, but it can also be rooted in a deep fear of confrontation rather than total disregard for the other person's feelings. People who are conflict-avoidant are more inclined to ghost because the thought of dealing with the fallout from a break-up or explaining their emotions feels too overwhelming.

> ## *Accidentally Unfiltered*
>
> I have been spending a fair bit of time on dating sites this year and was messaging one guy who I was interested in. I thought it was going great, but I kept wondering why at the end of each message he would sign off with his name. Turns out I was calling him the wrong name for two weeks, and he was hoping I would realise. He ended up ghosting me, despite me sending an apology message!

GHOSTING HURTS EVERYONE – EVEN THE GHOST

Being rejected in this way is cruel. It leaves you with no rationale, no guidelines for how to proceed, and often saddled with a heap of emotions to sort through on your own. If you suffer from any abandonment or self-esteem issues, being ghosted may bring them to the fore. You're left questioning what you did wrong, why this happened and then there are the feelings of stupidity. *How could I have trusted this person? Why didn't I see this coming? What's wrong with me?*

There are many reasons why ghosting is a shitty thing to do to someone, but it is also a shitty thing to do to yourself. Ghosting robs your partner of closure, and closure is an imperative part of accepting, understanding and moving past heartbreak. But what a lot of people don't reflect on when they ghost is that they may be hurting themselves too by increasing their own anxiety, avoiding important conversations and creating more prolonged drama and unrest.

We learn so much from having honest, vulnerable conversations, and denying yourself the opportunity to grow from these situations will do nothing for improving your communication and relationship skills. It will also leave you feeling nervous and guilty every time you look down at your phone and wonder whether that text message ping or missed call will be them demanding an explanation.

Now, don't get me wrong, I don't think every person you go on a date with requires a deep or considered level of closure. If you meet someone for a drink and there is no chemistry or spark, you don't need to text them to offer an explanation – you honestly don't owe them anything. Is it nice to send a 'Hey, nice to meet you, but I wasn't vibing it' text? Sure. Is it essential? No.

If this were Britt's chapter I know exactly what she would say: 'Treat other people the way you want to be treated'. If you would expect a courtesy text for closure after a first date, then you should also text them. But, maybe we're not so different after all, because I do agree with this in theory; I guess I would just never expect a text from someone I've spent minimal time and energy on.

Where the line becomes firm, in my opinion, is once you've been on several dates, shared an understanding of what you're looking for, bumped uglies, or led them to believe that your connection and investment in them has some longevity or is heading somewhere. If someone has invested their emotional energy in you because you led them to believe the relationship has real potential, then they deserve more than the silent treatment. Period.

SO YOU THINK YOU'VE BEEN GHOSTED...

Some forms of ghosting can be undeniably loud and clear, such as a 'Hey, are we still going for that drink tonight?' that gets left on 'read' until the end of time. Other situations can be far more muddied and it can be hard to tell initially if the other person is just busy, performing a soft fade or if they've gone full phantom.

Sometimes a love interest will do a soft fade to a ghost. This is exactly what it sounds like: a gentle de-escalation of contact until you're left with nothing at all. This tactic is marginally less hardcore than ghosting but equally as cowardly. If they have dramatically changed the frequency with which they reply; if it takes them three days to get back to you when it used to take them three minutes; if their texts are short and don't allow for a back-and-forth exchange; if they haven't tried to arrange a time to hang out or, worse, have missed a date without valid explanation or warning . . . you're getting ghosted. You will have an inkling after a few days, and after a week of no replies and/or zero effort, the soft fade will become pretty clear. After a fortnight? I hate to break it to you, but you've been ghosted.

OKAY, NOW WHAT?

1. Don't let it slide

Some people will tell you not to waste your energy engaging with a ghost. But I think 'fuck it'. If you're ABSOLUTELY sure you've been ghosted and you're feeling like hell, then call them out on it. I'd love to say take the high road and move on, but people need to know that their behaviour is crap and cowardly. Don't expect a reply – clearly that's not their strong suit – but there may be some solace in sending a text and letting them know how you feel.

There are some rules around this, though. No matter how much you might want to tell Casper to go fuck himself, don't. Also avoid passive-aggressive digs that won't make you feel any better. Remember, you're sending this final text for yourself, not for the ghost. It is irrelevant whether they reply; this text is for you to put a full stop on this chapter and move on. Acknowledging ghosting for what it is marks a line in the sand and is the first step to creating a little bit of closure for yourself. And hey, maybe it might mean that they change their behaviour, so that next time they're trying to cool things off with someone, they can find some words to express that.

Some self-help experts might advise against sending a final text on the grounds that it might be petty. But this is *Life Uncut* and we're realists! Go on, scratch the very last itch. It can be a simple 'Hi, I haven't heard from you in a while and can read between the lines. I would have really appreciated it if you could have shared with me where I stood instead of leaving me to figure it out from your silence. Take care. Please delete my number.'

If you didn't have closure before, then wham bam thank you ma'am! You do now!

2. Block their number

Even after being ghosted, it's normal to miss the other person – to wish things were different, to hope that they'll change their mind and come around. To feel that tiny spark of hope every time your phone pings and then the surge of disappointment when you see it's not them.

Don't prolong your own sadness or suffering by clinging on to that hope. Ghosting someone is deeply disrespectful – and someone who doesn't respect you doesn't deserve you. You are worthy of better, so instead of waiting around for a reply, take control and block their number.

3. Unsubscribe, unsubscribe, unsubscribe!

Blocking goes for social media, too. Unfriend them on Facebook, block their Instagram, unmatch them on dating apps – unsubscribe in every way! No stalking their stories to see where they are or who they are with! No looking at their Insta grid or checking their mate's Facebook for any new photos! CUT THEM OFF. Don't torture yourself by trying to look into their world! They have closed that world to you, and you need to accept that and move on.

This isn't just about preventing yourself from reaching out in a moment of weakness. This is so that they can't resurrect themselves and slide back in your DMs to fuck up all the hard work you've already done seeking closure. If someone ghosts you, get rid of them for good. You deserve better than a zombie.

4. Be kind to yourself

If this was someone you were seriously into and emotionally invested in, let yourself be sad. Have a cry, call your friends for a debrief and allow yourself time to grieve the relationship you wanted and the potential that you saw.

Ghosting sucks because it invalidates us and leaves us feeling like we did something wrong. You may never know why they decided to ghost you, so DO NOT blame yourself and allow someone else's shitty behaviour to define your self-worth. That kind of thinking won't get you anywhere.

Here is your mantra:

Just because someone else does not see my inherent value, that does not diminish it. I'm a fucking catch.

Now repeat.

HAPPINESS

It's what we all want – but is it a trap?

LAURA

SEE ALSO: IMPOSTOR SYNDROME, QUITTING, SOLITUDE, TIMELINES,
TOXIC POSITIVITY, UNCONDITIONAL LOVE, XPECTATIONS

Happiness. It's defined as 'the quality or state of being happy. Good fortune; pleasure; contentment; joy'.[11]

If you took a quick glance at almost any social media platform, you'd be bombarded with happy snaps, thigh gaps, #relationship-goals, butts and bits that defy gravity, and people living their best goddamn life. Strangers, influencers, your own mates – but in the world of highlight reels, FOMO and filters, what even *is* happiness?

Happiness is a tricky thing to pin down, because it means different things to different people. There is no formula, no 'If you do Y, multiply it by Z and add a little H, you'll get happy.'

There are, however, a few smartypants philosophers who agree on a couple of things. The first is that happiness is deeply rooted in perspective – in how you view your life and how you exercise gratitude. The second is that happiness is not a static emotion, so despite our society's fixation on 'being happy', you simply cannot be happy all the time; it is not a fixed state. (Unless you're a Teletubby.)

What I find fascinating is that, according to science, we are all predisposed to a certain amount of happiness. In fact, how happy you feel could be 50 per cent influenced by your genes and

91

50 per cent influenced by your circumstances, as well your perception and reaction to those circumstances.

Over the years we have been very lucky to speak with some truly incredible guests on the podcasts and have asked them to tell us what happiness means to them. One conversation that happened off mic that stuck with me deeply were the words of Shonel Bryant.[12] We interviewed Shonel in December 2021, and only one month after we spoke in January 2022 Shonel passed away. Shonel was a warm and compassionate thirty-seven-year old woman. She was a wife, a business owner, and a mother of two beautiful children Smith and Vogue – and she had also been diagnosed with triple-negative breast cancer that had metastasised throughout her body. When we spoke with Shonel on the podcast she knew she was dying, but it was her final wish to advocate the message to other young women to 'check your breasts'.

I asked Shonel what happiness meant to her, and she had this to say:

'Happiness is deeply rooted in love. Don't let happiness wash over you; let it seep deeply into your pores, nestle and find a home. Happiness is when you allow love to truly reach you. When you lean into people and moments that make you feel alive, you open yourself up to the gift that is life.

'Receive it, embody it, imprint the intricacies of how it makes you truly feel. These precious moments in time are what it's all about and they transcend everything else.'

I struggle to read Shonel's words without tears in my eyes – for Shonel, knowing that she had such a limited time left cut through all the shit that previously clouded her outlook on life, and what truly brought her happiness were the people in her life whom she loved beyond measure. I think of all the times that I've become bogged down by trivial crap (as we're all guilty of doing), consumed by things that don't matter, by my phone, by work stressors, by insignificant drama and then I think of the one thing that brings me the sort of deep connected happiness that makes life worthwhile – and Shonel is right; for me it is my family, my children, my friends. And as she said, it's rooted in love.

But unlike love, happiness does ebb and flow more rapidly as it is impacted by life events and our own shortcomings. Suffering, pain, loneliness and grief are all part of the human experience, and feeling these complex emotions gives us a greater and deeper sense of gratitude for times of happiness. Without winter, we would take summer for granted.

That beautiful expression of Shonel's – 'Don't let happiness wash over you' – is something that has stuck with me. How often are we all guilty of taking happiness for granted?

It made me think about one of the happiest moments of my life: when I held my daughter Marlie for the very first time. Looking at her puffy little squished-up newborn face, I knew my life had changed forever – and in that moment I felt a sort of happiness I had never experienced before. But then, after six weeks of sleep deprivation, as well as an infection from my episiotomy, my happiness was replaced with fleeting thoughts of loneliness and moments where I'd think to myself, *What have we done?* Some days were marred by exhaustion and fear, and on many of them I felt a lot less happy.

An example I think most of us can relate to is feeling unhappy and unappreciated at work, at some point in our careers. Think back to your last pay rise, the one that you were sure would make you feel appreciated, comfortable and, in turn, happier. How long did that happiness last? Six months? One year? How long did it take before you wanted more? This is known as the Hedonic Treadmill, the theory that people will repeatedly return to their baseline of happiness regardless of what happens to them.

Hugh van Cuylenburg from The Resilience Project spoke on the podcast about how we often think that we will 'reach happiness' when we obtain a certain thing or goal.[13] For example, you want a new car. You get the new car and you're ecstatic! You say, 'I'm going to keep this car clean and perfect.' That lasts a few months until the kids smoosh some crackers between the seats and you clip the wheel in a carpark after you've just yelled at your partner to stop criticising your driving. Pretty quickly the new car feels, well . . . less new. You pull up at the traffic lights and see a nicer car and all of a sudden you shift to, 'If I can get a car like that, a bigger car, with more . . .'

It can be easy to kick your own happiness down the road, constantly tethering it to some goal out in front of you. But by doing that you're only robbing yourself of the chance to feel more joy right here, right now.

WHY WE SHOULD CHOOSE CONTENTMENT

When we understand that happiness is an emotion much like anger and sadness, and that it comes and goes in much the same way, we have to ask ourselves, well, what is a static state that I should be gunning for if I want to be happier? And to that end, my friends, the answer is contentment. Unlike happiness, contentment is a mindset. It is grounded in acceptance, gratitude and purposefully finding a state of happiness with what you currently have – hopping off the Hedonistic Treadmill.

COMPARISON CULTURE

They say *comparison is the thief of joy*. Whoever 'they' are sure know their stuff.

What makes the happiness trap even harder in today's tech-driven society is that we live so much of our lives in an online world that only displays part of our lived reality. Sure, we are seeing more diversity online than ever before, and in so many areas, from race and disability, to sexuality, body inclusivity, skin positivity and also a wider range of emotions. In today's social media landscape discussions surrounding mental health are rapidly becoming destigmatised. Visibility is critically important in normalising the full scope of human emotions, in showing that it's okay to not be okay 100 per cent of the time – in fact, it's not only okay, it's also pretty normal.

However, Instagram still has a long way to go when it comes to showcasing an authentic window into people's lives. An area where it falls particularly short is the lack of representation when it comes to lifestyle. I don't see anyone posting photos of the less desirable things in life, such as being in debt, working a sixteen-hour shift, friendship break-ups, being dumped or broken-hearted, living in a crappy apartment with a couch the cat scratched holes in, or wearing clothes that are ten years old because who the fuck has the sort of money needed to stay on trend and up to date. Instagram is still highly geared towards aspirational living, and when you're in a challenging stage of life, feeling like everyone else has their shit together can be a real kick in the teeth.

This is not to say that comparisons are all bad. Comparing ourselves to others is part of human nature, and can have some positive and useful aspects, too. It can motivate us and keeps us striving to achieve our goals. But it's important to understand and be aware of our thoughts and feelings, and recognise when comparisons are playing a healthy motivating role in our lives, and when they are leaving us feeling chronically inferior.

FIVE THINGS YOU CAN DO NOW TO INCREASE HAPPINESS

1. Cleanse your social media and your news

We are all guilty of idly and unconsciously scrolling through our phones, and every day we are bombarded by content that is negatively geared, thanks to the news cycle, or content that shows us the curated version of how other people live their lives, thanks to social media. Being a conscious consumer of what you read and watch is the first step in making tangible progress towards happiness. Unfollow accounts that make you feel shitty about your life or situation. When you're finding the news too overwhelming, it's okay to switch off – we all need a break sometimes. And block influencers who feed into feelings of inadequacy and switch off when the news is too overwhelming – life's too short for this shit and you are responsible for the content you consume. So unfollow, unsubscribe, block!

2. Make connections, not comparisons

The next time you find yourself lost down an Insta hole, *stop*. Close it down and call someone you love instead, even if it's just to tell them how much you appreciate them or ask how their day is going. Choose to use that window of time in your day to strengthen an important relationship in your life.

Or, if you really want to give yourself the warm and fuzzies, a powerful tool for creating more happiness is writing a letter to someone in your life who you are truly grateful for. Whether it's old-fashioned pen and paper or an email, sit down and let them know the positive impact they have made on your life. Not only will it brighten their day, but you'll get a glow from thinking back on all the good things they've done for you and sharing that recognition. That's two people who are now feeling more content!

3. If you are going to compare, make it achievable

If comparison is an inevitable part of the human psyche, make sure that when you find yourself comparing your life with someone else's you do it with intention. Don't measure yourself against someone who is at the top of the mountain; consider yourself in relation to people who are a few rungs ahead of you and not far beyond your reach. Achievable comparisons can help propel us towards our goals and ambitions by showing us a clear path for improvement.

You could write down your role models, identify how they got to where they are and then map out how you might do the same. Or go deeper by finding a mentor who can actively guide you along your chosen path and share the lessons they've learned along the way.

4. Count your blessings

Hugh van Cuylenburg from The Resilience Project recommends writing down three things that went well for you every day before going to bed. Not the big things that you're grateful for, such as your family, job or partner, because these tend to get repetitive. Instead, as Hugh suggested, reflect on the smaller, more specific wins from your day, including those that were unexpected. The act of recording three things that went well for you that day can bring a sense of gratitude that leads to greater contentment.

5. Stop caring so much about what people think

When bestselling author Mark Manson joined us on *Life Uncut*, he shared this gem: 'You should give a fuck what people think – there's a name for people who don't, and that's a psychopath – but you should also have more important things in your life than what other people think.' So go out there and do the things that give you purpose and make you feel alive. Your life isn't truly yours if you're always caring about what other people think.

I

THE ICK

I want to like you, but you repulse me

LAURA

SEE ALSO: BOUNDARIES, DATING, QUITTING, RED FLAGS

A few years before meeting Matt, I started dating a guy in my outer friendship circle. On paper he was amazing: good-looking, funny, charming and keen for a relationship – DING DING! We spoke on the phone for hours, spent days sending each other dumb memes and had a lot in common. By the time we had gone on a couple of dates and he invited me back to his apartment, I was sure this new 'thing' we had going on was heading somewhere. And then . . . we had sex.

I remember waking up in the morning and rolling over to face him. He was asleep, breathing heavily through his open mouth and in that moment, I felt physically repulsed. Overnight, something had shifted in me and our almost-relationship had gone off like a bag of prawns in the sun.

Sure, the sex had been pretty average, but let's be real, I was single and in my twenties – I'd had my fair share of average shags in the past and had often still given things a second crack. This time, though, something deep inside me was utterly turned off. It made no sense: he was a GREAT guy, we got on well and he was genuinely into me . . . it all checked out. I was tempted to try to shake off my unease and work through it, but it was as if my emotions had been unplugged at the wall. It was too intense to ignore. When

I left his house, I knew we'd never go on another date – and we didn't. Over the next week or so our texts got further apart, and in the end, we lost contact.

At the time I didn't have a label for it, but looking back, it was a chronic case of The Ick.

LADIES AND LIFERS, WELCOME TO THE ICK

The Ick was first coined back in 1999 on the hit TV show *Ally McBeal*. Over a decade later, it made a comeback in an episode of the reality show *Love Island* ('Are they catching The Ick?') and, well, since then, it's become a TikTok trend and a dating phenomenon we simply cannot escape. The verrrrry reputable and reliable Urban Dictionary defines The Ick as:

'You THINK you like them but then you suddenly catch The Ick. From then on you can't look at the other person in the same way, you just progressively get more [and] more turned off by them, weirdly [and] maybe for no reason in particular. You cringeeeeee at the thought of you and them together.'[14]

If you've ever caught The Ick then you'll know there is no denying just how intense the repulsion can be.

I threw it out to the Lifers in our Facebook discussion group to find out what had given them The Ick in the past, and the answers varied from enlightening to confusing to downright hilarious. Here are just a few:

- ♥ During the deed he made eye contact and said, 'Good little girl.'
- ♥ Crocs.
- ♥ Without warning (or asking) a guy literally hacked up saliva and spat on my face the first time we had sex. Then told me we should isolate together if one of us got COVID.

- ♥ He said he was 'frightened' about a horror movie – 'That was rather frightening'. I never saw him again.
- ♥ 'Good morning' or 'good night' texts from someone I've just started talking to.
- ♥ I discovered they had personalised number plates that said . . . 'No Shame'.
- ♥ Went to a movie with a guy and he asked for ONE ticket to see *Spider-Man*, he then proceeded to pay for his own ticket with money from a Velcro wallet.
- ♥ Beach date: she sat and rolled around in the sand, then never brushed it off when she stood up, just walked around like a giant chicken schnitzel.
- ♥ Build-up of white matter around his mouth every time he kissed me.
- ♥ His favourite song was 'Let Me Entertain You', which he listened to all the time on repeat – and not in an ironic way.
- ♥ We went to breakfast, and it was going really well. We decided to go for a walk along the esplanade after. He walked so slow my great-grandmother could run rings around him. I left and didn't even need to power walk away from him. This was fourteen months ago – pretty sure he is still on his way back to the car. I have ADHD and immediately knew everything he did would annoy me.
- ♥ Every time my ex peed, he would lift his leg a little and let out loud farts, while leaving the door open. Every single time!
- ♥ I dated a guy who said, 'Oh my gosh, oh my gosh,' over and over every time he came.
- ♥ He had a convertible and would play his music SO loud. One day he came home saying some guys threw Macca's ice

cream cones at him while he was blasting Benny Benassi's 'Cinema' and he was stuck at the red lights covered in ice cream. When I replayed the images back in my mind ... I was done.

As the list above suggests, the reason for catching The Ick is so wildly different for each person. It could be a more superficial quality, such as nail-biting, teeth-sucking or snoring, or it could be a moral mismatch, such as discovering your date finds racist jokes funny (ewww, dump them!). You might be able to immediately identify the cause – their baby talk, how they leave their dirty undies inside their pants next to the shower – or sometimes, as it was with me, the exact cause isn't as obvious. You're coasting along, smitten, you text all day and spoon all night. Then, BAM!

You've probably broken up with someone because of The Ick and, I'm sorry to say it, there's a chance you've been dumped because of it, too. But how seriously should we take The Ick when it hits? And is it always a deal-breaker?

WHAT'S THE ICK TRYING TO TELL US?

According to relationship experts, The Ick is fundamentally different to just having doubts about a person. Relationship expert Liam Barnett, interviewed for the *Huffington Post*, defines it as 'something [your date] did or said which shows a certain human behaviour that, at times, is, and at times isn't, acceptable by social norms'.[15]

The thing you think has triggered The Ick can seem superficial but it can be a symbol of a deeper mismatch. At the start of a relationship, we're all putting our best self forward. Now, you're starting to get a slightly more warts-and-all insight into who they are ... and your gut doesn't like it!

We talk a lot about trusting your intuition on the podcast. Our instincts are SMART and, generally, we should listen to them, as they are our internal warning system telling us something is up. However, if you keep catching The Ick over trivial issues (for example, if the thought of dating a person who wears cargo pants makes your vagina dry up) it might be worth investigating why you keep getting turned off. Is it really about the pants, or are you finding excuses to not get serious? Is there something bigger at play here, like maybe a fear of commitment? Sometimes catching The Ick says more about the Ick-catcher than it does about the culprit.

If The Ick hits, it pays to stay vigilant and get curious. What are your instincts really trying to tell you?

ARE WE GENERATION ICK?

Well, maybe! We certainly are Generation Comparison – whether it's with our friends, our co-workers or millions of strangers on social media. I'm going out on a limb here to proclaim that The Ick is more prevalent than ever, and that is partly driven by the 'grass is always greener' mindset that comparison culture encourages. For example, how easy is it to fall into the trap of imagining that everyone else's relationship is more romantic, and that you are the only one whose partner farts in the kitchen and leaves their stinky sports shoes in the hallway? When we start to compare, we start to believe that a better option must be out there – and then we search, even subconsciously, for a reason to leave our current partner.

You can look at The Ick through three lenses:

1. Intuition: your inner compass is telling you something and you need to get out.
2. Insecurity: you might be looking for anything and everything as a justification, out of fear of commitment.

3. Impatience: you're expecting this human to be a level of perfection that you're not either.

According to Dr Raquel Peel, a psychology lecturer at the University of Queensland, The Ick can undermine your chance at love. 'One possibility is this is a self-defensive mechanism or strategy,' she wrote in a blog post for *The Conversation*, 'to protect against relationship failure, fear of commitment, fear of intimacy or rejection sensitivity.'[16]

It's important to try to avoid comparing your relationship, and your partner, to what you see around you. And it's equally crucial to avoid comparing your partner, or your relationship, to an earlier version of itself. Sure, they've probably changed, but you have too!

If you're in an 'opposites attract' relationship, The Ick can hit you harder. That outgoing, life-of-the-party guy you idolised doesn't seem as attractive when he's hungover and you want to go to the farmers' market.

WHAT LEVEL OF ICK ARE YOU?

How you respond to The Ick will depend on the stage of your relationship. From anecdotal evidence, The Ick seems to happen a lot in the early days of a relationship, but long-term partners aren't immune to The Ick either. If you're in the early days, it's easy to cut your losses if you want to. But if you're in a long-term relationship that was once fulfilling, it's worth slowing down and assessing the situation a little more closely before you make any rash decisions. Think about:

♥ What is it that's really making you feel this way?
♥ Where is it coming from?
♥ Is it something you can work on over time or is it a deal-breaker?

For instance, we've heard from podcast listeners who got The Ick from partners who didn't cover their mouth when they coughed or one girl who caught The Ick when she discovered that her boyfriend would stick his used floss to the shower wall. Neither of these issues represent major moral failings; both can be worked on! But if your partner has become lazy around the house, gets drunk every Saturday night or has vastly different political views to you, these sorts of Ick igniters could be relationship-enders. A negative shift in your partner's morals or behaviour is a very valid reason to be turned off – even instantly.

It's also worth zooming out to consider the other factors impacting your life (and your sex drive!). Is The Ick driven by resentment or exhaustion? Is it because you've just had a baby and your partner's not pulling their weight? Is there more at play here than one annoying habit? Are you drifting apart and lacking connection?

We can be quick to say that if you've caught The Ick the relationship is doomed, but it is possible to come back from these feelings if there is still a level of trust, respect and love at the foundation. It might be time to seek external help, such as speaking to a couple therapist. Unpacking why you suddenly feel turned off by your long-term partner can have so many different root causes that are unique to the relationship, however it's important to know that attraction ebbs and flows in all relationships. Feelings are not static and just because you've caught The Ick doesn't mean that you can't work through it and get back to a good place. Things that might seem to be in a downward spiral can always spiral back up – with work.

WHEN THE ICK MEANS THE END

If the feeling of repulsion is unwavering, no amount of willing yourself to feel different is going to change it, and there comes a point where you can't force yourself (regardless of how great they are on paper) to be around or intimate with someone you feel put off by. How honest should you be when you end it? Is it really going to be beneficial? So, they click their teeth when you kiss. You hate it, but someone else might not care. This is why I think it's best to keep it vague, simple and respectful. If this is someone you've only hung out with a few times then you can say something like: *It was nice meeting you. I had fun. I don't think it's working out.*

If you're in a long-term relationship, you can start with an honest conversation. Instead of leading with their annoying habit, talk about how it makes you feel deep down.

I don't feel respected.
I feel taken for granted.
I'm feeling like I'm not a priority.

Then there's always the chance your relationship has simply reached its expiry date. It might feel sudden to you, but is it really? Or has it been a slow burn that you've been ignoring? We've all been in, or observed, relationships that appear to end suddenly, but with hindsight, it's clear that one person (or both) had been ignoring the signs of trouble.

And the truth is, when we really want to be coupled, it can be easy to ignore those warning signs. *On paper they're great. Funny, attractive, ambitious. Okay, sure, they repulse me, but maybe I can get over that!* It's tempting to reason with yourself like this, but it rarely evolves that way. You'll be pushing a boulder up a hill trying to make a relationship work with someone you're just not that into.

SIDE NOTE: CAN YOU GET THE ICK IN A FRIENDSHIP?

The Ick can happen in any close relationship, not just one that is sexually intimate. There are things about your friends you might only discover over the years as relationships become closer. Or you might find that your friendship has changed – as we all do, when we grow through life. Maybe you're holding onto who your friend used to be, but the reality of it is very different.

It's a shift. A switch. An emotional whiplash. You suddenly realise you've become very different people.

For me, The Ick in a friendship is more similar to The Ick in a long-term relationship. It's usually more closely tied to drifting apart and becoming different people. You can usually pinpoint the trigger behind it if you try hard enough. There could be a subtle feeling, such as *I don't feel good when I'm around this person*. Or it could be like taking off blinkers: *This person is actually very negative/critical/judgemental.*

Friendships should have a feeling of stability and closeness. If you suddenly don't feel that way, think about why that might have changed. Then, read our chapter on boundaries!

I

IMPOSTOR SYNDROME

Will we ever feel as though we are good enough?

BRITT AND LAURA

SEE ALSO: HAPPINESS, WORTHINESS

BRITT: Have you ever felt like a fraud? Like you're not good enough? Have you doubted your success? Have you ever sat around waiting for someone to call you out or discover you're not qualified and ask what you're doing here? Have you felt as if your achievements are all down to dumb luck and at any moment you're going to lose it all?

Yeah, us too! It's actually A Thing. It even has a fancy name. The professionals call this feeling 'impostor syndrome' and it was first identified more than forty years ago by psychologists Pauline Rose Clance and Suzanne Imes. It affects more than 70 per cent of men and women so it's alarmingly common – though, interestingly, impostor syndrome disproportionately affects women and high-achieving people.[17]

I remember watching a TED talk by Mike Cannon-Brookes, the co-founder of Australian software company Atlassian. He's just forty-two years old and worth about $23 billion, yet he spoke about how he still attends conferences and doesn't understand why he is there or what he has to bring to the table. It blows my mind that someone who is so obviously accomplished can still feel like they haven't earned their success.

LAURA: I think impostor syndrome has double downsides. Internally, you feel like you're not good or skilled enough, then when you voice those concerns externally, people around you think you're crazy – or worse, it can come across as insincere humility.

The real 'science-y' definition of impostor syndrome is an internal experience of believing that you are not as competent as others perceive you to be.

It's funny that you say it disproportionately affects women, Britt. I recently read about a study that said that men apply for a job when they meet only 60 per cent of the qualifications, but women apply only if they meet 100 per cent of them.[18] As one *Forbes* article mentioned, 'Men are confident about their ability at 60 per cent, but women don't feel confident until they've checked off each item on the list.'[19]

B: I feel like this stat is framed in a way that suggests women need to have more confidence in themselves and their abilities – but when you're someone who struggles with feelings of impostor syndrome, saying 'be more confident' is as unhelpful as it is condescending. The same can be said for someone saying 'just be more positive' to a person suffering from anxiety.

L: So true. Plus, impostor syndrome can affect people in different phases of life and can show up in various realms of life, too. It is often attributed to work but it can materialise in many ways, including in relationships. Since having children I have seen how impostor syndrome affects mothers and how they perceive and assess their skills in terms of being 'a good mum'.

B: I have felt it a few times in my life, for sure. I often seem fairly confident from a distance, but on the inside I'm usually a hot mess, wondering how I have got to wherever it is I am at that moment. I have felt it in all aspects: love, friendship, business, the list goes on.

Probably the most intense feelings of impostor syndrome I have ever had stemmed from my experience on *The Bachelor*. From day one I was convinced I was going home. I said at the first cocktail party, 'Ugh, it's probably me leaving tonight. I haven't spoken to him, I don't think he has even noticed me and there are too many amazing women here.' I kept asking myself, *Why would he keep you here? There's no way it will be you at the end.* At the time, I had nothing to base this on. It's just how I felt. But there are always people who feel it's necessary to let you know how much they don't like you. The bullying starts and insults start rolling in.

Laura, what was your experience like on there? I mean, besides the happily-ever-after ending, of course!

L: In terms of the *Bachelor* experience I can wholeheartedly understand your feelings, Britt. Reality TV is a weird beast in which the public are able to weigh in on your 'worthiness' and Instagram comments come in thick and fast with every episode that airs. 'Laura is fake, I hope he picks Tara', 'She has a good body, but shame about her head', 'She has no lips . . . ewww'. If I didn't feel like an impostor when I signed up for the show, I certainly did after our season had finished, when Matt and I had been thrust out in the real world!

B: Some people on social media are brutal, and the public scrutiny makes the whole reality TV experience so much more challenging. You'd think that making it to the end would have increased my confidence and lessened the impostor syndrome somewhat. But then when Nick didn't pick me (or anyone), any confidence I'd held on to melted away faster than a snowman in the Sahara. And on top of that, yeah, all those keyboard warriors really took away any small amount I had left.

L: I totally agree, the *Bachelor* experience bred a whole host of insecurities that I didn't have when I went in. My biggest fear was that Matt would wake up one day and think, *Yeah, I am too good for this chick.*

B: Which is crazy because HE IS BATTING! (No offence, Matty!)

L: Haha! Speaking of impostor syndrome, why do compliments make us all feel so awkward?!

Coverage of impostor syndrome tends to focus on its downsides – for example, how it is debilitating and counterintuitive to growth and confidence. I think it can actually have some positive implications too, though. When I first quit my full-time job and started my jewellery business, ToniMay, I really struggled to say that I was a jewellery designer. Even after a decade in the industry, I still find the title 'jewellery designer' feels foreign to me. This can often be the case for those who take non-traditional routes into their chosen careers; I had never formally studied jewellery design so I felt like I was undeserving of the title, even though my label was thriving.

But impostor syndrome forced me to work harder, to upskill and to learn as much as I could about business and the jewellery industry. I was challenging myself and moving forward. If you're interested in personal growth and development, you will often push yourself into unexplored territories and roles. You aren't growing unless you're doing that. Impostor syndrome also keeps our egos in check. If you think you're the best and at the top of your industry, what motivator is there to keep improving and developing?

B: Impostor syndrome can be great if it keeps us striving and thriving.

I know I have felt inadequate before in love. Hard not to, with my history! Okay, this is a pretty crazy story, but one time, I met this guy overseas and we were dating for a few months before I realised he was a billionaire (well, he was from a family of billionaires). Before I made that accidental discovery (he definitely didn't let on) it was going so well; we were having a lot of fun and really liked each other. One day, after witnessing him drop six digits betting on a sporting match (which he lost), I decided to do a quick google of his name and immediately went down a rabbit hole, discovering the full extent of his family's fortune. I then of course did what any girl on a self-sabotaging mission would do: I dug deep into his social media, scrolling back until I finally found photos of what his exes looked like. Of course they were all supermodels in designer clothing, who didn't even seem real. Meanwhile, I was wearing scrubs daily and working in an emergency department at that time, which couldn't have been more different from the life he was used to.

Suddenly I was telling myself that I wasn't good enough for him, that I didn't fit into his life, and that he would discover that soon and judge me for it, even though this had never bothered me – or him – before. This all made me awkward as fuck, and I pulled away. What did he see in me?

But truth was, he was dating *me*. He was happy with *me*, regardless of my occupation or my wardrobe. What blew it, though, wasn't him, but it was me telling myself I wasn't enough. I sabotaged any hopes of that relationship succeeding because of my own self-doubt and insecurities. The thing is, impostor syndrome is not just modesty, humility or self-deprecation. It is the deep, genuine belief that you are not good enough. It can be debilitating and it took me a long time to learn to deal with it.

The feeling of not being good enough is more extreme than ever these days, thanks to social media's promotion of comparison culture through filters and highlights reels. It is hard to look at the endless images of 'perfection' and not feel less than. I don't think there would be a person on Earth who has looked at social media and not felt worse about themselves at some stage, even if only for a moment.

L: I have a bit of a theory about this. I think sometimes we focus too much on how other people's approaches to Instagram make us feel shitty. Yes, looking at other people's feeds and drawing comparisons leaves us feeling less than, but I actually think it has more to do with the content we post ourselves and how we engage with our own content. To me, that's more likely to create feelings of impostor syndrome.

For example, if you're only posting perfect photos of yourself, where your skin is smooth, you've resized and cinched your waist and your ass is defying gravity, your perception of your appearance can become distorted. When you look in the mirror, what you see simply can't match up to the fantasy version of yourself you've created online. Have you ever been on a date with someone who you've met online and thought to yourself, *I hope they think I look like my photos*? Have you ever heard someone say about another person, 'They're hotter on Instagram than in person'? Brutal, for sure, but it's this disparity between who we present as online and who we are in real life that can leave us feeling inadequate. We receive validation and approval for the curated version of ourselves but then it's much harder for us to feel authentic, like a true representation of who we are. We can get stuck on the hamster wheel of having to maintain an image that doesn't reflect what is genuine in real life.

For me, one of the biggest breakthroughs in dealing with impostor syndrome has been understanding the power of authenticity and vulnerability. When you better understand, accept and learn to love your flaws, they no longer have such a hold over you. Vulnerability strengthens connections and deepens relationships.

It is one thing to recognise that you are struggling with feelings of impostor syndrome, but talking about it openly and vulnerably with a close friend or romantic partner could be a good idea. This way you'll be arming yourself with an external voice who can talk some sense into you when negative thoughts creeps in.

Britt, how do you deal with feelings of impostor syndrome?

B: To be honest, I'm not sure I do! Haha, check me out, I'm even feeling like an impostor about how well I deal with impostor syndrome.

Seriously, though, I will probably always have these feelings but, ultimately, my dreams and desires are bigger than my fear of not being enough. This is what keeps me pushing forward and chasing those dreams. These days I am not overly scared of rejection, which also helps – I'm motivated more by a fear of not getting something I really want. This means I am able to keep putting myself out there. Of course rejection still sucks, it still hurts, I still cry, I still wonder why, but my motivation exceeds that.

I always aim to separate feelings from fact. It can be easy to *feel* like you are undeserving of your achievements or that you are out of your depth, but if you separate facts from feelings it can often help to draw a line between your insecurities and reality.

So I try to focus a lot on the positives and what I *have* achieved rather than what I haven't yet achieved. That's a great reminder that I am doing just fine. It's extra challenging as a woman but I'm getting better at owning the role I play in my success and kicking that negative self-talk in the ass. Sometimes it even helps to say it out loud: 'I'm proud of what I've accomplished and I deserve my successes.'

What else helps? Well, I try to avoid comparing myself to other people and just run my own race. I've learned to recognise that impostor syndrome often comes from feeling like you don't belong, and there are definitely going to be times in life when this is normal, such as starting a new job or joining a new social circle. I've discovered from experience that this is something that you can work through; it won't last forever.

Finally, if there's a quote that I live by it's this one: 'Only those that go too far can possibly find out how far one can go'. If you want to discover your true potential, you have to aim high!

J

JEALOUSY

When does jealousy become a relationship
deal-breaker – and the sign of a deeper issue?

LAURA

SEE ALSO: ATTACHMENT THEORY, BOUNDARIES,
EMOTIONAL CHEATING, GASLIGHTING, RED FLAGS, WORTHINESS

So, it's a standard Wednesday evening and you're scrolling idly through Instagram when you come across a girl whose profile you don't recognise. She's been liking your partner's Insta pics and her name keeps popping up in the comments section – a fire emoji here, a wink there – but she never seems to like any of the photos you're in . . . is it obsessive that you've noticed that? You've clicked through to her profile and looked at every photo dating back to 2018 but you're no closer to figuring out who this mystery women is. *How do they know each other? Is she single? Is she hotter than me? Who the fuck is she?*

That feeling right there? We've all felt it to varying degrees. It can rear its ugly green-eyed head in relationships, friendships, families and workplaces. We're talking about jealousy!

When Matt and I met on *The Bachelor*, it was the perfect petri dish for jealousy to spawn. I was single, of course, and totally committed to the experiment, and he . . . well, he was dating twenty-two women simultaneously.

I don't like to think of myself as a jealous person, but if there was ever an environment that was going to ignite the feeling, it was *The Bachelor*. Now it doesn't matter how self-assured you are, no one is immune to feeling it from time to time, and being on the show conjured up some pretty unhealthy insecurities in me. I still remember how amazing I felt after our first date together, during which we had shared the first kiss of the season. It felt special – until the very next day when Florence, whom I had become really close friends with in the mansion, went on a date with Matt and came home talking about what an amazing time they'd had and shared intimate details about their pash. This then became a daily occurrence for three months – whoever had been on a date that day would come back and unpack with the rest of the girls in the mansion.

The Bachelor is an environment designed to make you feel a little crazy (big emotions equal big ratings) and with feelings of jealousy comes the feeling of being a little unhinged. Considering the bizarre circumstances, I did a pretty good job of keeping the lid on my crazy. But I would be lying if I said there weren't times during filming where I felt the green eye-monster.

After filming ended, Matt and I had to keep our relationship under wraps for six months before the final episode aired, while on TV, our fledgling romance was put out there for public opinion. Hell, you could even use Sportsbet to vote on who you thought Matt would pick. Thousands of complete strangers weighed in on our relationship across social media, and although there was so much support for the two of us, as it is with reality TV, there were also a lot of unfavourable comments (for example, people commenting that Matt should have picked Tara or Elise instead of me). Because of this, there were days where self-doubt got the better of me and I found myself wondering whether I was good enough. But the comparisons didn't stop there. I remember opening an article from the *Daily Mail* that was a chronological list of all of Matt's ex-girlfriends – with photos! Can you imagine a news website listing all of your partner's exes?! The comments section was brutal, with people comparing me to Matt's exes (who, annoyingly, are all smoking hot).

When my self-confidence was at an all-time low post-show, I found myself questioning if Matt was 'dating down' by being with me. I was in a total comparison spiral. Was I jealous or insecure about the women who weren't even a part of Matt's life anymore? Had the show really made me that batshit crazy?

In part, yes.

There is a name for the sort of jealousy that is attributed to becoming slightly obsessed with your partner's ex or exes and it is called 'retroactive jealousy' – a pattern of obsessive thoughts relating to your partner's former relationship(s) or sexual history. If you've ever experienced this very unique flavour of jealousy, you might think it's something that you don't have a lot of control over, but ultimately it is a sure-fire way to sabotage your relationship and make yourself feel miserable in the process.

I've told you I'm not typically a jealous person, but that didn't stop me from having these feelings in this specific circumstance. Which is to say that maybe you're not someone who usually gets jealous either, but that doesn't mean it won't ever happen.

The truth is, we all have the capacity to feel jealous – especially in circumstances where our self-worth has been rocked or where we are navigating unfamiliar territory in a relationship. Jealousy creeps in when we have something to lose.

Nobody likes admitting to feeling jealous – it's a 'yucky' quality and we often worry that it's going to turn our partners off, or make us look like stage-five clingers, but being vulnerable and open can often have the opposite effect. For me, talking about my insecurities with Matt and speaking about jealousy actually brought us closer. He was patient, reassuring and consistent, which helped me work through my own shortcomings and feelings of inadequacy. Yes, he was supportive, but I still had to do the work.

Now, five years down the track I've met both of Matt's long-term exes. I've even been a guest at one of their weddings. Yes, they are both still smoking hot, and no, I no longer feel threatened in the slightest. But, looking back, I'm not ashamed to admit that I was. Like I said, feeling that way meant that I had something to lose; something that I cared about deeply.

AM I JEALOUS OR AM I ENVIOUS?

A lot of people confuse jealousy with envy, but there is a difference. Envy is when you covet something someone else has that you don't. For example, you can be envious of a colleague getting a promotion, or maybe your best friend falling pregnant when you're desperate for a baby. Jealousy, on the other hand, is a 'pre-emptive' emotion you experience when you already have something, but are afraid that it could be taken away. It surfaces whenever you feel threatened and comes from a deep-seated fear that maybe you will lose something that you love. It's a protective emotion – although maybe too protective.

With jealousy, we're trying to protect ourselves from feelings of pain and trauma and abandonment. Envy can be associated with wanting to gain material objects or value. Jealousy is more tied to relationships and people.

It's useful to know the difference between the two so that you can figure out which you might be experiencing, and figure out how to deal with that.

JEALOUSY STRADDLES TWO VERY POWERFUL EMOTIONS: TRUST AND SELF-WORTH

Chances are, unless you're an ethereal unicorn mermaid who's found enlightenment, you've probably experienced jealousy at some stage, and I'm willing to bet that it was probably in the context of a romantic relationship. Maybe you felt jealous for reasons that seemed warranted or maybe it came from feelings of inadequacy.

Either way, if left unchecked, jealousy is a simple and easy way to transform your relationship into a dumpster fire of insecurities!

A lot of people say jealousy is your shit and you have to work on it. I agree, but I also think you can find yourself in relationships that inflame your jealousy, and this is because the relationship itself is lacking in trust. When this happens, it's a two-person job to fix it – and it might not always be fixable.

Prior to my relationship with Matty I had a real doozy of a time dating. One of my relationships was the textbook definition of toxic. If you're a listener of the podcast you would be familiar with the story, but basically there was a lot of cheating by him, a whole lot of gaslighting and many, many tears (mostly mine). He visibly flirted with girls in front of me, refused to make our relationship public on social media and said it was because he thought that sort of thing was ridiculous. (Turns out it was because he was dating other women at the same time.)

I didn't trust him. Bottom line: I *shouldn't* have trusted him.

In a way, the jealousy that I felt was warranted. However, what wasn't warranted was the way I expressed that jealousy. When he would flirt with girls in front of me, instead of calling out his BS, I would feel frustrated with whoever the other woman was, and would strut over and insert myself with the sort of 'he's with me' vibe that screams 'unhealthy attachment'. Deep down I knew his behaviour was the problem, but accepting that meant leaving the relationship and I wasn't ready to walk away yet. So it was easier to get territorial and shift blame to the other girl for 'throwing herself at him' than to hold him accountable (or, better yet, hold myself accountable and GTF out of there).

Jealousy often stems from a lack of self-confidence – for example, a lingering fear that your partner will find someone 'better' than you. Knowing your self-worth is key.

The problem is, when you're in a jealousy spiral, it can be hard to separate fact from fiction, especially when your partner is telling you that you're imagining it. So, how can we start to break it down, boost our self-worth and bring some logic to our thinking?

WARRANTED OR UNWARRANTED?

If you're experiencing jealousy about something, then the first step in addressing this feeling should be to figure out why. What has prompted these feelings? It might help to ask yourself the following questions:

♥ Where are these feelings coming from and when did they start?
♥ Is your partner's behaviour making you feel insecure?
♥ Have you had negative experiences in past relationships?
♥ Do you trust your partner?
♥ Do you trust yourself?
♥ Are you basing your feelings on fact, or assumptions?
♥ What's your attachment style and how could it be fuelling these feelings?

Once you've pinpointed the source of your jealousy, figure out if these feelings are being driven by your own insecurities or if they are a by-product of the actions of your partner.

How do you achieve this? Through an honest and open conversation about how you're feeling.

Imagine this: you start dating someone who is close friends with a girl you've never met. They hang out frequently and text each other late into the night but you've never been introduced to her. You start wondering if you should feel weird about this friendship, and voice your feelings to your partner in a non-accusatory way. In a healthy relationship with good boundaries, your partner would probably respond with something like, 'Holy shit, I'm sorry you feel like that. Why don't we all go for dinner so you can get to know each other?' A more dickish response would be a total dismissal of your feelings ('You're being crazy, we're just friends') followed by them making basically zero effort to introduce the two of you.

At the end of the day, other people's actions can make us feel jealous, but we can't control other people. We only have agency over our own feelings and our reactions to whatever situation we've experienced.

Accidentally Unfiltered

I had been with my boyfriend for about four months. I had been cheated on in the past, but this felt like it was going well. Until I saw a text on his phone to someone else: 'I can't wait to see you this weekend! I've planned some really fun stuff, pack a warm jacket!'

I immediately felt my stomach drop. No way I was doing this again. So I ended it with him without a reason – I couldn't be bothered arguing about it and going through it again. He was shattered.

A few days later, as the weekend approached, jealousy and curiosity got the better of me. We had each other on 'Find My Friends' so I thought, 'I'll just go see what she is like.' Imagine my shock when I saw him with a young girl, and I mean young. Turns out she was his thirteen-year-old niece that stays with him sometimes! FML.

Happy to report we got back together after I admitted what I'd done. He thought it was ridiculous and hilarious but he also took me off 'Find My Friends'. Fair!

OKAY, YOU'RE OFFICIALLY JEALOUS. WHAT NEXT?

As someone who has experienced both warranted and unwarranted jealousy, there are useful steps you can take. They're not a magic cure but, over time, they can help to strengthen your sense of self.

- ♥ **Accept and validate.** Jealousy is normal, to a degree, but you need to figure out if it's you or them. Where are your feelings coming from and what is the trigger?
- ♥ **Open channels of communication.** Explain how you feel, even if it's not rational. 'I know you've done nothing wrong, but I feel like this . . .' Help them understand your behaviour and you can try to ease your insecurities together.
- ♥ **Resist the urge to dig and pry.** I know it's probably unrealistic to tell you to completely stay away from those dark corners of social media that are stoking your jealousy, but seriously, you've got to try. You have your own life to live, and spending hours lost in the Instagram feed of someone else is not the way to live it!
- ♥ **Be present in your relationship.** See above! Enjoy the here and now. And don't let the past intrude upon the present.
- ♥ **Innocent things sometimes look suspicious ... but that doesn't mean they are!** If you're inhabiting a jealousy mindset, even the most innocuous thing can look suspicious. It's important to remember that feelings are NOT facts.

And, after all that, if you really can't overcome these jealous feelings, it's on you to leave the relationship and find one you feel more secure in. This is where you have to back yourself. *I want more from a relationship. I want to feel safe, loved and valued.* Regardless of the catalyst for your feelings, you're in control of how you react to and act upon them. Having healthy boundaries and a strong sense of self-worth is critical to feeling confident in a relationship and to knowing when to leave a situation that compromises that.

I tried to control my toxic ex's behaviour with rules around what was acceptable and not, and it did absolutely nothing. It didn't stop him cheating or help me to cope with it. You can't force someone to change their behaviour if they're not motivated to do it.

WHAT IF YOUR PARTNER IS THE JEALOUS TYPE?

If your partner is plagued by unwarranted jealousy, you can offer them love, trust and compassion – but there is a limit. You do not have to minimise your life to make someone else feel more secure. You can help them to feel loved, but you're not obligated to constantly prove your innocence. Trust is mutually built.

If I had a partner who kept saying, 'I know you've done nothing wrong, but I still feel insecure . . .' I would get tired of that narrative eventually, too. It's a self-fulfilling prophecy. Most people want a partner who feels like an equal in the relationship, not someone who is constantly questioning their value.

There are also people out there who are intrinsically jealous, thanks to a variety of factors in their past that usually centre around violations of trust or a lack of control. But jealousy can be a sign of manipulative and coercive behaviour, and it goes without saying that that is deeply problematic and dangerous.

Jealousy is NOT a sign of how much your partner loves you. It has more to do with fear and control than it ever has to do with love. If someone is trying to implement rules around the way you can or can't behave (*You have to call me when you finish work, I don't want you hanging out with those friends, I want you to give me your passwords to your social media accounts*) it is not just a red flag, but a giant neon fuck-off sign that the relationship is not conducive to healthy boundaries.

THERE IS NO MAGIC CURE FOR JEALOUSY

Some people deal with these feelings by telling themselves, *I'll feel more secure when we live together* or *I'll be happier once they propose*, but kicking your jealousy down the road isn't a solution. And besides, things go wrong at all stages of a relationship, regardless of whether you're living together, married or even co-parenting. You've got to find a deeper level of trust together.

Accidentally Unfiltered

About five years ago I was in a situationship with a guy who had a girlfriend (long, long story and not my proudest moment). One day he gave me his Ticketek password to access some tickets he had bought, and I decided to try the password on his Instagram. Success! For months I would log on to his Instagram and delete photos he uploaded with his girlfriend, and unlike and delete all his comments on her posts. He eventually changed his password but to this day he has no idea it was me the entire time.

KINKS

Don't yuck my yum, baby!

BRITT AND LAURA

SEE ALSO: BOUNDARIES, DATING

LAURA: To kick this chapter off we went straight to the well of wisdom – the *Life Uncut* Facebook group – and asked a simple question: What is the kinkiest thing you've ever been asked to do in the bedroom? Here's some of what we got. Brace yourselves, because some of these are pretty out there!

- ♥ Someone once asked if they could fuck my feet.
- ♥ I got a guy to piss on me once. Never again, but it was funny to try.
- ♥ A guy I matched with on Bumble asked if he could spit in my mouth.
- ♥ I was asked to not swallow, but transfer his cum from my mouth to his, so he could taste it. Apparently it's called 'snowballing'.
- ♥ Twenty minutes into making out with a one-night stand, he asked me if I would 💩 in his 👄. He then got up and pulled a camping chair out of his closet with a hole cut in the seat and then lay down under it . . . face under the hole.
- ♥ A guy once asked me to bend him over and fit as many fingers as I could into his bum and jerk him off at the same time. Shit, I'm not that coordinated.

♥ I had sex with a 'looner', meaning he got off on balloons. He asked me to blow up a balloon while Skyping him. He was wanking while he watched the balloon get bigger, and the excitement for him came as it got close to bursting. I had to do it twice for him to reach orgasm and he was so grateful to me for doing it as he said most women just laugh at him.

♥ I had a six-month-old baby and this man I was casually dating wanted to dress up in a nappy and have me breast-feed him. Look . . . it wasn't for me.

♥ He asked me to fart on his tongue.

♥ 'Don't be scared,' he said, as he brought out a collar and a lead.

BRITT: What a way to start this chapter off! Talk about a baptism of fire!

Kinks: they're not really something we all talk about very openly, are they, yet they hold a major fascination. When we spoke with sexologist Chantelle Otten and a listener who had a few kinky fetishes, that episode shot straight to the top of the charts.[20] There is no doubt that people go crazy for kinks! I'm so interested to hear others talk about the weird, wonderful and unusual things they get up to behind closed doors – probably because I'm not into anything wild myself. But I guess you could say I'm kink-curious . . .

L: I think kinks are having a real renaissance at the moment, and the more sex positive we become as a society, the more commonplace it is to talk about the things that were once kept as dirty little secrets (that is, unless dirty little secrets are what get you off). But something that I didn't realise until I did a deep dive on the topic is that kink has been depicted through history, art and religion for thousands of years. There are historic artworks of ancient Greek gang bangs, Mozart wrote a song called *Leck mir den Arsch fein recht schön sauber* which translates to 'Lick me in the ass right well and clean' (google it, I am not making this shit up!) and even Cleopatra, one-time ruler of Ancient Egypt, had a very unorthodox sex toy. She would use a hollowed-out phallic dildo that was filled with live bees. The bees would buzz angrily around inside, causing the dildo to vibrate and bounce around. Even in a time long before AAA batteries, with some ingenuity, dirty desire found a way.

The history of kinks is also as chequered as it is long. Up until fairly recently, being kinky was considered a psychological disorder in need of medical treatment. In fact, sexual kinks were only removed from the *Diagnostic and Statistical Manual of Mental Disorders* – the guidebook for psychologists and psychiatrists – in 2013. When you think about the fact that less than a decade ago, people who enjoyed a good spanking were thought to have a mental illness, it's pretty wild to see how far we've come in terms of understanding, acceptance and conversation around kinks . . . and, I mean, who doesn't like a little spanking now and again?

B: I mean, I'm sure there are people out there who don't. Just like the time you famously declared on the podcast that 'everyone likes a finger in the bum' and again, not everyone does, haha!

Kink was taboo for such a long time, and although we're more accepting of it these days, represents the unknown for a lot of people. When we were doing research for our episode, it was surprising how many people came forward with their own harmless kinks but wanted to stay anonymous as they didn't want others to know they get freaky in the bedroom. I guess they didn't want anyone to make them feel ashamed of what gets them off.

Understanding the history of kinks and bringing the conversation out of the shadows does a lot to destigmatise the shame surrounding what gets your rocks off. It is also slowly starting to become more acceptable to talk about, thanks to big films like *Fifty Shades of Grey* coming out of Hollywood, and TV shows such as *Billions*, which portrays a main character having to navigate his kink obsessions. All this publicly highlights what kink looks like in a relationship and as a result, people are starting to be more open about their thoughts and desires. And I am here for it!

But, Laura, what is the difference between a kink, a fetish and a fantasy? I think it helps to get those straight quite early on.

L: Well, kinks are defined as a sexual activity that falls outside of sex that society traditionally considers 'acceptable'. So what is 'acceptable' sex? Some might call it vanilla, as it basically includes all the conventional stuff we think of when it comes to sexual activities like penile penetration, masturbation, hand jobs, blow jobs ... you get the picture. Now, 'vanilla' doesn't necessarily mean 'boring', it just means that it's pretty standard stuff in terms of what we're all doing between the sheets.

A kink can constitute anything that is thought to deviate from social norms when it comes to sex and arousal. It covers a wide scope of different activities that can include everything from urine play and bondage to having sex in public and even dirty talk. And what's super kinky for one person can seem pretty normal to someone else, so while the spectrum is broad, it's all really personal.

A fetish technically refers to a sexual desire in which arousal is linked to an object. This can be anything but is often a body part (hello, foot fetish). Fetishes differ to kinks in that for the person to get off and achieve sexual satisfaction, the object of desire needs to be present.

A fantasy, meanwhile, is just that: something made up in the mind. It can be any mental image that helps to bring about sexual desire and arousal. Some people like to play out their fantasies by role-playing, or opening up their relationships to another sexual partner, but more often than not fantasies remain in one's imagination. And, quite possibly, their browsing history.

I think it needs to be stated that having a kink or a fetish is nothing to be ashamed of. There's a reason why there are so many websites and even dating sites specifically for them!

Accidentally Unfiltered

I am an Adult Learning teacher. I had a fling with an older male colleague. He showed me how to use the wood lathe; it was very Patrick Swayze in *Ghost*.

One day at school, we played a game. I put a small bullet vibrator, that he controlled, down my pants while I taught a lesson. Things went awry. The vibrator failed and wouldn't stop! I nearly burnt my clit off that day.

After school, we fucked in the staffroom.

B: From everyone we spoke to when we were preparing our episode on kinks, the biggest barrier that most listeners were facing was that they didn't know how to bring up their kinks with their sexual partner. I mean, how do you ask your new boyfriend to pee on you, or suck your toes? How do you ask that girl you really like to handcuff you to a bed and smack you with a paddle? There is fear of judgement and also fear of rejection. But the thing is, how will you know if they're really your thing unless you give them a red-hot crack?

Lux Alptraum, sex expert and author of *Faking It: The Lies Women Tell About Sex – And the Truths They Reveal*, says: 'It can be very vulnerable to be open and say, "Hi, I want to explore this thing."' In an interview with Healthline, she mentions it can 'be nerve-wracking to be on the receiving end of a kink announcement, even if it ends up sounding hot to you. It can be a little scary because there may be a sense of pressure or "what if I do it badly or don't know what to do?"[21]

As with just about everything we've ever discussed on the pod, it's all about communication. You need to speak to your sexual partner openly about what you're thinking, feeling and wanting to try. Gauge their interest. See if you can dip your toes in the water. Chantelle Otten recommends raising the idea of something you'd like to try in a conversation outside the bedroom first – for example, in the car can be a good place as it's not high pressure and it's easy for you to both look elsewhere!

A way to establish whether you and your partner could be open to trying some kinks together is to take a quiz that identifies what you would both be interested or open to. One you can do alone or with your partner is kinktest.org.

We have surreptitiously scoured the internet for a list of kinks you might like to try. (And we can report that even googling kinks feels a little subversive – and hot.)

Bondage: Bondage is a form of restraint – pretty self-explanatory. Think being tied up, whether that's with kinky sex toys such as handcuffs or rope, or trying something as tame as you using a scarf, tie or T-shirt to restrain your partner's wrists when you're getting it on.

Dom/Sub: Dominance is one half of the DS (dominance and submission) in BDSM and is all about a consensual power exchange. With this particular kink, which is fairly common, the dominant partner derives sexual pleasure from taking control. The submissive partner allows their dominant partner to . . . well, dominate them.

Masochism/Sadism: Masochism is deriving pleasure from the high sensation most often referred to as pain, be that physical or emotional. So, if you enjoy being spanked, humiliated or spat on, you might be a masochist. The flip side of masochism is sadism, in which someone derives pleasure from inflicting pain of a physical or emotional nature.

Impact play: Impact play refers to the use of hands, paddles, whips, or whatever you have around your house to hit the body (maybe a spatula after whipping up a cake). If you've ever playfully spanked your partner during sex, that's impact play. For obvious reasons, it always requires consent and communication.

Orgasm control: Orgasm control means exactly what it sounds like – controlling and prolonging the timing of your orgasm. Typically, it's done by getting to the brink of orgasm, then stopping, slowing down, or lessening stimulation until your arousal levels drop. Then you get back to the edge of orgasm, and repeat as many times as you want or can stand.

The basic process of orgasm control can help your sexual interactions last longer. You can also use orgasm control to incorporate power-play dynamics into your sex, by having one person be in control of the other partner's orgasm. You can practise orgasm control alone, which is typically called edging, or you can practise it with a partner.

Age play: Age play is a form of role play in which one or both partners pretend to be (and get off on being) an age other than their own. Chances are you've already experienced what could be considered ultra-light age play if you've ever called a partner 'baby' in bed. Another common example is the 'daddy dominant–baby girl' setup. If you're calling someone 'daddy' in bed you're engaging in light age play. A more 'extreme' and less common example of age play is full-on role-playing, where one partner is turned on by wearing a diaper and acting like a baby.

Voyeurism and exhibitionism: A voyeur is someone who derives sexual pleasure from watching others get it on. When we speak about voyeurism from a kink perspective, we're talking about consensual voyeurism. Very important distinction! Exhibitionists enjoy being watched, and voyeurs enjoy watching, which makes these two kinks a common item on the menu at sex parties or kink events.

Foot fetishes: Foot fetishes are one of the most common fetishes out there, especially for heterosexual men. Someone with a foot fetish is literally turned on by feet – thinking about them, touching them, seeing them – and could potentially get off on all of the above. They often want to engage in foot worship, in which they treat their partner's foot like a holy object: kissing, caressing and massaging it. So even if you don't have a foot fetish, having a partner with one can be extremely enjoyable as it means there are potentially foot massages galore in store for you.

Urophilia: Urophilia is a fancy name for watersports, golden showers, or the more direct name, pee play. With this kink, people find urination sexually arousing. There are lots of things you can do with urine, though the most common way to enjoy pee play is to give or receive golden showers. A golden shower is letting someone shower you (or vice versa) with their pee. We had one of our listeners come on the podcast and speak very openly about her pee fetish and just how it goes down, why she likes it and logistically how it works. Yep, you have to get some tarps involved sometimes!

Role playing: Role playing is another common kink, involving people taking on characters outside of their day-to-day lives as part of a sex scene. This can be as simple as putting on a nurse's outfit and as elaborate as constructing an entire scene complete with fully realised characters! The sky is the limit! The most common examples include doctor or nurse and patient, boss and secretary, pool boy and rich housewife or college student and professor. But honestly, use your imagination.

A word on after-care: Even kinky folk need a cuddle! So check with each other how it was, whether you both liked it and felt comfortable, what you'd do differently next time. Don't just race off to the shower! Take the time for conversation afterwards to help ensure it's a positive experience.

L: I'll never forget when I was in my early twenties and the guy I was dating at the time decided to try dirty talk with me. Now, mind you, this was only the second man I had ever slept with and my sexual experiences at this point were pretty conservative. There wasn't any pre-warning, no warm-up, no conversation outside the bedroom – he just went for it.

'You're a dirty little slut. You're a whore.'

I was frozen. He kept asking for me to say I liked it – but I didn't.

Once he had finished he got up and went to the bathroom and I lay in bed and cried, thinking he really thought these degrading things about me. Had he brought up the idea beforehand and explained to me he was into dirty talk, I would have had a moment to get my head around it. Take this experience as your 101 for how *not* to introduce kinks into your relationship – don't just spring them on your partner. It turns out I actually really like dirty talk when it's with someone who makes me feel safe and secure.

If you want to try something new, bring it up before the pants come off so all parties feel respected and involved – and remember, once you're finished, the after-care is just as important as the preceding conversations. Recovering from a huge rush of endorphins can leave you feeling sad and depleted without the care and follow-up from the person you've been intimate with.

Accidentally Unfiltered

My first boyfriend and I once got into a frisky mood out in public. We thought we would attend to our needs and got down to some hanky panky (🐒-style 😂) in a public toilet on the ground floor of a five-star hotel. It was hot. A few minutes in, however, we heard a sudden clicking of the lock and the door was flung wide open. We were mid-action, staring into the eyes of the cleaner, who SCREAMED so loudly and slammed the bathroom door shut.

We were mortified. We waited a few minutes to see if the coast was clear – and it seemed to be. So we got back to business.

Big mistake. A minute later, the bathroom door was flung open for the second time, revealing two hotel security guards AND the cleaner. They waited while we dressed and then security escorted us from the hotel in silence. Needless to say we never had sex in a public toilet again.

No matter what you're into, kink is about consent, communication and compromise. Before trying any new sex act, obtaining enthusiastic, continuous consent from all parties involved is a must. Make sure you talk about safe limits and boundaries – pick a safe word if you need to. As you explore, your tastes and tolerances will likely change so it's important to keep a running dialogue about your limits. With all that established, it's just about having fun, getting off, and trying something new, so get out there and enjoy it, you kinky little thing!

THE KNOT

Is a wedding really the end goal?

LAURA

SEE ALSO: PENGUINS, TIMELINES, UNCONDITIONAL LOVE

I was never the little girl who dreamed of a big, white wedding. In fact I've always felt pretty apathetic towards the idea of a wedding – that is, until I met Matt.

As the child of multiple divorces, for me the whole concept of a big wedding used to sit a little bit uncomfortably. I always thought I'd end up eloping in Las Vegas in a sequinned dress. However, although the idea of a white wedding never got me buzzing, I've still always believed that marriage and monogamy were for me. So, who better, out of the two of us, to write a chapter on tying the knot than the one who's been engaged for three years and always thought they'd have a small nuptials, but instead is currently up to her eyeballs planning a wedding that's turning out to be ... er ... not so small after all.

I cannot tell you the number of questions our wonderful Lifers have sent in over the years that centre around weddings! Whether it be etiquette at a wedding, bridesmaid debacles or wedding disaster stories, we've heard them all ...

'HELP, can I not invite my friend's partner to my wedding?'

'How do I tell my friend she's not in my bridal party?'

'I'm engaged, but how do I know if they actually are The One – what do I do?'

Now, it's important to mention that getting married or even monogamy is certainly not for everyone; however, for a lot of our listeners, engagements, weddings and, in turn, marriages are still a fundamental part of so many relationships. When you're in the throes of dating, a proposal can seem like the ultimate goal – the point in your relationship at which you can relax with the comfort that you're in it, together, for the long haul. Which is exactly why there can be so much pressure to get to that point AND to get it right.

I remember Matt once saying to me that he wasn't someone who wanted to have a long engagement. Matt is traditional at heart and always saw himself getting engaged, having a wedding, and then popping out a couple of kids … in that exact order. Like I said, as I write this, we've now been engaged for three years, so that plan well and truly went out the window! When we were faced with the happy accident that was an unplanned pregnancy we decided to throw society's timelines in the bin and have never looked back.

We were on a babymoon in Fiji when Matt proposed. At the time, I was seven months pregnant with Marlie-Mae. I didn't know the proposal was coming, although looking back I should have. A few months earlier, he'd been showing me something on his phone when I noticed something I'd never seen before: a private photo vault app.

I pushed Matt for an answer because, of course, when your body is pulsating with pregnancy hormones and you find a rogue photo vault on your boyfriend's phone, your first thought is 'What the fuck is he hiding?', not 'Ooh, I bet he's secretly doing something thoughtful for me.'

Matt's sister Kate was having dinner with us that night, and when I continued to press him about the app despite him becoming increasingly squirmy, Kate took me aside and told me to pull my head in. 'Matt is trying to do something nice for you and you're going to ruin it for yourself!' she said. Resisting the urge to dig for answers took every fibre of being, but it turned out the vault had photos of the engagement ring in it, not topless photos of his ex . . . phew!

After Matt proposed in 2019, things got weird in the world. We had a baby, then there was that whole pandemic thing. Our original wedding date was right amid the second Sydney lockdown, so, instead of getting hitched we decided to have another baby.

Although we never intended to have a long engagement, it's worked out that way. But if everything from here goes to plan and there are no more false starts, we will be trotting down the aisle and into wedded bliss in November 2022, and although I maybe once felt apathetic towards the idea of a wedding, I'd be lying if I said I was anything short of excited for the day to finally come.

Attitudes towards marriages have changed dramatically over the years. Happily, there is now more freedom for people to choose what type of relationship they want – though that isn't to say that those decisions are completely free from judgement. Just yesterday my Uber driver asked me if I had children.

'Yes, two,' I replied.

He later asked me a question about my husband.

'Oh, I'm not married, but we are engaged,' I replied.

I could tell he seemed put out by this. I was pretty annoyed, too – first by the assumption that if I had children then I must be in a heterosexual relationship, and then came this: despite being a complete stranger he said, as though he had some sort of right to an explanation, 'So why are you not married?' This is not an isolated occurrence.

That's the thing about marriage: there are people with such strong views around the right way to do things that they think it's socially acceptable to challenge anyone who chooses to live life in a way that's at odds with their beliefs or traditions.

If I had a dollar for every time Matt and I have been asked when we are getting married, or why we aren't married yet – well, we'd be off on an all-expenses-paid trip to the Bahamas with a nanny and unlimited mojitos.

TICK-TOCK, IT'S THE MARRIAGE CLOCK

The pressure to put a ring on it still exists, but it is dissipating. The marriage rate in Australia has been steadily declining over time, reducing by 23.7 per cent over the two decades between 2000 and 2019.[22] At the same time, the median age of people getting married has been steadily increasing. People are less likely to rush into things these days and a contributing factor to that is the move away from religion.

In the past, religious ideologies had a stronghold over many communities in Australia. Less than sixty years ago, the idea of 'cohabiting' with a partner and having children without being married was socially radical, widely frowned upon and deemed to be 'living in sin'. Religion is becoming more and more a matter of personal and private choice, and as the church's influence over people and communities declines within Australia (a process known as secularisation), so does the expectation of marriage. Instead, people now feel freer to enter into marriage because they *want* to, not because they've been pressured into it. And just five years ago in 2017, the recognition of same-sex marriage was a major change to the way marriage has been viewed in Australia.

There are a whole bunch of other reasons why marriage isn't factoring as high on many people's agendas as it did with previous generations. Increased independence for women, changing views on monogamy, shifting gender roles within households and the destigmatisation of de facto relationships and divorce have all influenced the way in which marriage is perceived.

It's crazy to think that not so long ago, most couples only lived together for the first time after getting married. De facto relationships are now the norm, and for many people they're something of a road test of what married life might look like. It's not that millennials and Gen Z are rejecting the idea of marriage completely, but we're making more informed choices around the people that we want as life partners before making that particular commitment.

We also live in a time that celebrates personal growth, self-worth and education when it comes to navigating relationships and smoothing over issues that arise. I mean, Britt and I have an entire podcast about it! I love this modern model for romance because it allows for a more connected relationship where you can grow together. And if a marriage or relationship does end, we are slowly learning to reframe our perception of this, to see it not as a failure but as a transformative time for personal growth. If there were mistakes or toxicity within the relationship, you can learn not to repeat them in future, or if you just grew apart, you can value the time you did have together. It's all contributed to who you are and forms part of the narrative of your life, regardless of whether or not there's a ring involved.

BUT HOW DO YOU KNOW IF THEY'RE THE ONE?

Earlier in 2022 we interviewed human-connection specialist Mark Groves on the podcast.[23] Mark is a man well-versed in everything love and relationships, which is why I was surprised to hear that it was his own failed engagement in his twenties that led him on his quest to find answers to the question 'How do you know they're the one?'

Here's what Mark had to say:

'In my late twenties I had an engagement end. I was raised Catholic, and culture, religion and movies had all embedded this idea that I need to get married by twenty-five to twenty-seven and have kids by somewhere near to thirty and if you're not doing that, there is something wrong with you. And so here I was, right on time. At twenty-seven I got engaged, and it was this massive moment where I remember proposing and then it was this realisation that sometimes you meet a moment that you're taught to want and then you realise that you don't want it.'

For some people, the choice is easy and they feel nothing but elation leading up to the wedding day – however, for others there can be a certain amount of fear and anxiety surrounding the idea of choosing the partner that they're going to be with 'forever'. As Mark said, 'Some level of fear is normal, as it's uncertain. But the idea that one should go terrified towards marriage is not right. Having a high level of anxiety about anything is not great, anxiety being such a great indicator of us creating a future that we might not want.'

Mark had three questions for anyone unsure if their fiancé(e) is The One:

> ♥ If they left you tomorrow, would you be okay?
> ♥ Can you imagine what it would be like waiting at the altar for them, or walking down the aisle towards them? Does it make you happy, anxious or scared?
> ♥ Can someone else love them better?

WEDDING WITH A SIDE OF MARRIAGE

In my experience, there is another question that we should also be asking ourselves before we dive headfirst into holy matrimony: is it the allure of the wedding or the commitment of marriage that you're most drawn to?

We often receive questions from listeners of *Life Uncut* who are worried about their relationship status. Their friends are getting engaged but their own partner hasn't yet popped the question. They want to know: what can they do to nudge them?

Regardless of your age, you have to ask yourself:

Do you want them to propose because it's the next step in the relationship?

OR

Is the fact that everyone else is doing it giving you some wild FOMO . . . or both?

In one of my previous long-term relationships, I was really pushing for marriage – for all the wrong reasons. I wanted him to propose because I saw it as a symbol of a healthy relationship, despite knowing, deep down, that we didn't fit into that category. To me, marriage would be an affirmation that he was committed to our future. He wasn't.

I don't want anyone to think that I have a negatively skewed view of marriage – I don't. I like to think of myself as a realist. I believe that marriage is both a physical and spiritual commitment, a promise that binds your relationship and deepens your commitment to each other. There is something very cool about choosing someone to be your person and making the promise that you're going get up, day in, day out, and work on your relationship. However, marriage still comes with conditions. It's not an end goal, after which there will only be blissful contentment – in many ways, it's where the real work begins. Life continues after that memorable day when you tie the knot, and I feel that you both need to be prepared to support each other through everything that follows.

GETTING ON THE SAME PAGE

What if marriage is important to you, but your partner doesn't want to get married? This is another very common question.

First up, there is a big difference between a partner saying: I don't want to get married and I don't want to get married to YOU.

Perhaps your partner is a child of divorce (like me) and doesn't believe that a piece of paper is symbolic of commitment. But if they are committed, and all their other actions reflect that, is it worth throwing away your relationship? Is there something else you can do to ritualise your commitment? Can you exchange something else besides vows that means something to both of you?

It could also be a matter of timing – as in, they might be telling you that they're not *ready* to get married. According to one survey, millennials tend to prioritise achieving other life goals before getting married. First on the list is establishing and achieving financial independence.[24]

Choosing to live on your own timeline is incredibly freeing, especially when you choose that timeline together. Matt and I bought a house and had two kids before marriage – and now our girls will both get to be flower girls at the wedding. There is a good chance herding a couple of toddlers down the aisle is going to be chaos, and y'all know we thrive in chaos!

One of the biggest lessons that we've come to advocate on the podcast when people ask questions about marriage is that you have to make sure that both you and your partner are on the same page with what you want out of life. Do you both want kids? Do you want to live in the city or the country? Who is going to stay home and look after the kids if you have them? Who will do the cooking? Who will do the cleaning? How are you going to split finances? How many times a week can your in-laws visit? Honestly, the list goes on and on. And the best time for figuring out whether you're on the same page with what you want out of life? That is long before you walk down the aisle.

Accidentally Unfiltered

My sister got married a few years ago, and I was her maid of honour. She wore an amazing dress – a really special princess-style ballgown – and she had been on an exercise regime in the lead-up, so she was looking fierce. For some reason, even though she didn't need to, she decided to wear big, suck-you-in Spanx-style undies under her dress. Ceremony happens, and it is beautiful. Fast forward to the reception. We are sitting at dinner, and my sister looks really exhausted and red in the face. I ask her if she is okay, and she leans over and says she feels like her undies are cutting off her circulation, and she is struggling to breathe. So we go into the bathroom together, and she takes them off and instantly feels better. But now we have a dilemma . . . she doesn't want to 'freeball' at her own wedding. So I swapped undies with her! However, we did not take into consideration the wedding night! I spoke to my sister the next day and she said it was a good night EXCEPT she felt super awkward when her hubby pulled her (MY) undies off with his teeth when they got back to their hotel room! It is a secret that we have kept for years, and now I am sharing it with you as well!

P.S. I kept the Spanx!

YOU'RE GETTING HITCHED! WHO TO INVITE?

We recently received an email from a listener who was planning her wedding and found herself in a friendship dilemma. There was one girl in her friendship group who she didn't want to invite to her wedding. She didn't get along with this person or enjoy being around her anymore. Should she put her reservations aside and invite the whole group to the wedding, or leave the person she didn't enjoy spending time with off the guest list?

Super awkward! It comes down to the intensity of your feelings and your gut instinct. Personally, I wouldn't want anyone at my special day who had toxic energy – but are they really that bad to be around? If you've just grown apart and there's no bad blood, is it really going to affect you if she's in the background of your wedding pics? Is her presence really going to ruin your memories?

If it's a yes, then don't invite her. If it's a no, is it worth the conflict?

It's a big statement to exclude a single person from your friendship group. If you've had a huge argument with the person in question, you've got a very real reason to feel this way. If it's more that you don't mesh with them, I would still invite them, as, in my opinion, the drama surrounding not inviting them would be far more stressful.

Generally, I believe it's your big day, so you should do what is going to make YOU (and your partner) happy. This is how I'm trying to approach my wedding. However, I appreciate that for a lot of brides that is not always the case – especially if there are religious or cultural constraints. For so many people, weddings can be just as much about keeping the family happy as they are about the couple. I can't imagine the added challenges of organising a wedding when you have to take into consideration other people's wishes for your special day. If your wedding is being orchestrated to keep other people happy, then either you say 'fuck it' and do what feels right for you, or you make some compromises and accept that maybe you won't have the wedding that you desired, but know that ultimately it is about the marriage and your commitment. A wedding is just a day – but you have the rest of your life together to make up for it.

<u>Side note: How to be a good wedding guest</u>

- ♥ **Outfit overkill:** If Kendall Jenner has taught us anything, it's what NOT to wear to a wedding. Remember the dress she wore to a friend's wedding that looked like a couple of handkerchiefs tied together with a piece of dental floss? She looked like a smokeshow, sure, but it was the sort of dress that screamed, 'I've arrived!' It goes without saying that wedding guests should not be trying to upstage anyone. Leave that kind of jaw-dropping entrance to the bride, who has probably forked out a pretty penny to have you there. Oh . . . and don't wear all white. Jeez.

- ♥ **Gift giving:** Now this is a tricky (and divisive!) one. We had a big debate on the podcast about appropriate gifts for a wedding. We got to a point where we agreed that yes, you have to give a gift – and money is totally acceptable (and often preferred). We did a poll of podcast listeners to figure out just how much money you should be putting in the wishing well, and the answer was: $80 per person is the sweet spot. $50 is okay and $100 per person is generous – anything above that and you're a gold-star guest. Also, movie tickets and scratchies are not a vibe. If you've spent a BOMB getting to the wedding – hello, destination wedding! – or you get the couple a kick-arse engagement gift then maybe it's fine to forgo a present at the wedding, but don't you dare show up without a heartfelt card, you naughty peach.

- ♥ **All the extras:** If you're in a bridal party, weddings can be spendy! Don't we know it! There's the outfit, the hens' party, the gift, the travel, the accommodation … it's enough to make your bank balance wheeze. I've been in a bridal party before that cost a small fortune. This is where you need to have an honest conversation early on, and be realistic about what you can contribute. It's okay to say, 'I'd really love to be a part of your wedding, but can we talk budget?'.

♥ **Celebrating being single:** Attending a wedding when you're single can be tough, especially if you've just gone through a break-up or if you aren't living your best single life and are wanting a relationship. Go easy on yourself. It's okay to feel a little bit sad while being so happy for your friend at the same time. We are multifaceted humans! My advice? Weddings are great places to meet new people, as everyone is feeling the love bug! Just don't get really fucking drunk – but if you do, put your phone where you can't easily access it. The last thing you want to do is text your ex.

LONG DISTANCE

How the hell do you navigate it?

BRITT

SEE ALSO: LOVE LANGUAGES, NUDES, PENGUINS

Long-distance relationships suck. The end.

There are no two ways about it.

I am yet to meet anyone who says, 'Oh yes, I love my long-distance relationship, it's so easy and fulfilling!' (Except maybe my narcissist ex, who was living a double life, marrying someone else while also sleeping with multiple people. Long distance was the key there.) I'm willing to bet that any non-sociopathic person would rather be with their partner than be on the other side of the country or the world to them.

All but one of my relationships, both the serious and casual ones, have been long distance. Either I am very unlucky or I wasn't actually ready to be in a relationship and sought out these situations like I seek out the chunks of cookie dough in my ice cream. But it means I have had my fair share of experiences with them.

As most of our listeners will know, my most recent serious relationship with Jordan was also one that was mostly long distance, as he was constantly travelling around the world to compete in tennis tournaments.

In the past, I was drawn to these types of relationships for a few reasons. I think they worked for me because I was scared of letting anyone get too close to me. (Again, I'll direct you to previously mentioned experiences, such as dating a totally shady narcissist!) Distance was also a convenient excuse any time I wasn't too emotionally invested in seeing the person or actively developing a connection with them. The distance factor gave me an easy out and meant that I didn't have to make a whole lot of effort.

With Jordan, though? None of the above applied.

Until I met Jordan I didn't know a love like that could exist. I fell for him so deeply it honestly scared me to death. When he told me early on that he wanted a relationship, I went through my usual motions of being a little scared, wanting to run, not understanding why someone would want to get close to me. But when he told me he was going overseas for a year, that scared me even more. The thought of finding this person – this pure, beautiful, fun love – and then losing him wasn't an option. I didn't think twice. I gave him my heart and jumped headfirst into another long-distance relationship. But this time, the distance wasn't a convenient way out, or a safeguard against intimacy. It was a very real part of our relationship that we had to navigate every day. Our long-distance relationship certainly wasn't without its challenges, but it taught me to know when to be patient, when to be imaginative, when to be assertive and when to be kind. And, rather than holding me back, like pretty much every other long-distance relationship I have been in, it taught me how to change and how to grow. Even though our relationship ran its course, it was absolutely worth it.

HOW TO KNOW IF YOU SHOULD DO LONG DISTANCE

Are they worth it?
What if it is a waste of time?
Are they going to cheat on me?
If you've found yourself in a geographically challenged situation,

147

these are all questions that are probably racing through your head. To some degree, they are perfectly normal, but if you are genuinely worried or have reason to believe that your partner will cheat on you, then you might need to step back and ask yourself some hard questions about your relationship. Let's unpack these questions a little bit further.

Are they worth it?

If you ask me, you should know if they are worth it or not before you commit. Embarking on long distance is a big undertaking, so it's important to have a clear answer to this question from the outset, because the relationship is going to take up a lot of your emotional energy. It may not work out, but you need to at least have reason to believe it will and have plenty of hope, otherwise what is the point? If you are on the fence about whether they are worth it, then you need to ask yourself why you're not convinced. If it's really early days and you need a bit more time with them to feel confident, then that's something you can work on. But if there's anything else that's making you pause, then that's a bit of a red flag.

What if it is a waste of time?

If you are already worrying about the potential end of a relationship when you've only just entered it, you're setting yourself up for failure by bringing in too much negativity and pessimism. Sure, the relationship might not last forever, but that doesn't mean it was a waste of time. We can learn so much from every experience in life – the good, the bad and the ugly – and if you embrace your long-distance relationship with an open heart and a willingness to learn, you will be far better off. Even if it does end, you'll have gained knowledge about intimacy, commitment, love and – most importantly – about yourself. So, instead of freaking out about the future, try to live in the present and focus on how you feel about each other right now. Make your plans without assuming it is going to fail.

Are they going to cheat on me?

It's an uncomfortable truth that long distance makes it easier for a partner to be unfaithful. If you are worried about your partner cheating on you I can say right now with complete conviction: do not stay in that relationship. In fact, now might be a great time for you to reflect on why you don't trust your partner. Do you have a genuine reason to distrust them or are your concerns stemming from your own insecurities? Relationships are built on trust, and long-distance relationships absolutely depend on it.

Years and years ago, I was in a long-distance relationship in which, deep down, I didn't trust my partner. I was always worried about him cheating on me, but I buried those feelings and went on pretending everything was fine, when I was constantly riddled with anxiety, worrying about what he was doing, and thinking the worst. Turns out I had good reason to feel that way!

When I was with Jordan, I can honestly say there wasn't one single feeling, one single thought, that ever crept into my head about him doing the wrong thing by me. I just knew, deep in my bones, that he would never hurt me in that way. I trusted him with every inch of my body and that is why I was content in the relationship. Would it have been better if I had been able to spend every single day with him? Of course. But I trusted him, no matter what.

So next time you find yourself wondering if your partner is going to cheat on you, try to instead ask yourself if you trust them. If the answer is yes, then you've got to stick to that, and try not to let yourself get overwhelmed by hypotheticals.

Accidentally Unfiltered

After a year of long distance, I finally landed myself a great job in the same town as my partner. Ahead of the move, I was in the process of selling all of my furniture, including my modular couch. One day, two young guys came to collect it. As they picked up the first section of the couch, it dawned on me that I had left my vibrator on the floor underneath it, and suddenly, there it was on full display. Fortunately there were also a lot of cat toys under the couch, and while I don't think they could tell the difference between the two, I said pointedly, 'Wow, a lot of cat toys under here!' If they noticed they didn't say anything, but still, I was absolutely mortified. I played it cool as they carried the couch out the door, but the second they were outside loading it into the van, I quickly swiped the vibrator up and stashed it away. Fortunately there were no vibrators under the second section!

A FEW HOT TIPS FOR SUCCESS

Now you have established that you're okay with long distance, and you find yourself knee-deep in it, how do you make it work? Well, I have a bit of advice ...

♥ **Really good communication.** Stating the obvious, but communication is one of the most important factors when it comes to ensuring a healthy relationship of any kind. But in long distance it is literally all you have. You need to be open and honest with each other, check in on each other, and really listen to each other.

What that looks like is different for every relationship. Some couples need to call each other every day at the exact same time, or else they have a meltdown and think something is wrong. Other couples don't need that level of intensity and speak every other day. Both are fine! Sometimes not being in each other's face every day is healthy and gives you a chance to have new things to talk about. In my previous relationship, at first I thought it was important to establish a routine with our communication – speaking every night at the same time before bed, or whatever other time of the day worked – so this is what we did for the first half of the year. After spending some time together mid-year, that changed for us – we realised we didn't need to speak multiple times a day, every day. Some days a text was okay, other days a call, others a video call. I am still a big believer that video calls are important because you need to be able to see each other and not just rely on your voices for communication.

♥ **Make plans!** I can't stress this one enough. It is so important to have something to look forward to. Something to count down the days to, to talk about, to get excited about. This could be a weekend away, or the next time you see each other. It could be talking about when you will finally be together in person forever, when one of you will move cities, or maybe buying or renting a property together. Having a common goal and something you are working towards brings you together mentally and emotionally when you can't physically be together, and reassures you that you are both still on the same path.

♥ **Organise date nights.** You can still share a meal together over a video call – this became big throughout the COVID-19 lockdowns, but it doesn't just need to be a pandemic thing. Order the same meal and eat together, or even have a video date while you cook the same meal at the same time. This helps build connection and brings about a sense of normality.

♥ **Show desire.** You need to show each other you are attracted to each other. Otherwise what's the point in them being anything more than a friend or penpal? Obviously there needs to be a very large level of trust and communication because anything can be recorded, but sending nudes, sexting and phone sex (with video or without) are all things that allow you to demonstrate and maintain intimacy without physically being together. Technology these days is a wonderful thing.

♥ **Don't forget spontaneity.** To avoid boredom, you need to embrace the element of surprise! This might be sending them a gift or postcard, planning something without them knowing, or sending them a cheeky nude in the middle of their work day when you wouldn't normally contact them. If you always text or call, maybe send an email – if they're not used to seeing you in their email inbox, it will create a new level of excitement. In my relationship we were big on sending emails every so often just to keep each other on our toes, and I loved it when I'd see his name pop up on my screen!

Is a long-distance relationship going to be easy? No. Most definitely not. Will it be worth it? Only you can decide. But if this person is the love of your life, then yes, some short-term hard work is definitely worth it.

A healthy long-distance relationship takes time, dedication, commitment, communication and energy. There will be moments of pure bliss and moments of heartache, tears of happiness and tears of sadness. But it's important to remember not all good things come easily. If you share similar goals and know you would rather be physically apart than without each other entirely, jump right in! But if you feel that you and your partner are on different paths, or your values and plans don't align, then maybe it's worth thinking twice. Love alone isn't enough, and time is a precious commodity. Don't waste it if you know something isn't right. Be brave if it proves to be better to bid each other goodbye and know that you won't be leaving empty-handed. There are lessons in every chapter of life.

Accidentally Unfiltered

My new boyfriend and I are in a long-distance relationship and he was visiting me. On our last night together, we planned to have a relaxing bath with a few drinks, and decided to add some whipped cream and strawberries into the mix.

I was standing over the top of my boyfriend's face while he was lying in the bath, and he grabbed a strawberry and eyed off my pussy, as if to say, 'Can I put this up there?' I nodded and next thing I knew, there was a strawberry half up my vagina. As he went to get the strawberry out, he pushed it up my vagina. *Very far* up my vagina.

That's when I started to freak out. My boyfriend advised me to try pushing it out like I was giving birth to a baby. But how?! I've never given birth in my life! I started trying to push out this strawberry, and peed uncontrollably all over him, which then made me freak out even more.

He then looked me dead in the eyes while laughing and said, 'Oh, I love you,' to which I replied, 'Babe, I love you too, but there's a strawberry up my vagina!' He managed to eventually get the strawberry out and thankfully we didn't have to go to the ER that night. It's safe to say we won't be using strawberries in the sheets any time soon!

L

LOVE LANGUAGES

Are you speaking my language?

BRITT AND LAURA

SEE ALSO: ATTACHMENT THEORY,
CONFLICT RESOLUTION, LONG DISTANCE

BRITT: I've always wanted to be able to say that I am fluent in more than one language. In fact, I moved to Italy for a year to learn Italian – but perfecting how to order a great big plate of carbonara and glass of wine was about as far as I got. Since starting the podcast, however, I've now ticked being multilingual off the bucket list – that is, if the five love languages count!

My twenties were a confusing time for relationships. I didn't know what I wanted, who I was, what was right and what was wrong in a relationship. That definitely showed its ugly head in the relationships I did have! I accepted things I shouldn't have, in order to keep the peace and hold on to the 'love' I thought I was being offered. But when I learned about love languages and how they can affect your relationships, it literally changed everything.

LAURA: I also vividly remember when I first read about love languages. I had been in a relationship with my then boyfriend for two years and he had never bought me a present. Not a birthday present, not a Christmas present . . . NOT. A. SINGLE. THING. In two years!

Generally speaking, I'm not big on gift-giving or receiving, so at the start it didn't bother me, but as time went on it started to seem pretty weird. Was it laziness, lack of interest, or was he just not that into me? It wasn't until I read about love languages and I made him do the test that the penny massively dropped. Gift-giving did not even rate – he scored zero per cent.

Did discovering love languages fix our relationship? Of course not, but it helped me understand him a little better and why our love tanks were both so empty all the time.

The whole conversation around love languages is not new to the dating and relationship lexicon, so chances are you'll have heard of them before. But when we did our deep dive into them on *Life Uncut*, I realised that maybe we focus too much on our own love language when really the most important part is understanding our partner's, and how we can be mindful of our behaviour to suit their unique needs and wants. After all, is it any great shock that paying attention to a partner's desires and preferences and acting accordingly results in a happier, healthier relationship?

B: Let's do a quick little refresher on what they're all about. The premise of love languages is basically that different people show and receive love in different ways depending on their different personality traits. Go figure!

Gary Chapman, a Christian pastor and marriage counsellor, was the wise man who first conjured them up in 1992 in his aptly titled book *The Five Love Languages: How to express heartfelt commitment to your mate*. He explained the five universal ways that people show love and how they want to receive love back: gift-giving, physical touch, acts of service, words of affirmation and quality time.

There are a gazillion websites that offer different tests and quizzes to find out what yours are. You might even be able to guess your primary and secondary love languages just by reading the descriptions. Usually we know ourselves without having to do a test to figure out what is important to us, but if you are in a relationship, here is your homework: tonight when you're sitting on the couch, do a love language quiz with your partner. Because while understanding your own love language is important, as you said, Laura, understanding your partner's, so you can show them love in the way they like to receive it, is vital. And if you aren't in a relationship, that's okay, you can do this homework, too! You can figure out what is important to you and you can enter the next relationship more prepared than ever!

The five love languages

1. Words of affirmation

Do you like to be in constant contact with your partner throughout the day – messaging, chatting on social media, etc.? Is it important to you that your partner often tells you that they love you, encourages or compliments you? Then it sounds like your primary love language is words of affirmation.

2. Acts of service

Some people believe that actions speak louder than words, and if this rings true for you – if, for example, it matters to you that your partner does things that make your life easier, such as picking up your dry cleaning or making dinner for you when you're stressed – then your love language is likely to be acts of service.

3. Quality time

Do you feel the most valued, secure and happy in your relationship when you are spending time with your partner? And not just eating dinner in front of the TV together or bickering in the car on the way home from IKEA, but occasions when you're fully attuned to one another, listening, making eye contact, and deeply appreciating each other's presence? If so, then it probably won't come as a shock to find out that your love language is quality time. This one ranks highly for a lot of people.

4. Gifts

This is pretty straightforward: you feel loved when people give you 'visual symbols of love', as Chapman calls them. These visual symbols don't have to be expensive or flashy – it's all about the meaning of the item, and the thought that went into its selection. How does the gift make you feel? What does the gift represent about your relationship?

5. Physical touch

Holding hands, kissing, cuddling and sex are all forms of physical affection, and people with this as their love language value these gestures highly.

L: Most people like a little of each, but we usually have a primary and secondary love language that best suits us, and then we enjoy the others but to a lesser degree. Another interesting thing is that they aren't fixed. Depending on your relationship or the phase of life you're in, your love language can change to reflect what's going on.

For example, my love language used to be words of affirmation and physical touch. But, now that I have two wild little beasts careening around the house causing chaos, acts of service has jumped up the ranks to prime position. Don't get me wrong, I still love a cuddle on the couch and being told that I'm pretty, even when I have a half-eaten Cruskit smeared onto my jumper, but now I seriously value the things Matt does around the house that show he appreciates and cares for me. If you really want to get me turned on, don't tell me you love me, SHOW ME, and by that I mean put the laundry on a spin cycle, take the kids to day care and mop the kitchen floors. Nothing gets me randier than a clean house and Matty J holding a Spray n' Wipe bottle.

B: Oh god, don't get started on what goes on in your household when Matt cleans the fridge and takes out the recycling! Wild times.

I think it's interesting that you mentioned how love languages can change. My number-one love language is physical touch. I am such a physical person, even with friends, and when I am with my partner I like to be touching them in some capacity at all times. This obviously posed a real issue when I was dating Jordan and 90 per cent of our relationship was long distance. My love language shifted during that time due to the fact that he wasn't in the country – physical touch became less important and words of affirmation became critically important. I needed the texts, the kind words, the sweet nothings, the curiosity and interest in my day and life. Because, let's be real, that's all you really have in long-distance relationships. And what I needed and wanted changed without me really noticing. I am not quite sure if this is a permanent change or just one that happened because of the circumstances – I haven't yet dated again, so who knows if this change will stick!

What is Matt's love language?

L: Not the same as mine, which I learned the hard way. I had always assumed Matt's love languages were acts of service and words of affirmation but you know what they say about making assumptions, it makes an 'ass' out of 'u' and 'me'! When the two of us finally sat down and did our love language tests, Matt's dominant love language was actually physical touch.

Yikes, and here I was with two kids under two, touched out, and constantly saying, 'Can you stop touching me?' It's little wonder why his love cup had a hole in it! So even though I was cooking dinner, telling him how much I adored him, washing his stinky undies, helping him create logos for work and being supportive in other ways, what Matt really needed to feel special was more physical touch, more cuddles, more spooning, and well . . . giggity, you get the gist.

B: I'm glad you resolved that, but I don't need the mental image of 'giggity'.

To be fair though, I'm sure that's so common, where one person feels like they are trying so hard in a relationship – maybe you've just spent all day cleaning and organising the house for your partner, rushing around doing errands that you believe will make their life easier – but all the other person wants is to cuddle on the couch and have some quality time. See how the disconnect can happen? You're speaking two different languages, and ultimately both individuals can be left feeling unloved and misunderstood.

Sometimes we think we are showing love to our significant other, but, really, we are just acting in a way that reaffirms what *we* want from the relationship, without consciously trying to meet our partner's unique needs. It's common to receive love and give love in a different way to your partner, but learning their preferences and understanding what they value can help you make sure you're expressing love in a way that will be meaningful to them, which will, in turn, strengthen your relationship. It can also point you to the true cause of any conflicts, arguments or misunderstandings, so you can figure out if there's a glitch in the communication or something bigger and more serious is going on. Let's come back to quality time, because as we've said it's so important in any relationship. Laura, I know you and Matty spend so much time together – obviously living together, often working together, and you did *a lot* of isolation together over the past few years. I'm guessing that most of it may not be 'quality' because you're wrangling kids, scooping poop out of baths and working, but you do spend a lot of time around each other, meaning surely it's more important than ever to know each other's love languages! Where does this sit for you two and how do you manage to convert your time spent into quality time?

L: I think this is such a funny one, because as you said, Britt, it's so important in *every* relationship. Quality time doesn't have to be face to face – if you're doing long distance it can be over FaceTime – but it has to be time where you're making the other person your sole focus and priority. And, as we know, quality time is vastly different to quantity of time – you could spend every waking moment in the same room as your partner, but if they have their head stuck in the phone the whole time . . . well, you're going to be left feeling unsatisfied and unseen.

This is something Matt and I have to be so conscious of because yes, scooping our one-year-old's aquaturds out of the bath doesn't really scream 'Having a great time!'. So what we do is check in every day with each other once the kids are in bed – even if it's just an hour on the couch to decompress and talk through our days. It's our time to touch base with each other and carve out some QT! Without it, it's easy to feel unappreciated and resentful, as if you are low down on the other person's priority list.

At the end of the day, love languages are not going to resolve every issue in a relationship, but knowing yours and your partner's helps to keep each person's love tank full. When your love tank is full you're better equipped to deal with other issues that arise because your emotional needs are being met.

B: Totally, and I believe you should truly want to be making your partner's life easier, not harder. If your relationship is getting harder and harder for no reason, if your partner brings you more bad than good, you're probably in the wrong relationship. Check yourself, team. Reassess and either regress or progress!

And if you haven't yet dipped your toe in the love languages pool, what are you waiting for? You might be about to make some incredible discoveries!

MANIFESTING

How to go out and get what you want

BRITT

SEE ALSO: ADVENTURE, DATING

The word 'manifestation' is thrown around a lot these days. It's something we hear our friends talk about, it's the subject of bestselling books such as Rhonda Byrne's *The Secret* (which, mind you, has sold 35 million copies according to *USA Today*) and it is loved by celebrities such as Oprah and Will Smith. But what exactly is it? And why is everyone on the manifestation train?

FIRST, LET'S TALK ABOUT THE LAW OF ATTRACTION

Manifesting is a way of putting the Law of Attraction into practice. This 'law' is the ability to attract into our lives whatever we are expending the most energy thinking about. Essentially, like attracts like, and all of our thoughts manifest into reality eventually, whether that reality is desirable or ... not so much. So if you're constantly thinking negative thoughts, are always pessimistic and tend to feel like there is a cloud over your head, chances are you won't get out from under that cloud. On the other hand, if you focus more on positive thoughts, vibrate a happy and optimistic energy and have positive goals, you're more likely to find a way to achieve those goals.

I know at first glance this can seem a little far-fetched, and it definitely isn't as easy as just saying, 'Hey universe, I want one million dollars! Love you, k thanks bye.' It takes persistence and action. You need to be deliberately and determinedly working towards your goals at the same time as focusing your thoughts in their direction. That means successfully manifesting doesn't happen by just sitting at home and thinking good thoughts. If you want to meet the love of your life, it isn't going to happen by hanging out in your bedroom watching rom-coms and saying out loud, 'I am going to have that love, too! Thank you, universe, for giving me that all-consuming, sexy, romantic, top-tier, shout-from-the-rooftops love!' Trust me, your life-changing love definitely ain't waltzing into your house and falling in your lap by accident. Unless they're an attractive plumber that you called after you clogged the toilet – but, let's be real, the odds are not in your favour.

PUT OUT TO THE UNIVERSE WHAT YOU WANT TO RECEIVE

Where were we? Oh yeah, how to bring that sweet, sweet goodness into your life! First, you must form a specific goal and outcome. Be very clear about what you want and your intention behind it. The more definitive you can be, the easier it is to make something happen. Say you want to fall in love. (Welcome to the club.) Ask yourself, what *exactly* do you want in a partner? What do they look like? What do they enjoy doing? What are their goals? Are they funny? Adventurous? Family oriented? Will they share their food? (Do not, I repeat *do not*, underestimate the importance of food sharing.) The more exact you can be and the more detail you can identify, the better. Use your imagination! Picture them standing right in front of you! See them! Visualise them! To help you get clear and specific, here are some questions you can ask yourself:

- ♥ What ten words would you use to describe what you really want in a partner?
- ♥ What personality traits in another person help to bring out the very best in you?
- ♥ How do you want to be treated by a partner?
- ♥ What are the deal-breakers?
- ♥ What are the behaviours that you know you will simply never tolerate?
- ♥ Where do you see yourself in five years' and ten years' time?

You can say all this out loud or you can write it down wherever you like. I used to write things down in my phone's Notes app throughout the day, which means I still have a record, from years ago, of dreams that were realised! Some of these were small, everyday things, some were jobs I wanted. Recording your intentions, goals and desires will give you a strong sense of what you want, which makes it much easier to go out and find it. I remember when I decided to start the *Life Uncut* podcast with Laura, I opened my notebook and drew a picture. It was of two female stick figures (ponytails and all) standing outside. The sun was shining, we were smiling, there were birds, we were winning at life, and there were little dollar signs all around the picture in obscure places to indicate a certain level of success. Talk about detail, there was even a little bird flying past with money in its mouth! That was my way of saying, 'Look, Laura and I are happy, we are working hard on something we believe in that will one day be our job'. I still have that picture. Right from Day One of the podcast, I knew I had to believe in us, and see our success. And we made it happen! (I haven't seen the bird with the money yet, though.)

PUT YOURSELF IN THE PATH OF MAGIC

Now that you have been clear about what you want, you have to ask yourself, what am I doing to achieve this? What am I doing to meet this person I have told the universe that I want to meet? How do I live the life I want? You need to align your actions with your thoughts.

For example, if you dream about being with someone who is really athletic and into sport, are *you* playing sport? Have you joined a team? Or are you going along to sporting matches as a spectator? (Sitting in your living room playing solitaire doesn't count!) If you know that you want to be with someone really generous and kind, are you practising kindness and showing people you meet that you possess that quality as well? Could you be more generous? Maybe you are surrounding yourself with people who aren't so nice? Have you worked out that you want to be with someone who doesn't party or drink lots, but you're only going out to bars and clubs and parties to meet people? You need to actively put yourself in situations where you will meet like-minded people who are in line with what you want. Last, and super importantly, are you actually open to finding love? Really? Be honest with yourself. Are you putting yourself out there so that love is able to find you? If not, you may have some work to do to figure out what's holding you back before you can start manifesting with full force.

I actually have my own funny story about manifesting love. Very weird indeed! There I was, a hopeless romantic but very unlucky in love. One day I found myself in need of a new laptop, so off I went to buy one. I got it home, set it up, and then it asked me to select a picture as a screensaver. There were *so* many images to choose from but for some reason I picked the most boring, random picture of all: an empty screen with a yellow tennis ball in the middle of it. That was it. Nothing else, just one boring little tennis ball, all on its lonesome.

I wasn't even a tennis person. I played occasionally for fun, but I didn't really know the rules – I would just run around the court, swinging wildly and laughing uncontrollably. Anyhow, for whatever reason, I picked that tennis ball screensaver and got on with my life.

One month later I met Jordan, a professional tennis player. Go figure! He came into my life as fast and hard as Rafael Nadal's forehand (for those non-tennis-lovers playing at home, that's damn fast). Some experts in the field might say this was a subconscious manifestation. I knew I wanted a hard-working, motivated, funny, driven, independent, fit, sexy man (I don't ask for much!) and I often imagined what he would be like when I finally found him, so I feel like consciously that part was always there. The tennis part, though, that came subconsciously. Never in a million years would I have imagined that!

TEN WAYS TO MANIFEST YOUR DREAMS INTO REALITY

So, you've decided to give this manifesting thing a shot. But what comes next? Here are some ways to get you started:

1. **Practise gratitude every morning.** When you wake up, write something down that you are grateful for. Really think about what you are writing, and feel that gratitude at your core. It might help to write in a journal so you can keep a record of everything you are grateful for, but anywhere is fine, as long as you are putting it into words.
2. **Focus on what makes you happy.** When you are filled with genuine joy and contentment, you will have the strongest energy to manifest your dreams. Positivity breeds positivity!
3. **Accentuate the positive!** Let's be real: we all have negative thoughts from time to time. But it's amazing what a difference it can make if, every time you catch a negative thought running

through your mind, you immediately try to turn it into something positive. For example, next time you look in the mirror and want to say something negative about your body, stop yourself and instead think about how amazing your body is and what it does for you. For me, it was my legs – my quads, to be specific. I was always quite muscly from all the sports I played and I couldn't help the size of my quads, it was just my physique. But man, I hated them and I was so self-conscious about them. One day, though, I changed my train of thought and focused instead on how lucky I was to have legs that worked, legs that I could run, walk and swim with, and that got me from A to B without a second thought. By switching up that thought pattern I've been able to shift my attitude.

4. **Meditate daily.** Use this time to visualise the life you want to lead. For example, today, on my morning walk, I stopped and lay down on a bench in a park overlooking the ocean. I closed my eyes and felt the sun, heard the ocean, inhaled the salty air and thought about my life and what I wanted. I only did this for ten minutes but I immediately felt so much lighter and more positive.

5. **Remind yourself that good things are just around the corner.** By being open to new and exciting horizons, you are inviting happiness and fulfilment into your life. I put this into practice by carrying out a *21 Days of Abundance* meditation course with Deepak Chopra and loved it. It was food for my brain and soul, and provided me with clarity around what I am seeking and gratitude for what I already have. I recommend trying something like it – and it could be fun to do it with a group of friends so that you keep each other accountable throughout.

   One of my favourite stories about abundance involves Jim Carrey. I love that man. He's a brilliant actor, but he is truly convinced that he manifested his success. Carrey once told Oprah, 'I wrote myself a check for $10 million for "acting services rendered" and I gave myself five years . . . or three years, maybe. I dated it Thanksgiving 1995 and I put it in my wallet and I kept it there and it deteriorated and deteriorated. But then, just before Thanksgiving 1995, I found out that I was going to make $10 million on *Dumb and Dumber*.' Oprah then pointed out how 'visualisation works if you work hard' and Carrey agreed, saying, 'Well, yeah. That's the thing – you can't just visualise and then, you know, go eat a sandwich.' This is a prime example of writing it down, believing it, then working your butt off to achieve it.

6. **Don't forget: like attracts like.** If you are a force for good in this world, then good things will find their way back to you. Good begets good – and the same. Be a good human. Help others in some big or small way each day. Be the energy you want to receive.

7. **Accept responsibility for your own life.** Often, our instinct is to blame other people when things go wrong or don't work out, but you will feel much better and have more success when you realise that most issues start from within. Not all, of course, but you have a lot more control over your life than you probably realise. Is someone treating you badly? Sure, that is coming from them, but are you letting them treat you that way? Are there things you could be doing to change the situation that you're neglecting, or not being bold enough to try?

8. **Go after the thing that scares you.** You have NOTHING to lose! Go out there and seize the day! One of my favourite quotes is from T. S. Eliot: 'Only those who risk going too far can possibly find out how far one can go.' Read that again. Remember, it's an instant fail if you don't even try!

9. **Avoid the negativity and naysayers, and surround yourself with people who only lift you higher.** You are the product of those closest to you, so check in: are the people around you raising you up? Supporting you? Encouraging you? Are they happy, optimistic, inspiring people? Downers will be downers; don't let them drag you to their level.

10. **DREAM BIG!** We only get one crack at this life, and when you're old and you're on your deathbed, no one is going to say, 'Remember forty-five years ago when Sally moved overseas and tried to get that promotion but didn't? Silly Sally.' No one will remember – or care, for that matter. And nor will you look back and say, 'I wish I didn't try to get that promotion forty-five years ago. How embarrassing.' Lolcano. As if you will ever say that! But I bet you'll regret *not* going for it.

Live wild, hungry and hard, my friends.

MONEY

*'While money can't buy happiness, it certainly lets you choose your own form of misery.'**

LAURA

SEE ALSO: BOUNDARIES, WORTHINESS

When we were teenagers, most of us probably just assumed we'd own a home one day. I know I did. Then you enter your twenties, start gaining some independence and realise that life is fucking expensive. Once you take into account your weekly income, minus tax, then stack that against the deposit, the student debt, the rising cost of real estate, not to mention the annual inflation on a smashed avo brunch, it's enough to make your wallet weep.

So, let's talk about the thing that makes the world go 'round: money!

Since childhood, most of us have been conditioned to not discuss money. It's seen as impolite and intrusive. But not talking about money has left a lot of us pretty shit at dealing with it, to put it bluntly. Me included! After getting smacked with a $30K tax bill in my twenties after I started my first small business, I bloody wish someone had taught me more about money, and less about algebra.

Yes, money can make people uncomfortable. But thankfully, this attitude is shifting. According to research, millennials are more likely to be open about their finances than their parents.[25] We live

---

* Source unknown.

in a time that celebrates destigmatising difficult conversations, although that doesn't mean we need to post our bank statements on Facebook. We should, however, be able to talk about money with our closest friends and partners.

Money is also the second leading factor in relationship break-downs (after infidelity) – personal debt, financial abuse and lack of transparency when it comes to managing finances can all take a huge toll.[26]

When it comes to money I am far from an expert, so this chapter won't necessarily contain the financial wisdom that will whip you into shape as a savvy saver, but it may just be the conversation starter needed to set you in the right direction. Matt and I have very different money personalities – the man is a saver, a list-maker and the one who does all the planning when it comes to holidays. Me, on the other hand? I'm more of a 'how does it make me feel?' kind of girl. And more often than not, that kind of live-in-the-moment attitude has left me feeling . . . well, broke.

From the start of our relationship, Matt has had a positive influence on my spending habits and, although we are chalk and cheese when it comes to the way we approach it, money has never been an area of conflict in our relationship because we've always had honest and open conversations around it.

Early on we made a not-so-sexy budget and saving plan. It felt good from a relationship perspective that Matt was so keen to work together on saving money. It made me feel like he was really serious about the relationship. It certainly wasn't the budgeting that got me excited but, over time, what I didn't expect was just how damn satisfying it is to see small sacrifices turn into money in the bank. A budget is telling your money where to go, instead of looking at your bank balance wondering where the hell it all went.

On the podcast we spoke to award-winning financial adviser Victoria Devine, creator of the podcast *She's on the Money*, who is transforming the way millennials think about their finances.[27] She shared with us the most common questions millennials ask:

How do I save?
How do I invest?
How do I prioritise my savings to achieve my financial goal, especially as a woman?

Victoria spoke about how we have been conditioned to see success and money through a social media filter. For example, thanks to reality TV shows like *The Block* and the endless scroll of DIY renovation porn on Instagram, many people think the ultimate goal now is to buy a house and renovate – because, isn't that what everyone is doing these days? But what Victoria reiterated is that success is different to each person. It has to tie back to your core values, and what you want out of life. Spending money to keep up with the Joneses is only going to set you backwards in terms of your savings. 'You see the Dior bags on Instagram but you don't see the associated debt,' Victoria told us. 'Wealth generation and financial security is invisible and that's why it's so hard to prioritise in a world where Instagram is so massive.'

Now, we probably don't need an award-winning financial adviser to tell us that to achieve our money goals, well, we're going to have to make some sacrifices. It can be tough watching everyone else 'brunching it up' on social media (we'll cover money comparison later). But there's also a thrill to feeling financially literate and in control of your spending – checking your bank balance with the smug confidence of a saver feels very different to pre-emptively flinching when you open your banking app because you know it's not going to be a pretty sight.

One thing is for sure: as women, we have a responsibility to not pass the buck (pun intended!) when it comes to financial literacy. Even if you think you'll never understand money, you can learn – and you have to. For too long, anything to do with finance – investing, stocks, shares – has been misogynistically geared towards the man's domain. This imbalance only works to broaden the inequality of power between men and women in other facets of life. The more you learn, the more you'll understand – and the more you understand, the more confident you'll feel. Competence builds confidence. Take it from someone who used to go hard and blow their fortnightly pay check in the first five days, what you need is a budget and a plan.

So many of us are guilty of kicking our financial plans down the road. 'I'll save for a house when I'm in a relationship', 'I still have forty years before I retire, why do I need to start thinking about super?' – the list goes on. But you should never let your current age or relationship status dictate your ability to be financially stable, and it's never too early to start working towards your own goals, whether it's saving to start a business, go on a European holiday or buy a car.

But budgeting should also be about balancing, right? So, how do we maintain that brunchy lifestyle and not end up eating spam in retirement?

IS SOCIAL MEDIA SABOTAGING YOUR SAVINGS?

Social media can make us all a bit flighty, especially when it comes to money. We're quite happy with our apartment ... and then we see another Three Birds renovation. We think our car/wardrobe/ smartphone is just fine ... and then we clock someone else unveiling their spiffy upgrade.

According to research, half of millennials say social media makes them overspend. And in a survey by Allianz Life Insurance,

57 per cent of millennials reported making unplanned purchases because of what they saw on social media.[28] Sure, we should take responsibility for our own spending habits. But let's recognise that we're also at the mercy of a very savvy social media algorithm, designed to separate us from our cold hard cash.

According to Victoria Devine, it helps to stop and ask one question: *Why do I want to make that purchase?*

If you don't have a clear answer to that question, then it's likely you're just being influenced.

As someone who works in the social media landscape let me tell you this: 99 per cent of what you see online is utter bullshit. So many influencers lounging around with designer bags are living way beyond their actual means because they prioritise looking wealthy over actually being financially comfortable. Victoria confirmed this – she works with social media influencers who are 'living it large' online, but have amassed a lot of personal debt. They're sent free clothes, but the pressure to live up to a certain lifestyle means they're overspending on accessories so they can create great content to go with it. It's a vicious cycle!

A while back, we recorded an interview with entrepreneur Samantha Wills about her journey to building a jewellery empire. She made an amazing point: everyone feels like they need to start a small business because it seems like everyone else is doing it and it looks so easy. But the challenges and sacrifices that are necessary for running a start-up, the unflattering business side of things, never make it onto social media.

A QUICK NOTE ON THE SCARCITY MINDSET

The scarcity mindset is something that we often talk about in regards to relationships, but this can also be applied to money. A scarcity mindset is the belief that something is limited or hard to come by, that there simply isn't enough to go around.

In terms of dating, it can make us settle for someone who isn't right for us, because we're worried there are no – or few – other options. When it comes to careers, a scarcity mindset can stop us from chasing opportunities, because we're fearful we might lose what we've already achieved. Or, it can cause us to become excessive 'yes' people because we're worried that, if we don't prove our worth, we might lose out on future opportunities – or even our jobs.

As for money, when we're trapped in a mindset of scarcity, we're worried that there isn't enough 'pie' to go around, and it can stop us feeling pleased for other people. If someone else gets a big piece, what's left for us?

So, how do we combat it? It's important to be aware of your feelings and keep comparison and envy in check when it comes to money.

We all have to figure out our own financial journeys. Some people's will be infinitely harder than others due to life circumstances, disability, abuse or trauma – but there are also many institutions out there to help. If you have financial or credit card debt, you could speak to your bank or talk to a financial adviser. Whatever you do, it's so important to reach out for support. Too often we try to navigate money in a silo without leaning on the support structures that are around us.

LET'S TALK MONEY, HONEY!

So, I've already mentioned how money can be a real stressor in relationships, and when it comes to juggling emotions and moolah, there is no one size fits all.

In my twenties, I was fumbling my way through my career as a junior graphic designer. The pay was atrocious but I was doing all right, juggling life and expenses on my own. That was until I moved in with my then boyfriend who was on a much higher salary than me. We had never spoken about how we would split finances or how we would approach money, and at the time I was a chronic avoider of conversations that made me uncomfortable. My ex was on triple my salary, but the thing was, he still insisted that we split everything fifty-fifty, to the dollar. This meant that we were living in a rental I couldn't afford, and while he would go out to long work lunches with his co-workers, I would take canned tuna, beans and crackers to work because I needed to spend the remaining money in my bank account on public transport and contraception. At the time, I didn't feel confident enough to tell him that I didn't have enough money to sustain this lifestyle, which meant that the resentment built up quickly.

In my experience, money often doesn't become an issue until you're out of the honeymoon period. Everything is sustainable in the short term, but if you're on wildly different pages when it comes to how you approach finances, then, let me assure you, the cracks will start to show. Every couple's approach to money will vary; there is no right way or wrong way, but getting on the same page early is important.

Matt and I had a kid together before we had a joint bank account. This is partly because we were too lazy (and then too busy with a baby!) to organise one, but also because it worked ... until it didn't.

From the start, we split expenses equally because we have similar incomes. After our first child was born, however, things got a bit murky. Matt was still saving money each month while my bank account was taking a hit because I kept making extra purchases for the baby – things like nappies, formula, baby wipes.

It was always very clear that our money was shared, regardless of whether we had a joint account or not, so I wasn't upset that he had accumulated money while I had not, but any imbalance is an imbalance, and it never feels great. And besides, I wanted to contribute to our savings, and he wanted to contribute to the baby's expenses. But how could we keep track of it in a way that wouldn't drive us crazy?

I never imagined I'd combine all my money with another person's – it always sounded like a bad idea to me, especially after witnessing an unsuccessful example of shared finances with my mum and stepdad. But it's now what Matt and I do, and it works for us. It comes back to honesty, trust and confidence. He doesn't need to justify everything he buys, but we both know we're on the same page and working towards our future together. I still, however, have my own bank account with my 'secret money' as Matt jokingly calls it.

Victoria calls this secret money the 'fuck-off account', and recommends that everyone have some money set aside that is their personal financial safety net. This account gives you the confidence to be able to say 'fuck off' to whatever it is that you don't want to do, without being handcuffed to a situation because you need the money. It doesn't have to be a lot, but it should be enough to make you feel secure. According to Victoria, it's not (just) so you can leave a relationship that no longer serves you, it gives you the freedom to tell that toxic workplace to fuck off or to say no to a really difficult client. Having a fuck-off account protects you from having to do things you don't want to – or, to put a much more positive spin on it, you can also use the money to do something nice for your partner without them knowing.

Often in long-term relationships one person will naturally take a more involved role in overseeing finances. But you never know what's around the corner! We all need to know how to financially take care of ourselves. Talking about money together can be a bonding experience. It's not about a dollar number in the bank, it's about knowledge and freedom.

When one of you earns more

How can you equalise the playing field if you're bringing in quite different amounts of money? Well, learn from my mistakes. COMMUNICATE!

No relationship is identical, and what suits one couple will not suit another. The most important thing is to have an open, ongoing, honest conversation that is deeply rooted in respect for each other's financial situation. If you're in a relationship where you have shared finances, checking in frequently means that talking about money never becomes a taboo or uncomfortable topic. There are no surprises.

Our financial situations aren't fixed and guaranteed states, either. What if your income has dramatically shifted because you've had children, or you've been made redundant? If you're on a lower salary than your partner, going dollar for dollar on every purchase or bill is often not a fair way of contributing to the expenses that you jointly share. It leaves one person with less disposable income and ability to save, invest or use in other ways.

For so many couples who choose to have children, money is a huge consideration. Spending all day at home with a small child is tough. You lose sleep, your identity and, for a lot of primary carers, your income. If you're the one doing the full-time parenting while your partner works, see that as a full-time job. Think about how much it would cost if your child was in day care.

Doing a percentage split based on both your earnings is a much fairer way to set your budget, and it's what Victoria recommends to her clients if their incomes aren't on a similar level. It's about equity rather than equality. But if you have kids, don't forget to take into account the 'invisible load' that one parent takes on.

Quick tips for financial harmony

Talk about your priorities. Maybe your partner is a little bit fancy and really likes to spend their money on the good things in life. Maybe you're a bit more frugal and would prefer to focus on saving money. That doesn't make either of you good or bad but it does require honest communication. You'll have to work a bit harder to compromise, as your focuses are different.

Be honest about your income. You don't have to share your earnings on the first date, but once you're in a committed relationship, you should know how much your partner earns. Then you can get clear about what you can contribute and budget things such as holidays and dinners accordingly.

Set a sexy budget! Okay, so budgets aren't sexy. But if you're going to have a joint bank account with someone, you're going to need a budget. Maybe you want a fancy vacay every year, maybe you want to save a house or just have savings for a rainy day – it's important to be on the same page and have a clear plan you're both committed to.

Factor in fun. Even if you're focused on an important milestone, such as buying a house, it's still important to budget for the fun stuff. And 'fun stuff' doesn't always have to be extravagant, either – life's too short to feel guilty about a $5 coffee. Especially if that coffee date is a chance to connect with your partner.

Don't go all in! When you're in a committed relationship and merge your finances, it can seem really exciting – it's the next big step. But you don't have to go 'all in' to prove your love for them. A lot of financial advisers recommend having three bank accounts in a relationship: one joint and one for each of you. A level of financial independence is a good thing.

TALKING MONEY WITH YOUR MATES

It would be great if we could normalise talking about money with our friends in the same way that we talk about relationships – the disasters, the success stories and everything in between.

I think the reason so many of us think we're 'bad' with money is because we don't talk about it. And, if we don't talk about it how can we learn? With friends, you don't need to go into the nitty gritty of how much you earn (unless you want to). But a little more transparency would benefit all of us – especially if you feel any guilt or shame around your financial situation.

Picture the scene: you go for dinner with your mates and they've been ordering expensive cocktails all night. You've had a salad and a water because you're waiting for payday, but are too embarrassed to tell them that funds are tight. Now they want to split the bill. In a world where you and your friends communicated openly about budgets and money, it shouldn't have got to that point. You could have met them for happy hour instead, or hosted them at yours. And, to be honest, it should be completely fine to show up at a restaurant and tell everyone you need to keep a light financial footprint that evening, before you even start ordering. That way, everyone's across the situation, and you can all enjoy yourselves without getting caught out later.

As I said at the very beginning, financial stability and wealth accumulation are invisible, but so too is debt. We need to talk about money to make savings cool, but also to avoid situations where you feel you have to keep up with a lifestyle you can't afford.

There's also a flip side. If you just got a pay rise, bought a house, or kicked off your small business, you should be able to celebrate it with your mates and be proud of your monetary achievements, too. And it's not just about celebrating your friends' achievements, it's about acknowledging that women who are open and transparent about things like finance, salaries and pay are helping to create a more balanced, equal and open work environment for everyone – and that's never a bad thing. This is how, as women, we can learn to negotiate and value our worth and support others to do the same. Now go, live a prosperous life and google compound interest.

Disclaimer: The knowledge dropped in this chapter is general and should not be relied upon to make an investment or financial decision (obvs!). If in doubt, please consult a financial expert.

NARCISSISM

Notes on a life-changing dating experience

BRITT

SEE ALSO: GASLIGHTING, RED FLAGS, YESTERDAY

How do you recognise a narcissist? And no, that's not the opening line of a joke. I wish.

Is it the person on a dating app whose whole profile is nothing but topless selfie pictures, getting their flex on in the gym, all oiled up and pouting? (That's an instant swipe left for me, BTW, ew.) Or is it someone who talks about themselves non-stop on a first date while never asking about you? These people obviously have very inflated egos, but they're not necessarily narcissists. Sometimes I think we throw the term around too freely. Sure, maybe they are on the lower end of the narcissism spectrum, but more often than not this behaviour stems from underlying confidence issues rather than full-blown narcissism.

Narcissism is just that – something of a spectrum. At the extreme end is someone with narcissistic personality disorder (NPD), a mental health condition characterised by the Mayo Clinic as possessing some or all of the following traits:

♥ an exaggerated sense of self-importance
♥ a sense of entitlement and requiring constant, excessive admiration
♥ expecting to be recognised as superior even without achievements that warrant it

- ♥ exaggerating achievements and talents
- ♥ a preoccupation with fantasies about success, power, brilliance, beauty or the perfect mate
- ♥ a belief they are superior and can only associate with equally special people
- ♥ a tendency to monopolise conversations and belittle or look down on people they perceive as inferior
- ♥ an expectation of special favours and unquestioning compliance with their expectations
- ♥ taking advantage of others to get what they want
- ♥ having an inability or unwillingness to recognise the needs and feelings of others
- ♥ being envious of others and believing others envy them
- ♥ behaving in an arrogant or haughty manner, coming across as conceited, boastful and pretentious
- ♥ insisting on having the best of everything.[29]

But, also according to the Mayo Clinic, only around 1 per cent of the population is diagnosed with NPD. While most of us possess a few of the characteristics in that list to a small degree – we're human, after all – there are also some who tick all of these boxes. They're further along the spectrum and possess these desires and behaviours to a more excessive degree.

It is reported that these people are usually intelligent, charismatic, charming, suave, funny, attentive, generally speaking are more sexually attractive, and often very successful – all the qualities you might think you want in a partner. But there's a catch: these qualities in a narcissist are there to serve only one person: the narcissist themselves.

Unfortunately, narcissists can be easy to fall in love with. I know this because I loved one for years.

THEY SAY LOVE IS BLIND

When I met Luke* I had only been in one real, adult relationship before, a relationship of eight years with an amazing man. We were young, each other's first real love, and we were all we knew.

I met Luke not long after that relationship ended. He knew I was freshly single and it's probably why he 'picked' me, sensing (correctly) that I was vulnerable and emotional. We met at work one day and he was by far the most charming man I had ever encountered. He was five years older than me, highly intelligent, dressed impeccably and was already killing it in his career. As soon as he opened his mouth you could tell how charming he was; he had a way with words and always knew what to say. I swear he could have sold water to a fish.

We got into a relationship very quickly, which was at his insti-gation, although it's fair to say that we were pretty obsessed with each other. We spent every night together and he made me feel like I was the only thing that mattered. Within the first four weeks of our relationship he told me he loved me and that he wanted to be with me forever. He pulled out all the classics: 'What even was life before I met you!?' and 'I could never live without you now that I have you'. All that fairytale bullshit that everyone wants to hear. Thinking about it now makes me sick to my stomach.

Those early weeks were always spent at his place or mine. We never really went out anywhere for two reasons – first, because he just wanted to spend all his time with me at home and not share me with anyone else. So cute, right? Second, because he was reluctant for anyone at our work to know about our relationship, as he was worried it might seem weird or awkward or inappropriate. I couldn't have cared less, so everyone in my department knew about us, but only a few of his close colleagues did.

---

* Not his real name.

Right from the start, the contact was excessive – and it slowly intensified. I would often receive more than fifty messages a day from him, which came in multiple forms: texts from one of his two phones (personal and work), emails from one of his two email accounts (personal and work), phone calls and even letters. He also loved to pop in unexpectedly at work to see me. I was bombarded, but I loved it! I had someone who I knew was thinking about me all day and being so affectionate. What more could I want? It was an addictive level of adoration.

This, I now know, is called 'love bombing': being initially showered with gifts, compliments and attention, which begins a cycle of abuse whereby the love bomber then withholds the love and attention you've come to expect in order to manipulate you.

Luke had quickly become a big part of my life, and spent lots of time with my family and friends in those early weeks. But then he had to move away for work. It was just a few hours' drive, so we started doing long distance. Every two to three weekends we would see each other, either at his house or in nearby holiday accommodation that he would book for us. I found it strange that he often wanted to go away instead of spending the weekend at home, but he always said it was nice to be in a different environment. *Fair enough*, I thought.

He'd often cancel these weekends away at the last minute, though, and always said it was because of a work emergency. With his work this was believable.

I remember on one particular weekend, I had booked an amazing stay at a hotel on Sydney Harbour and tickets to climb the Harbour Bridge. It was ridiculously expensive, but I didn't care. I wanted to go all out for the man I loved.

I drove the five hours from where I was living to meet him in Sydney but just as I arrived he pulled the pin, saying, unsurprisingly, that something had come up at work. I ended up staying alone in the hotel. Fortunately, a friend was able to join me for BridgeClimb, but I remember the bitter disappointment like it was yesterday. I always received a bunch of beautiful messages or presents from him after this happened – he loved making grand romantic gestures – and despite the persistent feeling of disappointment from getting regularly let down, I would always forgive him. Somehow he always made up for it, with empty promises, gifts or words – sometimes all of the above.

As time went on, Luke started to get a little more possessive and controlling. He always seemed to know what I was doing or what I'd got up to the previous day before I had even told him, though I never understood how, because he didn't have any social media. Yep, none. That isn't necessarily a red flag, but in this day and age it *is* pretty unusual, especially for someone young, good-looking, successful and sociable.

One day I got a message from him that said, 'Britt, are you posting bikini photos on your social media?!' I had just gone for a surf with my friends and had put some pics on Instagram. But how had he known that? It had only been about thirty minutes since I posted them, and he didn't have Instagram. And anyway, so what?

When I said yes, he told me I needed to take them down immediately. I was shocked and couldn't figure out why he was asking me to do that, but he told me I would understand if I checked my email. In my inbox was a message he had forwarded me from some anonymous person. This person had sent him the photos of me from Instagram in my bikini, along with a pretty horrible list of all the things this person wanted to do to me, with some very derogatory terms thrown in. I'll let you use your imagination on that.

I was disgusted. Honestly, it was pretty scary. I couldn't believe someone would do this, or even how they would have gotten Luke's email address. But it shook me to think some weirdo was out there creeping on me like that, so I put my Instagram on private.

'How do you think this makes ME feel, hearing people say this about you and receiving these sorts of emails?' Luke yelled down the phone at me later that day. 'I shouldn't have to deal with that.'

He told me how unsafe it was and that I should delete my social media, so I did what he said. After a few months I felt safe enough to reactivate it, but kept it on private.

That was the start of the isolation.

Luke was always very protective of both his phones. They were stuck to him at all times. One day, as he was scrolling through his photo roll to show me a picture from work, I saw something flash past on the screen. I recognised it because it was me. I asked him what it was because I hadn't seen it before and I looked naked. He tried to brush me off and keep scrolling, saying it was nothing, but I demanded to see it.

I was right; it was in fact a picture of me from when we were having sex. I had never seen this, nor did I know about it existing or having been taken. I confronted him, shocked. What the hell was it and when had he taken it? Ever so calmly, he said, 'Babe, you know we took that! Remember? We spoke about it. I think we'd had a few drinks. You probably just forgot!' He eventually convinced me that that was exactly what happened, I'd agreed to it and everything in the world was as it should be.

That was the start of the gaslighting.

In two years, I had only met his family once, and it was pretty early on. At that time he said he wanted to introduce me to them as a close friend for now because his parents lived far away from us, they were going through a very messy divorce and the family dynamic wasn't very healthy or stable. On top of that his grandmother was dying and he didn't want to bring any extra stress into the family. He also told me that they still loved his ex-girlfriend of four years (who he broke up with only just before we met) so he wanted to give them time to get over that break-up and be in a position to accept and like me. Of course, I didn't want to upset his family so I agreed to this.

That was the start of the compulsive lying.

One day while I was at work I noticed an unknown number calling me. I now know that if I had answered that call it could have saved me a lot of time, pain, money, anxiety and heartbreak – but I was busy with a patient so I let the call go through to voicemail.

Later that night, I listened to the voicemail. It was a woman on the other end, and I will never forget that call that day: 'Hi Brittany, it's Emma* here, Luke's girlfriend. Just calling to say stay the fuck away from my boyfriend, you psycho bitch. He doesn't want anything to do with you and if you keep trying to see him, we're going to have a big fucking problem. Bye.' Or something very similar. You get the gist.

What. The. Actual. Fuck.

I stared into my phone with a mixture of fear and confusion, then quickly called Luke.

'Why the fuck have I just received a threatening phone call from someone claiming to be your girlfriend?! Who is that?'

He immediately sprang into action. 'Oh my gosh, Brittany, you need to block that number and never take her calls! That is my ex-girlfriend and she is *so* unstable. She is literally stalking me and she just can't move on or accept that it is over. I don't know what she is capable of, so please promise me you will never have contact with her.'

Wowzers. This woman was crazy and was stalking us both! Unbelievable. I promised Luke I would never have contact with her, but I saved her number and the voicemail message in case anything

---

* Not her real name.

happened and I needed it in the future as proof. Which, it turned out, I would.

I asked him to speak to her one last time, to write a really nice email explaining that he had moved on and was happy and in love with me, so she needed to leave us both alone or he'd have to contact the police. He ran the wording past me before emailing her, then showed me proof he had sent it. He was so sweet, making sure I knew that I was more important and that he would do anything to protect us.

That was the start of the manipulation.

Two years had passed since I had started dating Luke, and we were planning the rest of our lives together. We were talking marriage and babies (we had visited Tiffany & Co. to look at the perfect rings), he had convinced me to get a dog, decided on the names we'd give our kids and were in the process of choosing a house to buy together for when we finally could live together. Luke loved making plans for us and despite the concerns that would sometimes bubble up inside me – especially when my friends and family would ask me about discrepancies in his behaviour – it seemed our future was set.

SUDDENLY I SEE

One night I was having dinner with some male friends. Though I had no idea, they happened to also be friends with Luke; and likewise, Luke didn't know they knew me. This is what happens when you are kept a secret, I guess.

We were in the middle of dinner when one guy started talking about how great it was when they went to Luke's for dinner and his partner cooked for them. I knew immediately this was my Luke. But I'd never cooked for these guys at our place. I didn't even know they knew Luke. I'd only recently become friends with them.

It was like time stood still in that moment. Everything started to line up and the more they talked, the more the last two years started to make sense.

Feeling sick to my stomach, I gingerly inquired about this Luke they were speaking of and his partner. 'I think I know him. I thought he was single?' I asked, feigning ignorance in order to confirm what I knew was about to make me crumble into a thousand pieces.

'Oh no, he has a long-term partner,' one of my new friends told me. 'I think they might be getting married. They've been together six years or something.'

Six years. Getting married. That was all I heard. I must have looked like I had seen a ghost because immediately they asked me if I was okay. *Fuck it*, I thought, and I told them everything. I showed them photos and explained that I had in fact been with Luke for two years and that, as far as I knew, *we* were supposed to be getting married.

These guys didn't know what to say except, 'Sorry, we honestly had no idea.'

They sounded sympathetic but I'd had it; I threw my cutlery down and stormed out of the restaurant.

I called and texted Luke straightaway but for the first time ever, no answer or message back. It was obvious the boys' club had quickly given him a heads-up. So I messaged him: 'Call me immediately, or I'm going to find the other woman and tell her.'

Surprise surprise, he called me back immediately. But as I watched my phone ringing in my hand, I thought, *Screw you, why am I even giving you that option? I'm going to tell her anyway. Fuck it, I deserve an answer.*

It was so lucky that I had kept Emma's phone number from when she'd phoned me a year earlier. I found it and called her, nervous about what she was going to say. But we spoke that night for six hours, telling each other everything and swapping shocking stories. She was having a similar experience to mine: all the incon-sistencies from the past two years were finally making sense, too.

It was while we were on that phone call that we realised this story was even more crazy than we could have imagined. We were trying to send each other emails as evidence of our relationships with Luke and plans we were making. I was attempting to send Emma an email about a house Luke and I wanted to buy, which Luke had sent to me, saying, 'I think this house is perfect.' I asked Emma if she'd received my email, but nothing had come through. She told me she would send me a link to the listing for the house Luke was buying with her, but no email came through then either. Then it dawned on us: right in front of our eyes, our emails were being deleted from our inboxes. Luke had worked out we were in communication and was literally logged in to both our accounts simultaneously – accounts we'd never given him the passwords to – and deleting evidence. We couldn't believe what we were seeing.

Emma and I quickly agreed to change our passwords and forward any messages to a backup email address. Then we checked our 'blocked senders' pages to discover that we were in each other's blocked list. We hadn't even known each other's full names before this, yet here we were, blocked in each other's emails so that if we ever tried to write to each other, it would never get through. Luke had thought of everything to cover himself.

It was at that moment that I realised how he always managed to know what I was doing, what I was up to, who I was with. He was keeping tabs on me by accessing my personal information, and had been for who knows how long. Probably from the start. I felt so violated; my skin was crawling and I was completely nauseated. I wanted to lock myself in my room and never date again.

There were so many shattering revelations and realisations for me that night. Like that initial creepy stalker email that Luke had received about my bikini pictures and forwarded on to me? You guessed it: it was from Luke himself. I guess he had set up a secret Instagram account so he could follow me. Of course he couldn't introduce me to his family as his new girlfriend; he already had a girlfriend. (His grandmother is probably still alive, too.) And no, Emma never received that email telling her to leave us alone. Luke had sent it to a fake address. What's more, he'd done the same thing to her when she got wind that he had been seen with me. When she confronted him, he told her that I was a psycho stalker and that I was obsessed with him and would just turn up at his house and message him all the time. He said I was unhinged and that under no circumstances should she have contact with me, though of course she broke that rule on the day she called me.

For two years, Luke had been switching everything in his house each week before one of us arrived for the weekend: swapping our clothes, our cosmetics, the framed photos. That explained why I'd found pieces of clothing there that didn't belong to me; and yet every time, he was so good at manipulating me that somehow I'd end up apologising to him about it.

What was perhaps even more disturbing to learn from Emma was that not only had Luke set up a double life, but he had made his lives with both of us *identical*. He made us wear the same perfume. He'd buy us the same gifts. He wrote us the same letters and Christmas cards, word for word, with just a different name inserted at the top. He encouraged us to get the same dog; two Rhodesian ridgebacks in different cities (RIP Lilly x). We were buying the same house in Melbourne. He'd even taken us both to the same Tiffany store. The list goes on. There must have been such a thrill, such a sense of power for him in the audacity of his lies. I was broken, but mostly disgusted and embarrassed.

The moment I knew he was truly sociopathic was the first time we spoke after that (one of only two), and the first thing he said to me was, 'Well, Brittany, I hope you're happy. You could have kept this to yourself; you didn't have to tell her so that now I don't have either of you. You obviously wanted to ruin my life and you did, so congratulations.'

He was so disconnected from reality it was astounding. His words contained not a shred of empathy or responsibility for what he had done. He was somehow blaming *me*! Then he told me how hard it had been for him to manage all this for so long and that he was exhausted – as if he was expecting that I was going to be sympathetic.

At that moment he genuinely scared me. He wasn't normal.

DEALING WITH THE FALLOUT

So that's my story – well, the version that fits in this chapter and that is allowed to be told, anyway.

The feeling of embarrassment after this all came out was all-consuming. I couldn't bring myself to tell anyone for weeks – not even my family. How could I have been so stupid to have this man in my life for so long? How could I have loved someone capable of this? I know that no part of this was my fault, but that doesn't take away from the fact that, in that moment, I genuinely blamed myself. He was good at making me feel like that.

I saw him one more time after that night and I believe Emma did too. For me, it was quite traumatic. I bumped into him on the street one day and he admitted to everything, to creating identical lives with the both of us because he knew what sort of life he wanted but just couldn't decide which of us to have it with, because he loved us both. He confessed that he had also been with thirteen other women during the time we were together, though I was 'the only other girlfriend'. As if that would make me feel better.

The break-up and everything that ensued went on for quite a while. I developed insomnia and anxiety, experienced panic attacks and didn't trust anyone for a long time. I was so worried that he would seek revenge against me. In hindsight, I should have probably seen a therapist. But I buried it for a long time.

There were so many red flags throughout my relationship with Luke but I wouldn't have noticed them even if a gust of wind came and blew the flagpole directly into my eyeball. So, how did a seemingly intelligent and mostly normal woman get blindsided, gaslighted, manipulated and walked all over for two years, you ask? Great question.

Intelligence has nothing to do with it. Narcissists are very good at what they do. They are master manipulators and get off on control, power, humiliation and devotion. They are smart and charismatic and know how to slowly break you down and take over so that you don't even know it is happening.

If you have been unfortunate enough to experience something like this, I am truly sorry. But know that it is not your fault, nor should you blame yourself, punish yourself, hide yourself away or feel embarrassed. Please don't let a bad relationship stop you from moving forward. Since sharing my story on the podcast, so many women have reached out to me to ask how I moved on, because they never want to date or trust anyone again, and can't help taking their past into their current dates and their future. To this I say, please don't! An ex-partner like that has already taken so much from you in the past; don't let them continue to take even more of your future. Seek the help you need to be able to date and trust again, because there are plenty of good people out there in the world that you can only meet if you are available.

It took me longer than I would have liked to realise that I could turn this trauma into something positive. But I did! It was a catalyst for me travelling the world for three years, which gave me the space to grow and heal. It's what made me redefine relationships: what I want from them, what I deserve and how I'm willing to be treated. I believe everything happens for a reason, and that my experience with Luke shaped me in a significant way. Since then I've had a much clearer picture of who I am, and you better believe I now trust my gut instinct waaaay more.

The subject of narcissism is also what kindled my friendship with Laura, when one day at brunch we began sharing and bonding over what we'd gone through in our toxic past relationships. I believe that if women can join forces through empathy, good things truly can come from it. Even Emma and I forged a friendship. She'd lost six years of her life to Luke, yet she was amazingly supportive to me and, in a way, we went through this ordeal together.

We have just this one life, and we are in control of how we move forward and how we choose to perceive every situation. If you've been unfortunate enough to go through anything like this, I want you to move forward into the next chapter with an open heart and hope for the future. A beautiful life is waiting for you.

NUDES

How do you nail a nude pic? What are the rules around sending them and how do you stay safe in a digital age that makes sending saucy snaps easier than tying your shoelaces?

BRITT AND LAURA

SEE ALSO: BOUNDARIES, DATING, SITUATIONSHIPS

Accidentally Unfiltered

I was showing pictures of my long-distance boyfriend to my nana, who hadn't met him yet. Was scrolling through my camera roll and came across a nude of him showing everything ... erect ... everything! I tried to skip over this one as quickly as possible, hoping Nana's eyes were a bit slow, but that's when she said, 'Goodness, you are a lucky girl, aren't you?' I went redder than red and shrank ten sizes in my seat!

He's now my husband and Nana adored him when she did get to meet him!

BRITT: Laura, how nude was your most explicit nude?

LAURA: Geez! It's been a while since I've sent a nude. I mean, my birth video with Marlie's head crowning doesn't count, right? We ain't talking that kind of nude! If I were to put a rating on the nudes I've sent in the past, I'd say on average I'd sit at an M15+. I mean, they're spicy, but I also like to leave a bit to the imagination: a pair of lacy undies, a strategic hand placement blurring out tits and bits. I've always had reservations about sending a full monty and they are two-fold: What if this picture falls into the wrong hands? And what if the nude is, like, too much nude? It's not like there's a handbook (and trust me, we've looked).

The thing about nudes is that unless you nail the brief, they can fall short of achieving the desired outcome. I reckon most of us have received a nude or a dick pic that has left us not so much aroused, but more . . . speechless.

I still remember the very first dick pic I ever received. I was in a situationship with a guy in Bondi who I had been seeing for the better part of a year. We weren't exclusive, but we were spending A LOT of time together by the time he jetted overseas to LA for a work trip.

Our flirty texts became progressively sexier and while I was at work one day, he asked me to send him a topless photo from the office bathrooms. Logistically I couldn't get my head around how I was going to do it well. There's nothing sexy about fluorescent lighting and toilet cubicles! So instead I asked if he would send me one first. I didn't really want a picture of his manhood (each to their own, but seeing a picture of a penis isn't really my idea of a good time) but I needed to delay his request. Sure enough: ping! Thirty seconds later there was a picture message sitting in my inbox.

I sheepishly looked around, covered my screen with one hand and opened the text. There it was: an eye-popping dick pic. The photo was taken waist down in the reflection of his mirror, his fully erect penis in his hand, it was freshly shaved and rock hard. When I noticed the surfboard leaning up against the wall behind him,

I instantly recognised the room he was in. It was his bedroom in Bondi.

But wait ... he was more than 12,000 km away in LA. How could he be sending me a nude from home? That's when it dawned on me. I had been sent a recycled nude; a cock from the archives.

There I was thinking nudes were taken in the heat of the moment, spontaneous and sexy acts. It turns out Bondi Boy had a whole album of curated dicks ready to whip out whenever the opportunity presented itself. That's when I realised, there was more to this whole nudes business than wham bam thank you ma'am.

B: Haha, you wouldn't be the first to get a picture of a recycled penis! Some people keep folders of what they deem 'good pics' so that they're on hand in case of a dick pic emergency (although let's be real, there's never a time a dick pic would be an emergency).

It does take a bit of the romance out of it to think that someone could be sending you a nude that they have sent to someone else in the past, but there are other reasons people might bank a fire nude. Take it from me, I did long distance for quite a while. What if things are getting steamy in text, but you're at home in your ugly trackies feeling blah? A little preparation pays off! Sometimes you have to get creative to keep the spark alive!

It's funny to think that for our parents' generation, sending a sexy pic just wasn't an option. Thirty years ago, if you wanted to send a nude you would have had to take a roll of film to the photo shop, wait three days to have it developed and then stand in line while the fourteen-year-old boy behind the register, who was most definitely going home to tell his friends that he saw your hoo-ha, handed over your prints. It just didn't happen. Now with Snapchat, iPhones, Messenger, it's just so easy – TOO easy – to send explicit photos, and I don't think that's something we can just gloss over. Every time we take one, we have to ask ourselves:

who am I sending this picture to and what would be the consequences if it was made public?

L: Absolutely, I mean, I would hope that the consequences would fall on the person who was distributing the photo without consent. Revenge porn is a real thing and it's illegal. We've come a long way in that respect, and now people who distribute nudes without consent can be held accountable for their actions – but we know that it isn't a foolproof system, and there are shitty people out there who don't think twice about sharing explicit photos that were sent to them in confidence, whether it be in a boys' WhatsApp group or passed around at a party. Yes, it is illegal and there can be significant penalties, but ultimately that doesn't erase the damage it does to victims who have their most vulnerable photos used against them.

B: It's actually pretty shocking when you dig into the stats. I've read that an estimated one in ten Australians are taken advantage of or have their images used or shared around without their consent.[30] Not surprisingly, this disproportionately harms women from the ages of eighteen to forty-five, where the incidence is as high as one in *five*.

As I'm writing this, under the image-based abuse provisions, online trolls face penalties of up to $111,000 each time they post an intimate image of a person without consent. Since January 2022, websites and social media companies have twenty-four hours to comply with take-down notices.[31] It's a step that has been enforced to further try to support victims who have experienced image abuse. I think this is a step in the right direction, but I also think more severe punishments should be in place for people that share nudes of others without consent.

L: Consent has been thrust into the media landscape, into schools via sex education and into how we interact and engage when we send nudes digitally. Consent is an ongoing agreement, and just because you've sent a nude to someone doesn't mean that that image is theirs. YOU OWN YOUR NUDES, no one else, period.

While we are on it, Britt, another thing we can't overlook is what happens if you break up? Can you keep saucy snaps of your ex?

B: NO! Receiving a nude from someone you're intimate with or dating is a privilege. When you're no longer dating that person anymore, or you're no longer intimately with that person, you are no longer entitled to it. So, yeah, people who keep nudes of their exes are fucking creeps.

That's the issue with consent and nudes – so much of it relies on trust and the person you're sending it to doing the right thing and treating you with respect.

L: PREACH!

So, with some of the very serious and important stuff covered off . . . how the farkkkk can we all take good nudes? Isn't that the million-dollar question? Here's a round-up of the best advice we found by searching the deepest crevices of the interwebs. (We would really love for someone to see our search history after 'researching' this topic. We took one for the team there.)

1. Good lighting is everything. The number-one piece of advice centres around lighting. Natural light, such as afternoon sunshine or a warm globe lamp, seems to be our best bet. Harsh, cool downlights tend to be less flattering and can look a bit clinical. So if you're snapping away in the bathroom and you have the option of a heat light, go with that bad boy.

2. Keep editing to a minimum. If good light failed you then by all means do some light adjustment afterwards but don't go putting any crazy filters or skin smoothing on the photo. You want to seem like you casually took the world's greatest nude, like it was no biggie – not like you directed a *Playboy* editorial.

3. Clean your damn room! Think about the background, nothing is going to kill a boner or dry out a fanny faster than a pig sty. I once read a meme that said 'Clean your damn room. I don't need to judge you twice'. That stuck with me! Avoid things in the background that make you look a little less desirable, such as toilets, rubbish bins, piles of clothes on the floor, dirty mugs and dishes and pets. Poor Fido doesn't need to be in on this action.

4. Clean the mirror, too. Speaking of cleaning, clean your mirror! This is a really simple way for that pic to look better.

Word on the internet is that putting your mirror at a 70-degree angle can help make you look longer and more elegant. If you're doing a full body shot, placing one leg in front of the other with a hip slightly popped to the side will highlight your curves and show off your waist. If the only mirror you've got isn't going to do you any favours, a self-timer can be your best friend. Find a surface that will give you a nice angle and background and get snapping! Taking naked selfies can also be a fun way to send slightly more discreet shots, such as lying stomach-down on your bed with your knees slightly bent, and the curvature of your back dipping down to show off your butt. A little pout and bare shoulder action is always a bit of a tease.

5. Stay safe by remembering less is more (or, should we say, more is more). Think about who your recipient is and how much you feel comfortable sharing with that person. When someone you're sexting is asking you to send them something naughty, take a moment to decide if what you're sending is something you're happy about and whether you can trust them with it, or whether you're just doing it to appease the other person. If option 2 is springing to mind, skip the nude altogether. You have the control here so be smart, be savvy. You can be super creative and send provocative pictures without having to go full-blown explicit. Maybe you can put emojis over your private parts or maybe it's a strategic pose or crop. You also have every right to just politely decline. It comes down to *your* comfort zone and *your* boundaries. Don't let anyone persuade you otherwise.

6. Have fun and feel confident in your body. Finally, the best piece of advice for taking nudes is: practise! Find which angles best highlight the parts of your body and go with those. Nudes are not a one-size-fits-all situation, so have fun discovering what suits you and build your way up to bold!

Accidentally Unfiltered

Back in 2011/early 2012 I was one of the first people in my group to have an iPhone and loved sending nudes. I had a couple of apps I'd use to chuck filters on them before I sent them. Anyway, I came across a new one I hadn't heard of called Instagram and started editing my nudes in there. Lo and behold, a few days later I got a bizarre notification that someone 'liked' my post. It was then I realised Instagram was a social media platform NOT just a photo editing app. Absolutely mortifying.

B: Laura, remember when I took that one really spicy hot semi-nude photo? The one where the nude-photo gods had been shining down on me – the natural light was perfect, I had strategically placed a vase to cover the important bits, I had nailed the angle and I was just really feeling myself? Jordan had just moved overseas, so I did what I feel any woman that's about to send a topless photo to her new long-distance boyfriend would do and sent it to you first! 'Hi love. Just wanted to show you this because I think I nailed it. Thoughts? Should I send it?'

And in true best-friend hype-girl fashion, your reply was something along the lines of: 'Girl 👀👀👀🍑🍑🍑! Send immediately!'

So there you have it! If in doubt, get a friend's approval before sending out.

Accidentally Unfiltered

I was away on holidays and sending photos of my bum in cute undies to my boyfriend at the time. Little did I know my phone was syncing with our family computer back home. My photos were being uploaded to the cloud and my parents could see them! I was mortified when my sister told me!

OVERWHELM

*Almost anything will work again if
you unplug it and hit reset. Even you.*

BRITT AND LAURA

SEE ALSO: BOUNDARIES, TOXIC POSITIVITY, XPECTATIONS

BRITT: Ever felt like you're drowning but your feet are planted safely on dry land? Like you're gasping for air even though you're sitting outside, where oxygen is plentiful? Like your body is so tired, so exhausted and so run down you just want to shut off to the world, eat your weight in carbs and Netflix yourself into oblivion – even though you just woke up?

You're irritated, you're beyond stressed and you've got so much on your to-do list but you can't bring yourself to tick off even one box because WHERE DO YOU EVEN START!?

You, my friend, may be experiencing a case of The Overwhelm, and you certainly are not alone!

LAURA: Is it possible to feel overwhelmed by the fact that you're overwhelmed?

B: I think they call that overwhelmed squared, and no one's got time for that!

L: It's like in *10 Things I Hate About You* when Chastity says, 'I know you can be overwhelmed, and you can be underwhelmed, but can you ever just be whelmed?' And Bianca replies, 'I think you can in Europe.' Bloody great movie!

B: It feels almost cathartic for me that we are writing this chapter now because, as it happens, I'm just coming out the other side of one of these periods of overwhelm. I have been mired in the depths of heartbreak – one that was confusing and pretty unexpected but probably unavoidable.

What followed was a really dark period, filled with feelings of depression, of not wanting to get out of bed, of many tears and of not feeling like I could face the day. Even now, many months on, I often still find myself in tears. Work has been the busiest it has ever been, and that's amazing because I'm truly lucky to have a job I love, but some days it feels like we are chasing our tails to keep up. Then getting a very energetic Australian Shepherd puppy (damn, I really underestimated how much work that would be!), writing this book and enrolling at the National Institute of Dramatic Art has been a lot – and not all necessary. But I think that's how I have always dealt with things like heartbreak and stress, by filling my life to the brim with other things to take my mind off it and fill the empty space. And, well, I guess it all just became too much. Having said that, my pup Delilah has been the best thing for me!

Coming from a background of working in a hospital and then running a business, forced downtime is not something I was used to having that often, but radio work actually has built-in downtime because of scheduling – and it couldn't have come at a better time! I took myself off on a trip. I was actually supposed to write this chapter while I was away, but I couldn't bring myself to. I could not even force myself to open my laptop and type 'overwhelm' because I was so deep in it. I knew that I had a deadline but my brain and body just said, 'You need to take a break'.

I cried almost every day of the trip. Healing from heartbreak isn't linear, and mine certainly hasn't been. But here I am now, feeling slightly more revived and finally putting down my thoughts about these feelings that are unfortunately all too common. Maybe that little break, my mini 'shut-up shop', was exactly what I didn't know I needed. I'm thankful that the opportunity came up to head off and regroup, because I have no doubt I would have kept pushing my thoughts and feelings aside until absolute breaking point.

L: I think that's what happens when you're in the depths of overwhelm – despite the to-do list that is SCREAMING at you, it's impossible to feel productive when below the surface you're thrashing around, barely able to keep afloat.

Taking a break can feel impossible. And often it is physically impossible, which means it just keeps piling up. Depending on your set of circumstances you can't always say 'fuck it', go on a holiday or switch off from life, when there are responsibilities demanding attention, such as kids or other people to care for, work commitments, Zoom meetings, soccer practice, getting dinner on the table, unread emails, friends you keep rescheduling, pandemics you need to worry about . . .

We live in a society that glorifies being busy, and hustle culture is a currency that we flaunt as evidence of success. But at what cost?

B: Yeah, you never hear someone say, 'Oh, I don't have a lot going on in my life right now . . .'

L: Exactly! The answer to 'How have you been?' is almost always 'BUSY!'

B: 'Oh my god, I am so busy I am *drowning*!' is the standard.

L: I don't think I've ever felt as overwhelmed as I have at different points since becoming a mum. Now, I want to be careful when I say this, Britt, as I am fully aware that having children is not a prerequisite for feeling totally submerged – anyone can feel overwhelmed, at any stage of life. But for me, the relentlessness and the enormity of caring for two tiny humans has piled an added weight to the feeling.

I reckon every mother feels obligated to preface any negative observations about parenting with the statement, 'I love my children so much ...' Because we do. We love them completely, but can feel so shattered at the same time. So full and so empty. Being constantly pulled and pushed throughout the waking hours of the day, shadowed by the anxiety around whether you're going to get a decent sleep at night.

Motherhood marked a huge shift in my identity, but also a shift in priorities. People always tell you that your priorities change once you become a mother. I remember thinking that I was ready to sacrifice my social life, and I was. I willingly swapped nights out for mornings at the park, and going to the gym for strolls with the pram. But what I failed to fully understand before becoming a mum myself was just how far I would slip down my own list of priorities. Without ever being conscious of it, I found myself at the bottom.

Before children, your time is your own. You can make time to exercise when you want to, you can have sex in the loungeroom at 11 am if you want to, you can do date nights on a whim without thinking about the logistics of organising a babysitter, or feel guilty about leaving the kids when they've been at day care all week because you have to work. You can see your friends without considering sleep schedules, when you're exhausted you can have a sleep-in, and – sweet saviour! – you can finish a cup of coffee before it goes cold.

I soon realised that when all the things I could do for myself slipped down the list of priorities, so did I – and it's a feeling that is universal to mothers, probably all parents, especially those in the fog of the first few years with little babies.

What I've learned is that you can love your children fiercely and still need time to tend to yourself. You can be a wonderful mum, but being a mum is not all that you are. Putting everything before yourself doesn't make you a better mother, it makes you overwhelmed and resentful and it affects your ability to feel joy.

Britt, I love that even though this phase of our lives looks quite different for each of us we can both relate to the feeling of overwhelm for our own reasons. How would you say it manifested differently for you?

B: I mean, jeez, I am tired just *reading* that. That's the thing, parenting literally never ends!

But yes, I think it's such an important point that there is no official prerequisite for overwhelm. And in this day and age, there is no escaping it. Think about the last two years and what the world has been going through: there wasn't one person who wasn't affected by the COVID-19 pandemic in some way or another. Some in more extreme ways than others, but it touched everyone nonetheless. Job losses, death, illness, anxiety, separation from family, social isolation, cancelling important events – no birthdays, no weddings, no seeing family, no funerals or goodbyes, wondering 'Will it ever end?' and 'Will the world ever go back to normal?'

This obviously had a flow-on effect too: political unrest as the world lost trust in many of its leaders, financial worries with no end in sight, and epic lockdowns that no one should ever have to endure, especially with no toilet paper! And if these things weren't enough to get your anxiety boiling over, throw in some natural disasters because hey, it turns out global warming is a very real thing, and we are now facing flooding, fires, earthquakes and droughts in quick and unrelenting succession. Oh, and if all that had not quite broken you yet, the devastating war currently going on between Ukraine and Russia and the worry that it will spill over into World War Three sure will!

Overwhelm can stem from many other things, too: work responsibilities, relationship stressors, traumatic experiences, financial worries, political issues and health concerns, to name just some. And of course, it's not unusual to experience several of these things at once.

It just feels like there is nowhere for us to hide. No one is safe and this can make us feel so very small, powerless and helpless.

Before I took my recent two-week break, the ice beneath me was cracking. I was very emotional. My skin felt very thin: words, expressions, looks, keyboard warriors, even my own thoughts were penetrating my self-worth in a way they never usually do. Small, menial tasks seemed very daunting. I was losing passion for things I usually loved. I felt like my brain wasn't working. I was sad, snappy, exhausted and uninterested in life. Every time I went online, the news was beyond depressing.

And it's funny, Laura, you talk about how having kids has affected your feelings of overwhelm, because for me, you know what made it even worse? The fact I *don't* have kids.

Yep, I know it seems a little backwards, so hear me out! But I felt so guilty about feeling buried and exhausted when I *don't* have kids to run around after on top of everything else that parents have going on. I worried that I wasn't allowed to feel tired, emotional and sad, or to complain or voice my feelings, because at the end of the day, 'You don't know you're tired until you have kids!' Which is fair enough, to an extent. I've done my share of sleepless nights working on call in emergency departments, including a twenty-seven-hour non-stop shift once, so I have definitely felt those sleepless, exhausting nights – but it wasn't every night. So every time I wanted to express my exhaustion I wouldn't, because I feared the judgement of the people around me who would internally roll their eyes like, 'Girl, you have no idea. You have so much freedom and so much to be happy about.'

This feeling of it all being too much, of being overwhelmed, can strike anyone at any time. One person's feelings and situation do not invalidate those of someone else. None of us should compare our stresses and worries to someone else's, because they are all relative and are all valid.

L: One hundred per cent! I think it comes back to the idea of comparison, and toxic positivity creeps in here, too. Thinking, *I shouldn't be overwhelmed because So-and-So has it harder than me and they seem to be coping fine* does nothing to lessen stress, and only serves to invalidate your own feelings. Then, as you said, what usually happens is you end up feeling guilty for feeling this way on top of all that. So now you feel overwhelmed, bookended by guilt. Yuck.

Instead of being self-critical, it's in these moments that we need to have more compassion for ourselves. Our typical response to ever-growing workloads is to work harder, put in longer hours and *do* more, *be* more, *achieve* more – rather than to step back, work out what exactly is making us do this, and look for a solution or a new way of being.

SO, YOU'RE OVERWHELMED. JOIN THE CLUB. WHAT NOW?

Let's start with right now. Take a breath, and step away.

It can feel impossible to step away from your never-ending to-do list for fear that more time will get away from you and the pile will multiply even more. But remember that your ability to be productive or calm is compromised when you're deep in the overwhelm, and your concentration and focus more easily gives way to those overpowering feelings of fear and anxiety. So yes, you may be getting through it, or some of it, but you won't feel like you're doing a good job. And then the cycle continues!

So take a breath and count to ten. Then walk down the street, jump in a taxi, go to the airport and fly to Barbados (jokes . . . but also, that would be bloody nice!). Sometimes it's enough to breathe and shake it out, but ultimately you need to step back and properly assess what changes you can make so you don't feel like you're drowning. For example, can you delegate tasks, take half an hour to exercise each day or book the kids into a day of day care? There are always solutions! As we said, taking time away may seem counter-intuitive, but it will give you more mental space to refocus your energies and not be so weighed down by the burden.

Figure out what's stressing you the most

There are always one or two things that are taking up more space in your brain than others. Pinpoint what those things are, and try to find a way to tackle them that's manageable.

While it may be impossible to actually take these things out of the equation entirely, if it's just the dauting nature of the task at hand you might be able to reduce it to more achievable pieces. Lists can help break down a overwhelming job into smaller, less stressful and more achievable tasks.

Boundaries, baby! Get comfortable with saying no

You are allowed to put yourself back up the priority list. If you find yourself caught on the hamster wheel and you're taking on more and more responsibilities and tasks, ask yourself what is actually essential, what can you delegate and what can you say no to. And do your best not to let other people's expectations overwhelm you. Protecting your time and your space can give you a sense of control, which is especially important at these times. Saying no to things you aren't in a position to do will create space for things you need and *want* to do.

Perfect is the enemy of good

Most of us are guilty of being perfectionists every now and then. It's totally natural to a) want to do something well and b) have a slightly idealised vision of what 'doing something well' looks like. Perfectionism can lead us to make tasks bigger than they need to be, which can generate procrastination and stress. These things lead to overwhelm, which starts a vicious cycle because it then circles back to feeling even more overwhelmed and then *boom*: risk of breakdown, because you can't break free of the 'procrastinate–pile up–overwhelm–procrastinate' cycle.

Sheryl Sandberg, the American business executive known for her long tenure as COO of Facebook, famously said one of her favourite mottos is 'Done is better than perfect'. So true, Sheryl! To figure out when to stop, it can be helpful to ask yourself, 'What is the benefit of spending more time on this task?' If the answer is 'not much', stop what you are doing and be done with it.

When we cling to rigid ideas of how something needs to be or are perfectionist in our outlook, it can become difficult to delegate tasks and open up the to-do list. But the old saying 'if you want a job done right you have to do it yourself' can well and truly get in the bin. Instead, surround yourself with people who can lighten the load – which is where the next point comes in.

Ask for help

Often when we are overwhelmed, we feel like we *should* be okay, like we *should* be coping. But, truthfully, it's totally fine if you aren't. What that does mean, however, is that you need to learn how to ask for help. Communicating with those who love you, expressing to your manager, your partner and your friends that your tank is completely empty, will open up space for people to help you. And they will genuinely want to offer some support if they know you're struggling. You're not the Incredible Hulk! You don't have to carry the weight of your world on your own.

Speak to a professional

We love to say it! If you've tried many techniques for feeling overwhelmed, and you still aren't getting on top of it, that's cool. Help is close by! Maybe now is the time to think about speaking to a therapist or mental health professional. Therapy can help you identify what's causing your overwhelm and help you on your path to feeling better.

PENGUINS

And why they are better than soulmates

BRITT

SEE ALSO: CONFLICT RESOLUTION,
DATING, THE KNOT, LONG DISTANCE

Okay, I want to talk to you about penguins for a hot second. But before you think either you've picked up the wrong book or I've lost the plot, hear me out.

If you've followed *Life Uncut* for a little while, you will know I refer to penguins a lot. I don't just believe it is a beautiful analogy for being in a relationship, but I genuinely believe we can learn a lot from these adorable little creatures. You see, most penguins are monogamous. This means that male and female pairs (although not always male and female! See the story about Dotty and Zee a little further on) will mate exclusively with each other for the duration of mating season – and, in fact, some breeds will continue to mate for life.*

The grand romance begins with preparations. The male usually picks out a nice nesting site before then approaching a female, making sure he looks desirable. Once the location of the love shack is secure, the male penguin searches high and low for the perfect

---

* Before we get too deep into talking penguins and soulmates it is important to note that not *all* penguins mate for life. There are some slippery little suckers that like to keep their options open, but for the purpose of this chapter, and to keep my faith in true love, we will be concentrating on the penguins that *do* remain faithful for life. Okay, glad we cleared that up!

stone to present to his prospective female. This is the penguin version of a proposal. If the female accepts, they start to make a nest and the sexy time begins! After mating, it's egg-laying time – a single egg for female King and Emperor penguins, or two eggs for all other species of penguins. Each parent will take turns holding the eggs between their legs for warmth in their nest. Isn't that just so lovely?!

But wait, it gets better. There is a story that highlights penguins' long-term commitment to their relationships that is too moving not to share.

Dotty and Zee are two male Humboldt penguins at the Bremerhaven Zoo in Germany who have been together since 2006. They stayed by each other's side through the hard times, building a nest each year for their eggs and not understanding why they couldn't reproduce – but despite the struggle, their love survived. Then, finally, they adopted a chick together in 2009 after an egg was rejected from another female. They successfully looked after it, hatched it and raised their little one, their commitment never faltering.

This is why I love to use the expression 'penguins' rather than 'soulmates' or 'life partners'. It's darn cute and it brings less pressure with it than that sometimes-scary word 'soulmate', which suggests there is only one soul out there that is right for us; only one person we can truly connect with, who understands us and doesn't question what we do; only one person who we want to be with forever and who we don't question in return; only one person who will ignite a burning desire within us every single day; and only one relationship that is perfect for us.

The idea is magical, but honestly – and I hate to burst anyone's bubble – *I think not*. I'm a self-confessed romantic but the idea that out of the 7.9 billion people on this planet, we each only have one true soulmate, is something I just don't buy.

THE PROBLEM I HAVE WITH SOULMATES

Part of my objection is that the term 'soulmates' sets laughably high standards when we are looking for and dating our long-term partner. This promise that we will feel an insane spark the moment we meet and the relationship won't have any issues is simply unrealistic.

Falling for someone can be a slow burn; we don't *always* have to have that heart-stopping connection and intense lust from Day One, even though many people do. There are no rules, no right or wrong; connection is different for everyone. But when we set the bar so high that our expectation is to find an instant soulmate and nothing less, we are setting ourselves up to potentially miss out on something amazing that might take more time to develop.

Let me tell you about my first date with Jordan. It was the middle of the COVID-19 pandemic, with on-and-off lockdowns, and we booked a dinner that had a strict maximum timeslot of two hours. I have a no-dinner-on-the-first-date rule, a result of some disastrous dinner dates in the past. But on this occasion I was willing to break my own rule because the time limit gave me a clear way out. I needn't have worried, though, because the moment Jordan walked in I could tell how kind he was. I think it was his eyes . . . he has the kindest eyes. Some people just have that look about them. He was also the opposite of me: slightly reserved, a little nervous and fairly shy (not a feeling I know very well!). Regardless, I was totally drawn to him.

We were clearly having such a great time together that the lovely staff at the restaurant didn't kick us out once our two hours were up. I think they could tell it was a first date! (I *love* watching people when they are on a first date – there's nothing more endearing and interesting than witnessing two strangers navigate a first interaction. Throw in a little bit of lust from at least one party and you have yourself some spicy viewing!)

Anyway, six hours later we were finally kicked out because the restaurant was closing. We didn't even realise the time, were oblivious that people around us were slowly leaving – we were just really present with each other. I didn't want to leave. I'd been wanting to kiss him since about halfway through the evening, then as we were leaving I did and I didn't want to stop. I wanted to know him and be around him and was just so drawn to him.

Did I believe he was my soulmate that first night? No. But I very quickly knew that I wanted him in my life. I still have all of those feelings for him. But despite this, for us, unfortunately, love just wasn't enough on its own, and earlier in 2022 we decided to go our separate ways. That's the thing about penguins – they have a wonderful, deeply committed time together, but it's not always forever.

So, was it a flawless, smooth-sailing relationship with no ups and downs? Perfection with no arguments or differences? Always easy? The majority of the time I can say yes, it was, but anyone who says that their relationship has no ebbs and flows and is never challenging is telling you a porky pie. A perfectly perfect relationship doesn't exist. Relationships take work, even with someone we deem 'the one'. They require discussion, patience, understanding, commitment and compromise.

These harder moments are not only okay, but they are also a sign of a healthy relationship. Even Oprah says this, so it must be true! Instead of viewing disagreements and arguing as a negative thing, we should shine a different light on the situation. Conflict can be an opportunity to learn more about your partner – what makes them tick, what pisses them off, how each of you deals with things and how you can work together as a unit. Of course, when you're in the middle of it and your patience is wearing thin, there is steam coming out of your ears and you're about to hurl your partner's phone out the window it might be hard to see things this way. Just remember, it is impossible for two people to cruise through life having EXACTLY the same opinions and ideas about the world!

I think the term 'soulmates' works better if we broaden its meaning – after all, it's not our fault that we look at love and life through rose-coloured glasses. Hollywood and Disney perpetuate ideas of fireworks and happily-ever-afters. But I would like you to look at the concept of a soulmate in a different way.

Meeting a soulmate should be about connecting with someone at the right time. I think we meet many people over the course of our life that could fit this description. A soulmate is someone who sees you for you, who is imperfectly perfect and who sees, hears and loves every part of you, annoying little flaws and all.

The belief that there may be an even 'better' soulmate for you out in the world somewhere can be detrimental to your current relationship. It can create this grass-is-greener mindset that you shouldn't stay put even though your current partner is amazing – because what if there is someone better?!

This doesn't mean you should settle for less than you deserve, of course, and the only person who can decide what to do in your individual situation is you. But appreciating your partner for who they are, thinking about the things they bring to your relationship and how they make you feel, and remembering that there is no one person who will tick every single box and be extraordinary in every way can actually be a huge relief. We all have our flaws and anyone who tells you they don't isn't being truthful.

The reason I prefer the term 'penguin' over 'soulmate' is that soulmate, for me, is so definitive, so final. There's no room for error; no room to change your mind. Penguin is cute. It means that right now we can't imagine life with anyone else. Right now, we choose each other.

I look forward to the next chapter in my search for my next penguin. The person who will understand me, love me just as I am, and be moving in the same direction as I am. Let's take the pressure off ourselves to find 'the one', and start to enjoy the process a little, hey?! After all, it's the journey, not the destination.

PREGNANCY LOSS

One in five women will experience miscarriage – so why aren't we talking about it?

LAURA

SEE ALSO: FERTILITY, TIMELINES, TOXIC POSITIVITY, VISIBILITY

I was sitting at my desk, unable to ignore the dull pain in my abdomen. It was a perfectly ordinary Tuesday in the office. The printer was broken; Amy, who sits across from me, was talking about going away to Jervis Bay for the weekend.

Everything was normal . . . except I was miscarrying.

That's the thing about pregnancy loss: so often it happens in secret. It happens to women at Woolworths picking up pasta sauce, to women at work wrestling with deadlines, to women in line for the school pick-up – all these women carrying on as they undergo personal tragedy. Mothers quietly grieving the babies that they never got to hold, some of them ashamed that their bodies failed them, tormenting themselves with the question, *What is wrong with me?*

Like a lot of women, I had never really thought about my fertility. I had spent the whole of my twenties so focused on *not* getting pregnant that I'd never even considered how difficult having a healthy pregnancy could be. I certainly didn't think I would ever experience a miscarriage – let alone two. It's a mothers' group no one wants to be a part of, and yet there is something comforting and healing in talking about pregnancy loss. Hearing other women share their own stories was what put an end to the shame and stigma for me. I stopped trying to make sense of it, stopped blaming myself and was able to accept that I wasn't damaged goods, and understand that for a lot of women, miscarriage is a common and inextricable part of their journey to motherhood.

Matt and I had been dating for a year when I first found out I was pregnant. We had spoken about our future – getting married, having kids – but all of that was a safe five years away.

I was on a solo work trip to Bali when I started feeling a little off. I chalked it up to Bali Belly, but I also couldn't remember exactly when my last period was, so I thought I'd better just get a pregnancy test to check – not really believing that I could be pregnant.

I'd just finished dinner in my hotel and the pregnancy test I'd bought earlier in the day from a little pharmacy on Jalan Legian was on the counter. I took the stick out of the paper, peed in the plastic cup and sat there scrolling Instagram, expecting a single line to show up.

I remember looking down and seeing the faintest mirage of a second line. I held it up to the light to inspect it closer, trying to make out if I was imagining it – then as more time passed, the line grew darker.

I was pregnant.

The reality of those two little lines smashed me in the face like a freight train. I sat there on the cold floor of the bathroom and cried and cried. I cried because I didn't know how Matt would react to the news. I cried because in a single moment my life had careened off course again (see Timelines). And I cried because there was no doubt in my mind that I was keeping this baby.

I decided that I wanted to tell Matt in person, as this didn't feel like the sort of news that could be delivered over the phone – so for two weeks I walked around Bali with this heavy secret.

When I arrived back in Sydney, Matt picked me up from the airport. I was overcome with a mix of nerves and morning sickness, unsure what his reaction was going to be. I barely got the words out.

'I have something I need to tell you—'

He cut me off with the biggest, stupidest grin across his face. Somehow he just instinctively knew. 'You're pregnant!' he said, combusting into laughter.

In that moment, I understood that 'unplanned' is not synonymous with 'unwanted'. The weight and the fear around being pregnant lifted and it was one of the happiest days of our lives.

Over the next six weeks everything changed. Our five-year plan went out the window but we were so excited. We were going to be parents, and we were all in. The world didn't know yet, most of our friends didn't know yet – but we knew.

Weeks passed and we still mostly kept the news to ourselves, waiting for the elusive three-month mark before we told everyone the good news. When I woke up one morning with a dull throbbing ache in my side and a little bit of blood, I dismissed it as some spotting and didn't think the worst. I had read that some women can have bleeding in early pregnancy and so I wasn't overly alarmed. I had a shower, ate some breakfast and went to work.

A couple of hours rolled by and the bleeding got heavier. As I sat at my computer replying to customer emails, I realised I was miscarrying.

IT'S OKAY TO GRIEVE A PREGNANCY THAT WASN'T PLANNED

For me, losing a baby that was a happy accident was a unique sort of loss; it's emotional whiplash. It's hard to reconcile how you can be so sad about losing something that you hadn't been 'trying' for. I felt alone and I felt broken, which was compounded by the fact that

I didn't know anyone apart from my mum who had experienced pregnancy loss. I also found it hard to explain to friends and colleagues why I wasn't myself, and why I needed to have time off work. I wasn't sick; I was grieving. But very few people had even known I was pregnant.

On one hand I wasn't prepared for how sad I would feel in the weeks after it happened, but then there was also the physical pain, something I was equally ill-equipped for. I had scoured the internet for information, I had even googled 'How to stop a miscarriage' while sitting at my desk that afternoon at work. It felt silly and futile but my body was doing things I had no control over. As the cramping and bleeding increased, all hope disappeared and I didn't know what to do. Going to Emergency felt too extreme, waiting to see the GP felt too controlled – but there was no in between.

After the doctor confirmed what I already knew, I was told very matter-of-factly that I would have 'period-like' cramps and pass some clotting. But it is one thing to hear that and another to live it: to feel the weight of those clots drop out of you, what was once the hope of a baby, and then flush it down the toilet. This is the ugly side of miscarriage. As a society we don't like to talk about women bleeding, so the physical aftermath of miscarriage gets even less airtime than the emotional one.

There are stories just like mine all around us, held and carried by women in every workplace, friendship group, family and mothers' group – women who have experienced pregnancy loss. One in five pregnancies end in miscarriage and I remember reading this statistic over and over and thinking, *WHERE THE HELL are all these women?!* No doubt they are asking the same question, too.

It was only after I started talking about my miscarriage that other women who I was close to shared their own experiences. Listening to them, I felt less alone, and I hated my body a little less knowing that other women had shared the same feeling of their body having betrayed them.

WHY THE SECRECY? WHY THE SHAME?

It's the secrecy that makes miscarriage feel so stigmatised and leaves women feeling isolated. Silence is ingrained in us; it's enmeshed in every conversation that centres around early pregnancy. Women are told not to share their happy news in the first few weeks until they're medically given 'the all clear' and until the screenings that help determine foetal abnormalities have been passed. If you've made it out of the woods of the first trimester, the likelihood of miscarriage is statistically lower.

If we really unpack what this implies, it says 'You shouldn't share the good news that you're pregnant until it's safe. That way you won't have to share your bad news if things go wrong.' Keeping miscarriage a secret gives the impression that it's rare and taboo, when in fact it's so common.

Denying women the opportunity to talk about the early weeks of pregnancy also denies women the opportunity to talk about pregnancy loss. It insinuates that miscarriage is something to be kept hidden, something to be ashamed of. And where there is shame, there is also self-blame – maybe it was that glass of wine I drank, maybe it was the abortion I had ten years earlier, maybe I deserved this, maybe it's because I ate soft cheese, or because I lifted that heavy suitcase, or because there is something wrong with me. The maybes are endless.

PREGNANCY AFTER LOSS

After my first miscarriage, something fundamentally shifted in both Matt and me. The sadness I felt from losing our baby at eight weeks made it so clear to me how much I wanted to start a family. We couldn't just flick back to the five-year timeline, so we fast-tracked the baby-making.

We have since brought two little girls into the world. I feel so incredibly grateful to be a mum to my maniacal toddler Marlie-Mae and to Lola, who we fondly call Melon. Pregnancy after miscarriage is weird and crazy wonderful. It brings with it all the joy, but also a niggling anxiety that something might go wrong and the painful reality that it could. And in the years between having my two little girls I also experienced my second miscarriage.

Sometimes it can feel as though Instagram is an endless scroll of perfect pregnancy announcements and gender reveals. Comparison culture is rife and it chips away at our self-worth, especially in the motherhood space. When you're in the trenches of fertility struggles, you can find yourself thinking that everyone else has it so fucking easy. But talking about pregnancy loss is the first step to destigmatising it. Putting your hand up and saying, 'Me too, I'm a part of that club no one talks about,' is a warm embrace to anyone who finds themselves grappling with pregnancy loss, and feeling as though their body couldn't make a home for the baby that was so desperately wanted.

To anyone reading this who is in the trenches, I want you to know it's not your fault. So many things have to go right to bring a pregnancy to full term; only one thing has to go wrong for it to end in miscarriage. You're not broken, you're not defective and most importantly you're not alone.

QUITTING

Whether it's saying goodbye to a relationship, a job or even a friendship, quitting doesn't equate to failure

LAURA

SEE ALSO: BROKEN HEARTS, HAPPINESS, THE ICK, PENGUINS, TIMELINES, XPECTATIONS

I'll never forget the time I refused to let a boyfriend break up with me ... while he was in the middle of it. We were in a long-term relationship and I'd done everything I could that I thought would make him happy – I'd moved cities to be with him and enrolled in a postgraduate university degree I didn't want to do. I wasn't happy, but I was desperately in love and determined to make it work, so when we pulled into the driveway one afternoon in my Hyundai Getz and he turned to me in the driver's seat and said 'I don't want to do this anymore. I don't want to be with you', I was in complete denial. I doubled down. I convinced him we should try again.

We absolutely shouldn't have, but despite that, we stayed together for another turbulent two years and the whole time it was like pushing a wheelbarrow of manure up a hill – tiring ... and shit.

Now, I don't regret my stubbornness, because ultimately that relationship served up some cracking life lessons, but I would have saved myself a lot of heartbreak had I taken that earlier exit.

I was convinced that he was my person and had told everyone that we were going to spend our lives together. That's the issue with the idea of a soulmate: it lulls you into the conviction that there is only one person for you, so when things don't go to plan, you're more inclined to keep resuscitating a dead relationship. I was scared that I'd never love anyone like this again, and that breaking up would constitute a massive failure. I was so immobile in my views around where my life was supposed to be that I couldn't see that, really, it was what we both needed.

It's easy to see with hindsight that that relationship was not right for me, and walking away from it, as crushing as it was at the time, was not a failure but a stepping stone that moved both our lives in the right direction. It links back to one of the core messages from our podcast: the biggest 'failures' in our lives can lead to our greatest moments of growth. Heartbreaks, fuck-ups and failings can build resilience and courage.

WHY WE JUST CAN'T QUIT

The word 'quit' has a bad reputation. We quit a job because we can't stick it out, we quit a sport because we aren't good enough, we quit a relationship because we can't make it work. All of these narratives suggest that the issue lies with us not being patient, skilled or resilient enough when, in actual fact, although they're often painful to make, these can be empowering decisions that mark the start of a new chapter.

Often we are too worried about other people's opinions of us, or are too rigid in our own expectations for ourselves, that it's difficult to loosen our grip, and so we swim against the current. But what if we flip that script on its head and consider how quitting can also be a kick-arse act of self-love and empowerment? You leave a relationship because you know you want better for yourself. You leave a career to make room for a new opportunity. You leave a friendship because it no longer builds you up.

When you're deep in the pain and fear of losing something that you love, you can't see what is waiting for you beyond the loss. There have been people and situations that I have clung to so fiercely I felt like I was losing my sense of self. What would I be left with after it was over? Who would I be without them?

Whether you're clinging to a lover, a job or even a friendship, it can be helpful to ask these questions:

> *What am I scared of losing? Is it a person or part of my identity?*
> *What did they add to my life?*
> *And how could I replace that feeling, even if I don't have that person or job in my life anymore?*

When it comes to studying, I'm not the slightest bit ashamed to tell you that I'm a postgraduate dropout. The only reason I enrolled in this degree was because I had moved to a small country town for the guy I wouldn't let break up with me. I was fresh out of my undergraduate degree and jobs in this small town were limited, so I thought the next best thing would be to continue my education with a master's degree in fine art history.

I was eight weeks out from graduating when I made an appointment to speak to one of the student advisers because, even though my grades were great, I was fucking hating the degree. I had zero passion for the course, but at that point I felt like I had to just grit my teeth and see it through. Quitting often feels even harder to justify to ourselves because of the sunk cost of pouring our time, energy and money into things. I felt like I had no other choice but to finish the degree and move into the field that I had spent five years of my life studying.

I sat down at the desk across from the adviser, a middle-aged woman in a bright floral singlet, and burst into tears. I explained my situation, thinking she was going to say, 'Stick it out, it's only eight more weeks and then you'll be a postgrad. It will be great on your resumé.' Instead, she looked at me for a moment and said, 'If you hate the course and the content, you'll very likely hate a career in this field, too. Five years is a long time studying something you aren't passionate about – but a lifetime working in it is even longer.'

It was the push I needed. I un-enrolled that afternoon and moved to Sydney three weeks later.

Quitting my master's made me realise that I had never wanted to work in a career that centred around theory, and it freed up my time so I could figure out what I was passionate about. I was no longer writing a thesis or studying for eight hours a day and so I got thrifty and started making jewellery to sell at Bondi Markets as a way to pay the rent. Jewellery was always something that had been a hobby of mine, but I had never put any energy into thinking it could be a career.

I wish I could say that it was an easy, linear path from walking out of the student adviser's office to becoming a jewellery designer, but it wasn't. Quitting postgraduate studies was the kickstarter, but I went on to work as a graphic designer for four years because a girl's gotta eat (and pay bills!). It wasn't until I'd saved up a bit of money that I took another leap of faith and quit my safe but uninspiring graphic design job that I finally had the confidence to give my own jewellery label ToniMay a red-hot crack.

Walking away from a situation that is genuinely making you miserable, particularly when you do it without the security of having the next thing locked in, can be absolutely petrifying, but it can also open you up to discovering more about yourself and your purpose. I realise it's not always possible to be able to quit jobs or degrees without having a next step in place - maybe you have kids, a mortgage, or people who depend on you, and these are all things that you have to weigh up against your own circumstances – but if you're doing something that doesn't align with your core values and doesn't make you happy, just remember that walking away can sometimes be the much braver thing than sticking it out. By making space, new opportunities can fall into place.

Like I said, running my own small business hasn't always been smooth sailing. The journey has been peppered with failures and setbacks but ToniMay is now a thriving company and is stocked in more than sixty boutiques across Australia.

For me, the act of quitting freed up my time and energy for creativity to flow – and what I learned is that for every moment you double down on something that's not working out, you are forgoing other potentially valuable opportunities. Sometimes you have to leave a situation to make space to thrive.

QUIT YOUR EGO WHILE YOU'RE AT IT

When it comes to quitting, I have learned that you need to leave your ego out of it. When we involve ego in our decision-making, it makes it harder to get to the core of what is authentic to us. Ruminating on what other people think of us can hold us back from making decisions that will allow us to grow and achieve in a way that truly defines what success is to our individual needs.

Maybe you want to leave your job and backpack around Peru but your parents think that's crazy. Maybe you are in a loveless relationship but you're scared of being alone or don't think you can do better. Maybe you secretly dream of starring in a Broadway musical but you're too embarrassed that you'll suck. Well, the truth is, if you don't even try you've already lost. And isn't that the scariest part of quitting? Losing!

When you focus on protecting your ego, you focus on the wrong questions, like, 'Am I a failure?' or 'Am I good enough?' Instead, ask yourself, 'What do I need to be happy?'

OUR QUEST FOR CLOSURE

Closure is a natural human need. We like to bundle things up, to make sense of them, and then pack them away in our minds to move forward. If only life was that orderly. Letting go of something that was once important to us can be really bloody hard, which is why most people feel they need a 'full stop' in order to truly close out the chapter. But does chasing closure really help? And, in the case of a relationship ending, do we always need closure in order to move on?

I reckon you can blame romantic comedies for our obsession with closure. Rachel drunkenly telling Ross, 'And that, my friend, is what they call closure,' on *Friends* or Berger breaking up with Carrie via Post-it note on *Sex and the City*, followed by Carrie's frantic obsession to find out why.

Our desire for closure falls on a spectrum. If you've only been on one date with someone, you might not be overly fussed if they ghost you. But if you've been working for a company for seven years and you're a star employee, you'll likely be shook to the core if you're called into the office on a typical Thursday and made redundant.

Sitting in the not knowing

At the end of the day, the vast majority of us tend to search for concrete reasons why a relationship (or any situation) might have ended. Generally, there are two paths we take:

1. We seek a reason directly from the source, and if that doesn't happen ...
2. We assume the reason without any evidence.

The truth is, both can send us on a self-hating spiral. Sure, hearing directly from a partner about why they dumped you can stop you from assuming the worst (e.g. 'They never loved me in the first place.'). But the truth can be a hard pill to swallow, too (e.g. 'I did love you but I've fallen out of love with you.').

Often with closure we never get the full story anyway; we get the fragments that the other person wants us to know, the version of the story that is the least hurtful or the most palatable to swallow. Humans are complex and hearts are messy. We all have a right to end relationships and change our minds (without being bailed up in a Hyundai for an hour until we've been badgered into submission).

Does that mean it's wrong to seek closure if you're on the receiving end of that decision? Of course not. But you have to go in with realistic expectations. The other person may not give you an answer, or it could be vague and not very satisfying. Then it's on you to get to a place of acceptance. As American author Zig Ziglar famously said, 'Your value doesn't decrease based on someone's inability to see your worth'.

At some stage in life, a situation – whether it's a work situation, a friendship or a romantic relationship – is going to end without explanation. And, despite that ambiguity, life goes on. You may not be able to control what is happening around you, but you can control your reaction to it. Adversities, failures and setbacks in life can break you, or they can make you – and that is the one thing that you can control.

HOW TO END ON A HIGH

Whether you choose to quit a relationship, a job, a friendship or social media, you can create your own closure. You don't have to set fire to all your sweet memories (although if you think it will help, grab some sticks for the bonfire), declare you hate your boss or delete your accounts forever. It comes down to mindset and perspective.

Follow the signs. Did you really not see it coming? Instead of looking at the end, the final nail in the coffin, look at what came before it. What were the signs? Follow the roadmap backwards and look for clues. Closure can come from recognising red flags that you didn't want to see at the time. When you look at things with the beauty of hindsight you can often see where things started to come undone.

Stalk less, heal more. In the case of romantic relationships, regardless of whether you were the dumper or the dumpee, now is the time to focus on YOU. It's not the time to spend every waking hour keeping tabs on your ex-partner. If there are kids involved, you obviously can't completely cut your ex out of your life, but you can – and should – put boundaries in place to help you move forward. This is a time during which self-care is critical, and let me tell you, self-care does not involve feverishly scrolling through the Instagram profile of a random girl your ex was tagged in a photo with, trying to figure out who she is and how they met. Put the phone down. Go for a long walk or eat a tray of Tim Tams or do both at the same time – whatever self-care looks like for you, do it.

Go back to the source. Why was that relationship or situation a source of happiness for you? Think about how it made you feel: confident? Valued? Purposeful? Part of a larger community? How can you find a new source of this in your life? Or, even better, more than one source, so your happiness is not tied to one person or passion.

Be patient. Time really does heal. It's so obvious that it's almost obnoxious to include it, but there is a reason that everyone says it. Frustratingly, there are no real shortcuts or hacks or ways to speed it up. You've just got to sit in your sadness for a while, and it's important to do that – but remember, things will get better.

Good things don't always last forever. Just because something ends doesn't mean it was a failure. Even things that were once incredible don't always last forever or turn out how we planned. A job can be a stepping stone in your career. A relationship can help you to grow into the next version of yourself.

Genuine closure is when you can look back on any relationship, romantic or platonic, without harbouring resentment, judgement or sadness and think: *I wish them well.* Looking back fondly on the parts that you cherished, acknowledging the challenges that made you resilient, and finding a deep appreciation for ourselves in the moments that stretch us beyond our limits to a place where new limits are created.

SIDE NOTE: SAYING SAYONARA TO A FRIENDSHIP

One question that crops up again and again during our 'Ask Uncut' segment on the podcast is how to deal with an ebbing friendship. It's never an easy situation, especially if it's a long-term friendship, but it happens a lot. And that's totally understandable – people change, grow and evolve. You don't always stay on the same page forever.

A friendship doesn't have to end in a blow-up, either – it can be a soft fade. Maybe you stay in contact with them, catch up with them every now and again, but they're no longer your ride-or-die. That's totally fine, too. Trying to force something just because you have a history isn't going to make you or them feel good in each other's company.

Maintaining long-term friendships with people who know your history comes with pros and cons. There can be an amazing level of comfort and familiarity, and a strength to your friendship that is totally unique. But on the other hand, sometimes friends you've known forever have trouble acknowledging when you've changed. It's easy for old friends to put you in a box – still seeing you as the shy teenager you used to be, when you've grown into a confident woman with a life of her own. Or still thinking you're the girl who laughs off her terrible romantic decisions, when, this time around, your break-up has hit you hard.

If the friendship is one you want to salvage, then it's worth having an honest conversation about how you're feeling. Something along the lines of, 'Hey, I don't feel like you're respecting me. I love you, but this isn't working for me right now.' If they refuse to acknowledge what you're telling them, or nothing changes, start rounding out your life with other hobbies or friendships that uplift and fulfil you.

Life is short and time is valuable, so don't spend it with people who make you feel bad about yourself. The best long-term friendships are with people who allow you to evolve and grow – they see you for who you are today, as well as loving you for who you used to be. If a friendship feels like it's constraining you, silencing you or shrinking you, then it's okay to walk away.

RED FLAGS

Why is it we can tell the difference between twenty-eight shades of red lipstick but we can't spot a red flag even when it's whipping us ferociously in the face?

BRITT

SEE ALSO: CONFLICT RESOLUTION, EMOTIONAL CHEATING, GASLIGHTING, JEALOUSY, NARCISSISM

Ah, our old friend the red flag. It's been used in a variety of contexts since the eighteenth century, from marking the start of military battles to indicating that our beaches aren't safe for swimming, but it's always signified the same thing: danger.

In dating lingo it's a marker that something someone is doing is problematic, or a bit of a warning that things aren't quite right. Red flags can also indicate that the person in question might not be capable of a healthy relationship and if you continue down that path, you'll potentially end up in an emotional hazard zone.

I swear to god I have been like a bull for the best part of my adult life: I see a red flag and I run *towards* it, not away from it. But red flags are supposed to teach you lessons – you know, each time you've been in an unsuccessful relationship that sent up red flags from the beginning, ideally you would take note of those warnings, stash those lessons away and apply those lessons learned to your next relationship.

Note my use of the word 'ideally'. I haven't always followed my own advice here, and I know I'm not alone. But it's so, so important to know what your 'danger' signs are, how to recognise them, and what to do next.

Before we get into that, though, it's worth mentioning that not all red flags mean you need to jump ship immediately. Sometimes they can serve as a reminder to re-examine your priorities and communicate them with your partner to find a way forward. The way forward can also depend on other things, such as the severity of the issues, your own relationship deal-breakers, attachment styles and dating histories on both sides. That said, there are some very obvious red flags that should never, ever be ignored or tolerated, no matter the situation.

THE BIGGIES

Physical abuse

Any kind of physical abuse should be taken very seriously, says psychotherapist and relationship expert Ken Page. 'If you feel physically scared by how the person is, or if they've ever behaved in ways that are physically abusive or threatening, that's it. Give it an absolute, 100% no,' he says.[32] I couldn't agree more.

I also understand that it is not always as simple as getting up and leaving. Leaving a relationship can sometimes be a very complex operation that needs to be handled with care and often requires assistance – especially since, sadly, the time leading up to and just after leaving a violent relationship can be the most dangerous for the person leaving. There are many people and organisations that are able to help, though. Are you able to reach out to a family member or a friend? Is there a safe place you can go? We have listed some resources at the back of this book.

Verbal and/or emotional abuse

Along with physical abuse, nobody should have to tolerate verbal and emotional abuse, confirms psychotherapist Annette Nuñez. 'In a healthy relationship you support and encourage one another,' Nuñez says. 'Anybody that makes you feel like you're the problem, you're crazy, or you're causing them to act a certain way – those are all red flags.'[33] Verbal and emotional abuse can include threats, coercion and intimidating or demeaning comments. Again, support services are available for anyone experiencing this; we have included some resources at the back of this book.

Fighting and anger problems

No relationship is perfect, but no relationship should be filled with arguments and anger either. There will always be ups and downs – that's actually relatively healthy – but they shouldn't be constant and triggered by small, insignificant things, especially at the beginning of a relationship. If they are, you need to reconsider.

The ways in which people handle and engage in an argument also speaks volumes. If your person becomes unnecessarily angry, flies into a rage, scares you when they are mad, has frequent explosive outbursts or switches moods quickly (happy one minute, angry the next), this shows an inability to regulate emotions. This is unpleasant and even frightening to be around, and ultimately is going to make a healthy relationship challenging. Your partner will need to seek help to properly deal with their anger issues.

Narcissism

A whole variety of traits and behaviours can fall under the banner of narcissism, but generally speaking, anything that makes you think your partner might possess a superiority complex is a red flag. Perhaps it's a lack of empathy or self-accountability, or perhaps it's an overinflated sense of entitlement. Remember that narcissism is a spectrum, and even if someone doesn't tick all the boxes for Narcissistic Personality Disorder (NPD), they can still possess narcissistic traits. According to Page, if you notice that somehow everything ends up becoming about your partner, this indicates they're not going to have the ability to truly see you.

After being in a relationship with a narcissist for a few years, I can categorically say that now, even a whiff of narcissism leads to a giant NO from me. I don't believe much good comes from dating this kind of person. And not to brag, but I can now sniff out a narcissist like a pig foraging for a truffle, and will happily run in the other direction.

Gaslighting

This type of manipulation is used to assert control over another human being and involves making someone feel crazy by denying the truth, even when it is right in front of them. It is unfortunately more common than you'd think, which is why we've devoted a whole chapter to it (see page 77). Being gaslighted can feel very destabilising and make someone question their own sanity, but in reality, it's just someone lying to you, trying to control your relationship.

Gaslighting is fucked. The end.

Emotional unavailability

There are many ways for a partner to be emotionally unavailable. Maybe they only want to see you when it's convenient for them. Or maybe they only contact you when they want something, take ages to respond to a message or aren't putting in any effort in general.

When someone has difficulty talking about feelings, or says they don't want a relationship, these are also pretty clear signs that they may be emotionally unavailable.

Emotional unavailability doesn't need to signal the end of a relationship, but it is something you need to talk about as a couple to see if you can move forward. And if, in the course of those talks, someone tells you they don't want you, that they don't have time for you, they aren't prioritising you or would prefer not to open up to you, *listen to them*. They are telling you loud and clear what they want, and unfortunately, it's not a relationship with you. It is so important in these situations that we don't do the old, 'I hear what you're saying but if I could just show you how great I am and do everything for you and in the meantime put all my needs aside, you'll change your mind and want me and we will live happily ever after'. Spoiler alert: that doesn't work!

Accidentally Unfiltered

I went on a date with a guy I used to bang many years ago and who is now circling back. I was pretty sunburnt on my front from being at the beach the day before. We ended up having great sex and he came all over my stomach and chest. For some reason we didn't clean it up straight after and just lay in bed, exhausted and chatting away, which meant the cum eventually dried all over me (I know, gross). All of a sudden, he looks at me and goes 'Holy shit, are you okay?! Your chest!' I look down to see what looks like red hives in the form of a bloody snail trail across my chest, everywhere he came. I panicked for a minute and then said, 'OMG I'm allergic to your cum! It must be a sign, you should probably leave.' We then had a laugh and had sex again (if that isn't toxic behaviour – literally avoiding red flags – then I don't know what is!). Afterwards, I washed the cum off, took a couple of antihistamines and applied lotion for sensitive skin onto the redness. After a few hours the hives had gone down, and, thankfully, everything was fine!

THE GREY AREAS

Now, not all flags are as big, red and serious as the ones above. Maybe you're not impressed by how they speak to their mum, or maybe they don't like dogs whereas you adore them and want to adopt one. Maybe they wear socks with sandals and like to eat anchovies with tomato sauce on toast. The fact is, there are many other red – or let's say pink – flags that may jump out at you while on the hunt for your penguin. Too many of them to run through here!

What some people feel are deal-breakers are perfectly fine to others. It is often very subjective. In fact, a turn-off for one person could be an attraction for someone else. The most common example that comes to mind here is having children. One person may not want kids, whereas their prospective partner might really want them. This is a deal-breaker for many people as it completely changes the course of their existence. But to someone else who doesn't have strong feelings either way about children, this is not so much of a problem and something that can be sorted out as a couple with a few, dare I say it, adult conversations.

Red-flag dilemmas come up a lot in discussions among the *Life Uncut* community because it can be so hard to know where to draw the line on what you're willing to put up with, and for some of these things it's just not black and white. Ultimately, every individual has to decide for themselves.

The best thing you can do is know yourself, and know what you want and what you're looking for. Be crystal clear on your non-negotiables.

In fact, let's start right now! I want you to take a few minutes to think about your top ten non-negotiables, and write them down here:

1.

2.

3.

4.

5.

6.

7.

8.

9.

10.

This is now something you can refer back to in the future. Maybe you're confused about your relationship, wondering if this is the right person for you, or if you should stay or leave. Revisit this list, and if any of your non-negotiables make an appearance in your relationship you need to address that. Is it something that you can discuss with your partner? Something you can change? If the answers are no, sadly it might be time to cut the ropes and let that ship sail.

For me, I know I have a few deal-breakers. Some are small, some larger, but they are all subjective. Smoking is a big one for me: I just don't like it. The smell, the look, the taste, the fact that it is so bad for you. Drug use and partying every weekend (nothing wrong with partying every weekend, but for me it doesn't fit with my lifestyle). Excessive swearing, particularly the C-word: gross. Not treating other people well: if you don't have a mutual respect for whomever you're speaking to, I don't want to be around you. People should be treated equally. And the last is not having a personal drive or work ethic: it doesn't matter what you're doing as long as you are following whatever dreams you may have or are working hard and are happy in your job. There are definitely more, but for quality control and word count purposes I have noted just a few.

If you're still on the lookout for the love of your life . . .

Don't give up! They are out there! Keep putting yourself out there, but remember your non-negotiables. That's why we write them down, so we can be sure we know what we want. We have to be clear with our intentions. Don't settle for less than you know you deserve and don't settle for things you know you aren't okay with. A lifetime is a long time to live alongside someone who isn't in alignment with you.

And remember: the beginning of a relationship should be the honeymoon stage; the best, most exciting and loved-up time in your relationship. If it is tumultuous at the start, where do you have to go? Certainly not up.

SITUATIONSHIPS

*What they are, the pros and cons, and when
you may need to vacate the building*

BRITT

SEE ALSO: BROKEN HEARTS, DATING,
GHOSTING, NUDES, XPECTATIONS

How many terms can we come up with for 'casual' dating, you ask?
Well, as it turns out, lots. But a situationship is a little more than
that. It's a relatively new term for something that most of us would
have experienced at some point: it's basically a relationship, minus
the label of A Relationship. It's the new 'friends with benefits' except
that you might go on romantic dates from time to time, making it
a more down-the-track version of casually dating. And it can feel
pretty damn exhausting if you're like me and have been in more
situationships that never eventuated into anything, than actual
relationships.

HOW DO YOU KNOW IF YOU'RE IN ONE
(AND HOW DID YOU GET THERE)?

Dating apps have a lot to answer for in all this, if you ask me.
They've created a realm of choice at the swipe of a finger and with
it, the reluctance to commit in case the next person's profile is ever
so slightly better. You have a feeling that the grass may be greener
but you don't necessarily know for sure, and you won't ever know for

sure if you decide to commit to the person directly in front of you – so you feel like you'd better keep your options open just in case.

There's a lot of crossover between the early stages of dating someone and a situationship, so it can sometimes be tricky to definitively pinpoint them – and everyone's individual circumstances vary, of course. But here are some pretty tell-tale signs that you've just touched down in situationship town:

♥ There's no evolution of the relationship. This can present in a lot of different ways but if, for example, you don't really know any of their friends, haven't met their family after quite some time and realise that their work colleagues have absolutely no clue who you are, you could be in a situationship.

♥ The two of you only make plans at the last minute or only for a very short-term future. Conversations are much more grounded in the present, centring around questions such as 'What do you feel like for dinner?' or 'What do you want to watch on Netflix?' These things suggest that you don't see yourselves actually spending time together in the long term.

♥ The other person can be really inconsistent. One week they might want to see you three times, the next they're so silent you can only assume they've accidentally got stuck up a tree without their phone while rescuing a litter of kittens for an elderly woman. This can also drift into the excuse territory: responses like 'Work's really busy', 'I'll let you know' or 'Let's play it by ear' ('PBE', as I like to call it), with no follow-through are a sign that this sitch is more in the 'non-committal' category.

♥ It's not exclusive. If they're doing the horizontal dance of love with someone else or going on dates with other people, yeah, spoiler . . . things aren't looking good.

Sounding familiar? If so, and you were hoping to transition this shapeless thing into a relationship, you'd better speak now or forever hold your peace.

Accidentally Unfiltered

I forgot this memory existed because I had buried it so deep. A while ago I had started dating a new guy. I really liked him, and we were a few dates in. We had slept together before, but on this particular day, I decided I was going to perform the best blowjob of all time. He had a monster schlong, but I had faith in myself and thought my throat was MUCH longer than it is. I was naked and went for it, shoved the whole thing down. It immediately made me gag and vomit all the Thai we'd had before. My mouth was full of vomit, but I didn't want to spit it on him, so I jumped off the bed in the direction of the bathroom. But on the way, my foot got caught in the cord of his lamp, bringing it crashing to the floor, along with the bedside table. I made it to the toilet and safely threw up (chuffed with myself!) but several items of furniture were casualties. The poor guy didn't know what had happened – he had just stared as I ran away mid-blow job and destroyed everything around me.

REASONS TO JUMP ABOARD THE SITUATIONSHIP

At times, having a relationship that doesn't (yet) have a label can be cool. It can give you the time to get to know someone before you decide whether or not you want to be in a committed relationship;

a type of 'try before you buy' scenario. Here's a list of reasons why situationships can sometimes be a good thing:

♥ You have more freedom to make decisions for yourself. You get to act without having to factor in the emotions of someone else as much as you would have to if you were in a committed relationship. This allows you to make choices that better suit you (in a not-so-selfish way), things that will improve your life without hurting the feelings of another person.

♥ They can be convenient for certain times or stages in your life. I had most of my situationships while I was travelling. During my three years away I was always on the move – a few months here, a few months there – being a transient little social butterfly. A relationship wouldn't have worked, nor was it what I wanted. Enter situationships!

♥ If you're craving intimacy and connection but don't want to have a committed relationship, a situationship can kind of tick all the boxes and give you some great sex, nice companionship and a relatively stress-free environment where you aren't constantly thinking, *Where is this all going? I wonder if they're involved with anyone else? Do they like me? Should I double text them? Why did I snort when I laughed?* Some people find this really fun and sexually liberating!

♥ Sometimes in life you meet someone who you just click with. It is easy, sexy, you get along like a house on fire – but you don't want anything more. These can still be really loving, beautiful and rewarding relationships as such, because at the end of the day they still are a type of relationship, and they can be a fun, sexually rewarding, transformative time of your life!

Accidentally Unfiltered

Info you need to know: I'm a fool who hasn't figured out how to remove the speed-dial contacts from the touch-screen console in my car. Christmas Eve rolled around last year, and I met up with an old flame in my hometown. We organised a sneaky rendezvous around midnight in my car (because as if we were going to meet up at our parents' houses to bang). He turned the music right down to zero because the pause button wasn't working, and he didn't want to listen to 'Welcome to the Jungle' during coital. Fair call. Anyway, in the middle of doing the naughty, he accidentally bumped the touch screen, but he didn't think anything of it and kept going. I looked over and saw it was in the middle of an active call and immediately hung up. In short, we had called my EX-BOYFRIEND in the middle of sex on Christmas Eve and my ex had answered. FML.

WHERE THE PROBLEMS TEND TO ARISE...

♥ When one person develops stronger feelings than the other. Stereotypically (thank you, Hollywood rom-coms) this is often the woman (if we're talking a hetero relationship) and anecdotally I would agree with this. I have seen this happen with friends and, let's be real, myself too. But there is a reason! Science! Man, I love science (says the girl with the science degree)! Science backs me up here. Physiologically, there's some brain chemistry magic going on when we become intimate with someone. The 'bonding' hormone known as oxytocin is released in our brain every time we have sex, cuddle or are intimate. Various scientific studies have shown that there are higher amounts of oxytocin floating around in the brains of women when compared to men.[34] Scientists believe that this was an evolutionary thing to make us bond to our 'mates', enabling us to procreate and continue the human race. Now it's just a *bit* bloody annoying that we can sleep with someone and have our brains fill with chemicals that make us think we might be good together! WHAT IS THIS SORCERY?! All this can make you feel pretty vulnerable and emotionally exposed, especially if you're the one who has developed deeper feelings for the other person.

♥ When you start to expect too much. If you have an expectation of support from someone that you're in a situationship with, you'll potentially feel really disappointed and let down if that support isn't there when you need it. Sometimes we have a bad day and want to vent about it to the person that we are spending a lot of time and being intimate with. Maybe you experience the passing of a loved one or have an argument with a friend and hope that the person who woke up in your bed that morning will be there for you – but the nature of a situationship makes that unlikely. They're not there for the good AND the bad, like in actual relationships, but sometimes it's easy to forget that.

♥ When being in situationship after situationship with no real progress starts to feel pretty damn exhausting. Your confidence can take a hit, and emotionally, you're just cooked! It takes so much energy to start seeing someone new – telling your story, asking questions, showing up for them, etc. I reached the point where I stopped telling my family or people beyond my close friends who I was spending time with because it so rarely actually went anywhere and it was exhausting and kind of demoralising having to tell people yet again that things didn't work out.

Sometimes you reach a point where you just need to step back, and take a breather and reassess.

♥ Being in these situations can leave us feeling as if we are consistently going through break-ups, but we don't really have the 'validation' for being upset or sad because it wasn't defined as a relationship. Well, I am here to validate you: you can be upset! You're allowed to feel exhausted, confused and deflated. You're actually going through more break-ups than anyone. I was once in a situationship that spanned a few *years*! We acted like we were together but we never officially were. At the beginning, that worked and we saw other people because we were both looking for our penguin. But then feelings developed, because SCIENCE, and we had to abort the mission because we just weren't right for each other. And I don't care what anyone says: that was a break-up. We never had the title but I tell you what, my heart said otherwise.

Accidentally Unfiltered

Going back about ten years ago to my younger, naive self, I had managed to get myself into a bit of a situation with a professional sports player I'd been seeing off and on for close to two years. I had major feelings for him, but it just never seemed to be the right time and he never seemed to want to commit. I wanted a relationship and would get sick of it, venture off for a while and then manage to stumble back into the situationship because of a) insane chemistry b) even hotter sex. Anyway, I was in my final year of study for midwifery doing my labour and birthing placement, when I was assigned to a woman in labour. I nearly died when I walked into the room only to find this guy who I was secretly in love with, supporting his long-term girlfriend in labour. Not only could I not say anything, but I had to spend the next eight hours with them being professional and then went on to deliver his baby while my heart was shattering into a million pieces.

RUN, DON'T WALK (IF YOU WANT TO): THE ART OF ESCAPING

The hardest thing can be working out whether you even want to be in a situationship. If you're genuinely keen on having one, cool! That's amazing for you. It's a good idea to establish that that's what it is and set some clear boundaries and expectations early on, or whenever the subject comes up. Being transparent about things like whether you're hooking up with other people, whether you're going to spend time together that isn't sexual (like going on dates) and establishing what kind of arrangement works for you will help things in the future. Make sure everyone involved knows what it is and what to expect.

It's so important to remember that if your feelings change after you've said you're okay with a situationship (like they did for me), that's okay! It is normal for feelings to develop. If this happens to you, I would suggest being honest and open about it. Talk to the other person, because maybe they've caught feelings too and you can head into something more official. Tell them the truth. (In a palatable manner of course – none of this 'I can't live without you and want to lock you in my basement' business. That's just a mood killer.) If nothing's changed on their side it might be a good idea for you to bid your farewells before hearts get broken. We say this about just about everything: communication is the key!

And, on the flip side, don't be scared to call it a day if your situationship is no longer servicing you. It is as simple as saying, 'Hey, I really care about you and we've had the best time but I think we are looking for different things now', and then off you trot into the sunset, margarita in hand, in search of . . . well, probably your next margarita.

Accidentally Unfiltered

I've been seeing this guy casually for a few months. He lives with his parents an hour away and I live by myself. He usually comes over to mine but this one time his parents were away, and he invited me over. So I drove to his and that night we ended up getting super pissy with him and his mates. We hopped into bed and as we started getting jiggy with it, I remembered I had my period, so quickly ran into the bathroom to take out my tampon. Being the drunk bitch I was and there being NO bin in the bathroom, I wrapped the tampon up and put it into the toilet paper basket next to the toilet. Woke up in the morning super scattered and had to work at 8 am, so I quickly collected my shit and ran out the door. On the way home I remembered I had left a BLOODY TAMPON SITTING ON THE TOP OF THE TOILET PAPER BASKET OF HIS PARENTS' HOUSE. I almost fucking died. Thank god he invited me over again a few days later. I got there and went straight to the bathroom, saw the tampon still sitting where I left it, grabbed it and disposed of it. MISSION COMPLETE! The bastard and his parents will never know how much of a grub I truly am. Massive win, loving life!

SOLITUDE

Why being alone does not mean you're lonely

BRITT

SEE ALSO: ADVENTURE, HAPPINESS, TIMELINES, YESTERDAY

When you think of the word 'solitude', what comes to mind? Do you consider it in a positive light or does the idea make you sad? Do you link it to loneliness?

From the outside, solitude and loneliness might look a lot alike, but dig a little deeper and you'll find they are markedly different. Loneliness is a negative state – a lonely person feels that something is missing from their life – whereas solitude is a state of being alone without feeling lonely.

I recently heard a TED talk by cultural historian Fay Bound Alberti who said, 'Before 1800, there was no word for loneliness in the English language. There was something called "oneliness" and there were lonely places, but both simply meant the state of being alone. There was no corresponding emotional lack.' It seems that over the last few centuries, our understanding of the emotional impact of being by ourselves has evolved.

It *is* possible to be with people and still feel lonely. Perhaps that is the worst form of loneliness, when you are surrounded by people but still feel like it is just you fighting the good fight. Even though other people might be physically present, that doesn't necessarily translate to feeling loved and supported. I have been there and at some stage we probably all have. On reflection, I think it has a lot to do with the way we speak to ourselves; the negative self-talk. If you constantly tell yourself, *You are on your own, no one cares about you, no one wants you* then you are going to start to actually believe it, even if it simply isn't true.

Not long ago, when I was going through a hard time, my therapist pulled me up on something I said. Without thinking, I'd told her, 'No one wants to be a part of my life. No one wants to stay.' She stopped me and said, 'Why do you speak like that? Of course people do, you just haven't met the right ones yet. And not everyone we meet stays. YOU don't want everyone you meet to stay either! You have to be more conscious of your choice of words.' And she couldn't have been more right.

Loneliness is a state of mind that can make you feel unwanted, undesirable and empty. It's associated with isolation, a lack of social skills, introversion and depression. When you're in a state of being lonely, you crave human connection but because of your sad state of mind it can be really hard to actually develop that type of connection. A vicious cycle indeed.

Solitude, on the other hand, involves being in a positive state when you are on your own. It is desirable: your company alone is enough and you can recharge. Being alone can be incredibly empowering, invigorating, educational and uplifting. I say this with complete confidence and experience because I was a lone soldier for a very long time, in every way possible.

Being pretty much single for the better part of ten years, I really learned to love my alone time. I had to. But it wasn't always like that; it was something I had to learn, something I was forced to learn after failed relationships and a touch of the blues. There was a period of time where I was really, really sad. All the time. I could never work out why. From the outside I had a great life, but on the inside I felt flat, sad, lonely, hurt, confused and isolated. I had some ridiculous thoughts, the ones we all experience at some stage. You know, the *Why aren't I good enough for anyone?* and *Why doesn't anyone love me?* and the old *I am never dating again!* HA. Cute. If only I knew. There I was, cruising around, doing life on my own, feeling lonely but at the same time not wanting to meet people. What a conundrum!

So I moved to a new city. I travelled alone. And I eventually fell in love with my own company, my own routine, my own journey. I was on my own schedule, accountable to no one and I did what made me happy whenever I wanted to. There was no one to judge me, no one else to think or worry about, no one to disappoint or try to impress. Just me running my own race. Freedom. Silence. Space. Alone with so many thoughts. And I bloody loved it.

Don't get me wrong, I still did fun things with friends and travelled a lot with my sister Sheri, but I didn't really get close to anyone for a long time and I believe that this played a huge part in finding happiness on my own. I grew as a person so much after I discovered that, hey, hanging out with myself isn't so bad!

I've learned so much from being on my own for so many years – including living alone, which I've done for a long time. First, I've noticed I never really let myself linger in the lonely feeling. I have since realised this is why I had always worked so much and was constantly on the go, because that is the way I manage negative, sad feelings. I just make myself ridiculously busy so I don't have time to acknowledge and confront the emotions I'm experiencing. Is that the right way to go about it? I don't think so. It is just a bandaid, really, but at times it's been what I've needed to get me through. That being said, I find as I get older that I don't need to do this anymore. I don't need to run myself into the ground to avoid acknowledging that I am on my own. (Mind you, as mentioned earlier, I still do tend to do this when I am stressed or avoiding feelings, but I manage it much better.) Now, I love nothing more than lying on the couch for hours binge-watching Netflix!

Secondly, once I got used to my own company I realised how many amazing benefits there were to it. Solitude gave me confidence in knowing that I was always going to have my own back. I became so fiercely independent! If I wanted something done, I just had to go out there and figure it out for myself – no one was going to help me or serve it to me on a platter. I think independence is such an underrated characteristic and is a very sexy trait to have in a partner. The ability to be content in yourself regardless of being in a relationship is an amazing attribute. People stay in detrimental relationships because they are scared of being on their own; they would rather be unhappy than alone. Instead, in my opinion, we should be basking in our independence and our own company and should spend periods when we're single focusing on making ourselves better people. This will not just benefit those already around us, but also will make us better equipped to embrace our next relationship when it comes our way. I know I would rather be late to the get-married-and-settle-down party and arrive with the right person than show up when everyone else does, but with the wrong person who wants to leave early. Making peace with being on your own might just be the key to finding your happily ever after. You picking up what I am putting down?

Solitude also brings other positives, such as:

- ♥ giving us space to 'pause' all the noise
- ♥ helping provide calmness and clarity
- ♥ helping us sort out our priorities
- ♥ refocusing us on what's important

♥ relaxing and de-stressing us, particularly if we are introverts
♥ helping us work out who we are and what we want from life.

Of course, you can have too much of any good thing, and time alone is no exception. For example, it's interesting to look at the effects of the COVID-19 pandemic. According to an October 2021 report commissioned by Telstra in conjunction with YouGov and Dr Michelle Lim, 27 per cent of surveyed Australians felt lonely for the first time during lockdown, and 38 per cent felt lonelier in lockdown than they had ever felt before.[35] Human beings are naturally social creatures – we learn social cues and socialisation and develop fundamental parts of our personalities by being around other people.[36] We were never supposed to spend extended periods of time alone.

Having said that, building time for a reasonable amount of solitude into our busy lives allows us to find balance. Extroverted people live primarily for socialising, whereas introverted people tolerate being alone much better – and both ultimately need a certain amount of solitude to find harmony. Do the work to figure out the level that works best for you. I am an introverted extrovert, which means that I do very well on my own, but mainly when my mind is in a positive state. For me, I recharge from alone time, as opposed to extroverts, who gain energy from being surrounded by other people. I could go two weeks without speaking to another human and be just fine, which is a weird thing to say (and maybe hard to believe) considering my job is to talk non-stop on multiple platforms! But I think it's why I love my alone time so much. I expend so much energy talking all day, being 'on' and energetic for my job, that I NEED that down time to reset. Besides, have you heard my laugh? Mate, that is exhausting in itself!

Solitude is more a state of mind than an actual physical circumstance and it reminds us that we are more than the sum of our reactions to other people and encounters. You can find solitude in meditation, going for a walk around the block, locking yourself away somewhere peaceful with just paper and pen, or embarking on a Vipassana retreat and spending days with yourself surrounded by others quietly doing the same. The point I'm making is that finding time to recharge through solitude doesn't mean you have to spend six months camping alone in the Amazon jungle. It can be done in small bursts, too. However you choose to experience it, it will teach you to become a better observer of your life and see things as they really are.

Remember, solitude is something you choose. Loneliness is imposed on you by others. But nothing lasts forever.

T

TIMELINES

Why society's plan for you can get in the goddamn bin

LAURA

SEE ALSO: ADVENTURE, FERTILITY, HAPPINESS, THE KNOT,
PREGNANCY LOSS, QUITTING, SOLITUDE, XPECTATIONS

I have this memory of being fifteen years old and sitting on my bedroom floor, writing a letter to my older self about what I wanted to achieve by the time I turned thirty. At thirty, I'd be married to Bradley Thomas (my boyfriend at the time). We'd have two green-eyed kids and live in a two-storey house in Lake Illawarra. At thirty, I'd be an adult, and adults have their shit together. Instead, at thirty, I was freshly single and living in a share house with no kids, no savings, no clear direction – and, by society's standards, a bit of a hot mess.

If you're an OG listener to the podcast you will know that I don't even really like the TV series *Friends* (I know, the audacity), but there's an episode titled 'The One Where They All Turn Thirty', where, at Rachel's thirtieth birthday party, she tells everyone she has a plan to have her first baby by the time she's thirty-five. She says she'd like to know the guy for a year-and-a-half before getting married. But in order to do that, she needs a year to plan the wedding and a year to be married before she gets pregnant, so she's already screwed as she would need to know the guy already.

Now I might prefer me some *Seinfeld*, but even I can relate to this feeling. We've been conditioned to place certain milestones along a 'one-size-fits-all' timeline, and society has this funny way of making women in particular feel that if we aren't meeting these milestones 'on time', we are failing. 'I don't know how you're still single!' 'When do you think you'll have kids?' 'Are you going to freeze your eggs?' These are the sorts of comments that women in their thirties hear every single day. Regardless of everything we may have achieved by the time we hit the somewhat random milestone of being alive for three decades, we are largely measured by the 'success' of our personal lives. If we're not married, having children or smashing goals in our careers it can feel as though we're careering wildly towards our 'best-before' date.

The problem is, when we pit ourselves against arbitrary timelines we can fall into a vicious cycle of feeling unaccomplished, unsuccessful, guilty and inadequate. We start questioning why we aren't where we are 'supposed' to be. At best, these artificial timelines can leave women feeling like they're failing when actually they're doing more than fine. At worst, they pressure women into settling for less, romantically and professionally, fearing that the clock will run out before they are able to meet these expectations.

Often the epicentre of the conversation about timelines and expectations on women is the decision to have children – a decision that, like for a lot of women, was not linear for me.

Something I haven't shared on the podcast, and something that is deeply personal around my journey to having children, is the decision I made more than a decade ago to not have a baby.

I was twenty-four and had been dating my boyfriend at the time for a little over a year. He was a kind and funny man, and provided a sort of comfort I hadn't experienced before. Things were moving quickly: we had just moved in together and got a cat, and in a lot of ways we were setting up our lives to 'settle down'. I was so wrapped up in the excitement of being wanted by someone else and building a life with that person that I hadn't consciously weighed up whether or not it was the life I wanted.

I was at work one day when the smell of someone's aftershave sent a wave of nausea through my body. I bolted to the bathroom and brought up the half a croissant and coffee I'd just eaten. *How weird*, I thought as I made my way back from the bathroom. I'd never really experienced anything like that before. When I told my colleague, a woman in her late thirties, what had just happened she joked, 'Are you sure you're not pregnant?'

It hit me like a tonne of bricks.

I couldn't even wait until I got home to check. I bought a pregnancy test on my lunchbreak and sat in a public bathroom, looking down at the two little lines on the stick.

I was pregnant. And I was devastated.

Sitting, crying, in that cubicle, I felt numb. I wasn't ready to have a kid. I wasn't ready to be a mum.

The next two weeks were a dark blur of shame, regret and embarrassment. I had always said that I'd never have an abortion, and up until that point I had believed it. But I had never actually been faced with the possibility of having a child when I wasn't ready, with a man I wasn't even sure I wanted to have kids with. Even though I was in a relationship that seemed perfectly on track, something in me felt completely broken and trapped.

I booked myself into the clinic before I had worked up the courage to tell my partner, and when I finally did tell him I was clear on the decision I needed to make. However, leaving the clinic still felt shameful. What I came to understand over the next few months and years was that a lot of my shame was wrapped up in my fear of what other people would think of me if they knew. In particular, it was a fear of being thought of as irresponsible or reckless.

Having an abortion was a difficult decision, and one that weighed heavily on me, but in the end, it was absolutely the right choice for me. Where I thought I might feel regret, the overwhelming emotion I felt was relief. I knew at that time I was not equipped to be a mum to a baby that I didn't want and wasn't emotionally, psychologically or financially ready for. But having an abortion in my twenties changed my feelings towards having children. It made me a better mum now in my mid-thirties because it made me think about exactly the sort of mum I wanted to be.

Those two little lines forced me to consider what I wanted for myself, and the years that followed were hugely transformative. While other friends were settling down, getting married and starting families, I broke up with my boyfriend, travelled and expanded my business. I grew as a person and really discovered who I was at my core. I made a LOT of relationship mistakes, worked through my co-dependency issues and lived life on my own terms – a life I never would have lived had I become a mum at twenty-four. For some people the path is clear, and for others it's peppered with landmines and lessons.

All this being said, for women, there is one aspect of life where time actually is a factor: fertility. Yes, it's true that there is a finite window during which a woman can fall pregnant, but this doesn't mean you need to derail the rest of your life by settling for a partner who isn't right for you or turning down an opportunity at work because you're worried you'll miss out on having children. It's important to understand your fertility so that hopefully you can make the choices that will allow you to live a life free from fear of missing out. And besides, starting a family comes in many shapes and forms – there's IVF, egg-freezing, adopting, etc. So remember that next time Aunt Nancy starts lecturing you about your fertility being a ticking time bomb.

HOW TO LIVE LIFE ON YOUR OWN TERMS

If I could give you one piece of advice when it comes to timelines, it's that, even if other people don't understand your choices or the path you're on, you have to trust and back yourself. It's perfectly okay to change your mind in pursuit of living a life that truly satisfies the deepest corners of your heart. Pivoting your life is not failure; it is growth.

I am no self-help guru but I *have* gathered a few lessons over the past couple of decades and look, I'm a generous woman, so I'm going to share them with you!

1. Figure out what truly matters to you

Choosing to live outside the expectations of traditional timelines can mean different things to different people, but at its core it means that you are choosing to live in a way that is meaningful and fulfilling *to you*. You can't define your life and give it direction until you work out what you believe matters the most. Take some time to understand your core values and what brings you joy. What do you actually want out of life?

And remember that figuring out what you really want and what really matters is not a linear journey. Your purpose might change several times over the coming years. It's not always as easy as sitting down with a pen and paper and collecting your thoughts; it can take time, fuck-ups and false starts. Use those mistakes as lessons to direct you towards what truly gives you purpose.

2. Set some goals

Just because you're kicking society's timeline to the kerb doesn't mean that you don't have any goals or ambitions. Write down some short-, medium- and long-term goals. Make them specific and then plot out different ways that you can go about achieving these goals. Take some time to think about the actions you can take to get there. Set yourself small targets and track your progress in order to hold yourself accountable.

3. Dump your scarcity mindset

When we approach life with a scarcity mindset based on the idea that there isn't enough to go around – *I'm never going to meet someone, I am going to be single forever, I won't find anyone better than this, it's too hard to start again* – we limit ourselves to what opportunities are available to us. Scarcity thinking often leads to settling for less – staying in a loveless relationship, for example, or having kids with someone who isn't right for you because you're too scared that nothing more rewarding exists out there for you. It's that fear of going back to zero and starting all over again that is holding you back.

4. Cut out toxic people

If you take anything from this list, let this be the biggest one: you attract what you surround yourself with. If you continue to surround yourself with toxic people and relationships, you can expect more toxicity in your life. Toxic people take it upon themselves to interfere in your business. They're the ones pointing out your flaws, making you feel inferior or telling you how you 'should be' living your life. Unsubscribe from that shit.

5. Consider your past and the lessons you've learned

Sometimes we need to look back on how far we've come and appreciate all that we have achieved in order to feel less overwhelmed by where we are heading. The things that have happened in our past shape us in many ways, but they do not need to define our future.

So unpack the lessons and the learnings in areas where life did not go according to plan and work on forgiving yourself for decisions you made or things that happened. Once you can look back on the path that you've already trodden you can create a clearer road towards your own goals, aligned with your values and lessons.

6. Stop holding yourself back

Sometimes it is our own self-limiting beliefs and fears that keep us trapped, stagnant and unhappy, subscribing to the pressure of societal timelines, even though we ourselves are unfulfilled. Living life on your own terms isn't just about doing what you want when you want – it's about finding the meaning, purpose, love for others and value in your life by reconnecting with your own core beliefs and values; knowing yourself and living life for yourself, free from the judgement of family, friends, strangers and our own self-imposed timelines.

7. Take responsibility for your own happiness

Finally, remember that building a life that authentically aligns with your goals and the things that bring you joy comes down to *you*. Even if those around you don't understand or are creating challenges, no one is accountable for how you spend your time on this planet except you. So get to it!

T

TOXIC POSITIVITY

*'Seize the morning, seize the day' – but what if
I don't want to?*

BRITT

SEE ALSO: HAPPINESS, OVERWHELM,
PREGNANCY LOSS, VISIBILITY, XPECTATIONS

How often do you wake up in the morning and hop on to social media, ready for some funny cat memes or cute pics of friends' babies, only to be immediately confronted by an array of sickly sweet posts of quotes telling you to be happy no matter what? You know the kind: 'Live, laugh, love', 'Be positive' and, my personal favourite, 'Good vibes only'.

These mantras are well-meaning, of course, and designed to be uplifting. And hey, sometimes they work! Sometimes I read these affirmations, so beautifully positioned in an elegant italic font over a perfect sunset or a girl in a bikini, and they inspire me to spring out of bed, look in the mirror and say to myself, 'I CAN live, laugh and love!' before dashing off and wringing every last drop of positivity out of my day.

But sometimes that is not my immediate reaction to that endless scroll of uplift. Sometimes those posts make me roll back over and bury my head in the pillow. Sometimes they make me feel even worse because I'm not sure I can live, laugh and love all day, every day.

It is everywhere we look: this messaging that pressures us into thinking we aren't allowed to feel bad or sad or have any sort of negative emotions because we only get this one life and It! Shouldn't! Be! Wasted! What many people may not realise is that these non-stop good vibes can end up creating … well, not-so-good vibes. Why? A little thing called toxic positivity, my friends.

Toxic positivity is essentially the pressure to maintain a positive attitude, even when dealing with a distressing or tough situation. Toxic positivity can be defined as 'the excessive and ineffective over-generalization of a happy, optimistic state across all situations'.[37] Or, as clinical psychologist Natalie Dattilo puts it, it's like having too many scoops of ice cream.[38] While it feels great to begin with, overdo it and you'll start to feel sick – and you definitely won't enjoy having it shoved in your face when you're not in the mood for ice cream.

The truth is, humans are flawed. We get jealous, disappointed, angry, needy, upset, furious, inconsolable, resentful and greedy. And sometimes life can just straight-up suck. By pretending that we're feeling 'positive vibes all day', we don't allow ourselves to live in a genuine way. We are *supposed* to experience emotions. Suppressing the existence of certain feelings can send us into a state of denial and repression.

According to the Canadian Mental Health Association, here are some signs that your positive attitude might be turning toxic:

♥ You dismiss or brush off feelings that aren't 'positive'.
♥ You feel guilt or shame for experiencing 'negative' emotions.
♥ You avoid or hide from uncomfortable feelings.
♥ You only focus on the positive aspects of a painful situation.[39]

Most of us have learned to ignore or dismiss our negative feelings. Instead of opening up about our sadness, fear or anger about something, we're told to look on the bright side, to keep our chin up, stay calm and get on with it, so that's what we feel we must do. During the early COVID-19 lockdowns we were even getting schooled on how we needed to optimise our lives from home: get more shit done, turn that side hustle into a business and generally use all our newfound free time to better ourselves. In a PANDEMIC. I mean, come on! Talk about crazily unrealistic.

When it comes to emotions, I believe that we should feel *all* of them; the good and the bad. Yes, feelings can sometimes be messy and uncomfortable, but guess what? So can life! And when we really need to, we have to be able to scream from the rooftops, 'I AM NOT FUCKING OKAY!'

A FEW GOOD REASONS TO EMBRACE EMOTION, NOT BURY IT

1. Suppressing sad or negative feelings can be bad for your mental and physical health. Fact.

The thing is, ignoring the deep, burning, uncomfortable feelings won't make them disappear. They won't pack their suitcases and move on. At best, they'll go on vacay, but they will always come back, either looking and feeling exactly the same, or having multiplied while you were busy burying your head in the sand.

In fact, studies from Healthline show that suppressing emotions can lead to increased anxiety and depression, sleep disruption and overall worsening of mental health.[40] Told you it was a fact!

On the other hand, accepting discomfort and understanding where your feelings are coming from and why you're having them can help you work through your emotions and speed up the healing process. Nobody's got time for elevated levels of stress and emotional torment, amirite?! Think how cathartic it can feel to have a solid cry, or even scream at the top of your lungs while hitting your pillow. There's power in that release.

2. Emotions are data

Have you ever really stopped to think about where emotions come from and why? They are actually sent from our bodies to help us, to guide us, to give us important information – hence we shouldn't ignore them. They aren't just random sensations; they provide useful data that can help us understand life.

Emotions guide our decision-making, help us develop empathy and are even necessary for survival. Have you ever had a gut feeling that you were in a dangerous situation? That's your emotions sending you a warning – one that's important to listen to. Knowing these feelings are there is one thing, learning to trust them and act on them is another kettle of fish. A fine artform, if you will!

I am a very optimistic person. I typically focus on the positives in a situation and tend to believe that things will work out. But that isn't always the reality. Being positive and optimistic can give us hope, sure, but we still need to acknowledge the risks and potential downsides of a situation. Optimism needs to go hand in hand with realism. In short: there's nothing wrong with choosing to see your glass as half full, just be aware that it can spill or be consumed at any time.

3. Pain leads to growth

Not a single person on this planet gets through life with nothing bad happening to them. Fact. Life is full of false starts, detours and obstacles to overcome. And the past few years have, for pretty much all of us, been notably obstacle-filled – some of which we jumped over, some of which we dodged just in time and others we ploughed right into. It's totally normal to respond to life's ups and downs with a range of emotions. In fact, it's an important part of being human.

So, what can feeling all the feelings do for you? It can lead to learning, growing and changing. And hey, change is as good as a holiday and everyone loves a holiday! Here are some traditionally not-so-nice states of being, and the unexpected upsides to experiencing them.

Anger: Needless to say, extreme or chronic anger can be detrimental to our wellbeing and to the wellbeing of others, but low levels of anger can help us move forward in a positive manner. It can encourage us to confront the uncomfortable and explore issues we may not have realised were even there, or that we were avoiding until they boiled over in a revealing moment of rage.[41]

Sadness: Moderate levels of sadness can trigger more effort and motivation to deal with challenges. When I think about the times I have been most sad or down, I've always ended up having a 'Fuck it!' or an 'I'll show them!' moment, and channelled my sadness into a determination to remedy the situation. I find motivation on the back end of it and always come out on top!

Sadness can also improve your judgement. Joseph Forgas, professor of psychology at UNSW, tells us that people are more likely to make misjudgements due to biases when they're happy.[42] They say that sad moods reduce common judgemental biases – for example, the assumption that a very sexy, attractive and overall aesthetically pleasing face is likely to come with other positive traits, such as kindness or intelligence. This most certainly is not the case! Having some sadness allows you to take the time to weigh up people and situations. This sounds complex, I know. But the more you think about it the more it makes sense.

Grief: 'There are *benefits* to grief?!' I hear you say. It's true. Grief is horrible; it makes us want to curl into a ball in bed and stay there forever. It is painful, confusing, raw and can last a long time. But if we dig deep, there are a few things we can take from grief. It can help us to appreciate life's fleeting beauty and our place in this big wide universe, and it shines a light on what is most important to us. We learn to re-evaluate and are stronger moving forward.

4. Getting vulnerable helps us connect

We cannot empathise and fully support others if we refuse to acknowledge anything but happiness and positivity. Recognising and giving space to our messier and more challenging feelings is how we can truly connect with one another. Think about a time when a friend has turned to you in a moment of need. How did it feel to be there for them, to provide a shoulder to cry on? Did it bring you closer together? Did it make you feel confident that you would be able to reach out to them in the same way if you needed to? Sharing the bad times as well as the good promotes trust and empathy.

On the flip side, it might only be when you're on the receiving end of some toxic positivity that you realise you've been dishing it out yourself. I used to be that person throwing out the upbeat sentiments, thinking I was helping when actually I was probably dismissing other people's real and valid feelings of sadness and pain. The encouraging words are often the ones we reach for when confronted with someone else's unhappiness, because *damn* that can be uncomfortable and it's so hard to know what to say.

But what I've learned is that people don't necessarily want answers and solutions. You don't need to 'fix' anything for them. Just create the space for them to talk, then listen, acknowledge and validate their feelings. Rather than leaping to find some silver linings, let them know you can see that massive, shitty black cloud hanging over them and you'll be there to walk with them through the hurricane.

5. Forced and constant compulsory happiness maintains oppression

This is something I read that's really stuck with me. It's a big sentence so let me try to explain it a little further.

I really fell into a rabbit hole when researching this topic. I was fascinated by how happiness could possibly bring about negativity. Seems contradictory, doesn't it?

But a society that is interested in pursuing 'good vibes only' is a society that ignores the realities of injustice, discrimination and inequality. These are issues that need urgent, serious and ongoing attention, and genuinely engaging with them requires a certain level of discomfort. To even consider choosing to ignore these injustices is indicative of immense privilege and proof in itself that things need to change. And for change to happen it's essential that everyone plays their part, and the first step is acknowledging that the world isn't all sunshine and lollipops.

By harnessing a broader spectrum of mental states, we can create a world in which more people find contentment, belonging and peace.

WE ARE NOT 'FINE' – AND THAT'S FINE!

The older I get, the happier I am to share life's downs as well as its ups, and present the full picture. That's one of the reasons we wanted to create the *Life Uncut* podcast in the first place – unfiltered, baby! Laura and I knew there was a need for other women to hear about the messy, confusing, embarrassing and unexpected aspects of romance and dating (and life in general), because we needed to hear it, too.

I've also learned that every success is laced with failure, and that's what makes the success taste sweeter. When the shit hits the fan, the only way out of it is through it – but who knows what will be waiting for you on the other side. You don't know unless you try. How boring it would be to walk through life with no falls, no scrapes of the knees, no Disney bandaids needed.

So consider this your reminder to remove that filter, welcome those emotions – and punch that Good Vibes Only cushion all the way to the rubbish bin where you can set it on fire. Possibly along with your ex's love letters. 😊

UNCONDITIONAL LOVE

The heart wants what the heart wants, but that doesn't mean the heart knows what's good for it

LAURA

SEE ALSO: BOUNDARIES, HAPPINESS, THE KNOT, PENGUINS

Picture this: it's Sunday morning. Your partner stayed out all night again, after they promised they'd be home at a reasonable time. They said their phone battery went flat, but your intuition is raging and you know it's more likely that they switched it off. You're angry, but not surprised – your partner can often be unreliable like that.

The relationship oscillates between incredible highs and the shittiest lows. Your friends are always saying that they think you deserve better and on paper, it sounds like an obvious decision. You should end it.

But there's one reason that keeps you there. You can't bring yourself to give up on the relationship because . . .

YOU. LOVE. THEM!

We tend to overestimate what love can do for us. Pop culture, and particularly rom-coms, have led us down the garden path when it comes to our expectations around love. They have instilled in us a belief that, if you love someone hard enough, fiercely enough, in the end it simply has to work out, even if everything else indicates otherwise. It sounds whimsical and romantic, this 'love conquers all' ideology, but when we believe that love alone is enough to sustain a relationship, we're more likely to ignore other fundamental values

273

that are critically important. Values that we can sometimes sacrifice because of love, such as respect, commitment, trust and kindness. Ask yourself this: have you ever stayed in a relationship long past its expiration date simply because you were in love?

When I was nineteen I was out at a bar and I locked eyes with a man across the room. It was electric and the definition of love at first sight. I went home that night and said to my mum, 'I met the man I am going to marry tonight.' A pretty bold conviction considering we hadn't spoken a single word and I didn't even know his name. Six months passed and I had almost forgotten the man from the bar, until I saw him again. This time he came up to me, we chatted, and I knew I was in trouble. I was head-over-fucking-heels in love.

My love for this man was instant and all-consuming. He, on the other hand, took longer to fall as hard as I had, but after a year of casually dating he did, and when he did it was big and exciting in an 'us vs the world' sort of way. However, despite how grand our love for each other felt, our relationship was turbulent from the get-go. It was long-distance, for a start, which we navigated terribly. We wanted different things out of life and would end up in weekly arguments about trivial shit that mostly came back to our fundamental lack of compatibility. We broke up and got back together numerous times, but despite all this, we were always drawn back to each other, convinced that we were meant to be together forever. Yes, we loved each other 'unconditionally' and at the time it felt incomprehensible that we wouldn't work out in the long run, but that quickly became an excuse for not addressing any of our issues properly. It was messy, it was painful. And it went on for SIX YEARS.

What I came to realise after we finally split for good is that just because you love someone and they love you doesn't mean that you're good for each other, nor does it mean that you belong together.

We've grown up with the idea of 'unconditional love' being the gold standard of romantic relationships. But let's take a moment to break down that concept:

Unconditional love: A love without conditions.

Conditions: The circumstances or factors affecting the ways in which people live or work.

In summary: Loving someone no matter how incompatible the relationship is, how they spend their time or how they treat you.

It's pretty normal to think you want unconditional love. But what we really want is love *with conditions* – a set of standards that you're both going to work towards. A love that is rooted in respect, kindness, compassion, consistency and honesty.

If you love someone unconditionally, then technically they can treat you like shit – and vice versa – because you've promised to love each other anyway. This sort of love might be one thing in parent–children relationships, but as far as romantic relationships go, it is toxic AF.

LOVE DOES NOT EQUAL HAPPINESS – REPEAT THAT FOR ME

Breaking up with someone that you're still in love with sounds unfathomable. But if the relationship is moving in circles; if you're having the same arguments over and over again; if your life values don't align, then you might need to hear the wise words of Mark Manson: 'While love may make you feel better about your relationship problems, it doesn't actually *solve* any of your relationship problems.'[43]

Ask yourself if any of these potential deal-breakers sound applicable:

♥ You want vastly different things out of your futures (e.g. one of you wants kids and the other doesn't).

♥ You have different core beliefs, whether they be political, religious, or values-based.

♥ Your partner is constantly trying to change you.

♥ Your partner doesn't like any of your friends.

♥ You don't have any shared interests.

♥ You're trying to make it work long-distance.

♥ One of you just isn't happy!

♥ You feel disrespected.

Depending on what phase of life you're in, some things may be more pressing than others. For example, if you're twenty-two and you're dating someone whose life goals don't align with yours, it might not be a big deal to you and that's okay! You've got plenty of time to figure out what you want in life. But if you're in your mid-thirties and you know you want to start a family, but the person you're in love with wants to live their life childless by choice, mutual love may not be enough to overcome the sacrifices that either person will have to make. Ask yourself this: how much are you willing to compromise and sacrifice before you lose yourself in the name of unconditional love?

Love is one of the most euphoric and intoxicating feelings in the world. Interestingly, it has also been linked to behaviours associated with addiction, such as dependency, withdrawals and cravings. This happens because the dopamine reward system in your brain is activated by romantic love. We can get hooked on the high that love brings, but like Mark Manson said, love doesn't fix or offset relationship issues. It can convince you, for a while, that every-thing will be okay, but if you've got recurring issues or deep-seated problems in your relationship, then love won't make that go away.

This is going to make me sound like a cranky old cynic, but hear me out. Love is rare(ish), but it's not (that) rare, either. We have the ability to love different people throughout our lifetime: we can love people who we are compatible with, and we can love people who are terrible for us – and anyone in between. We are made to manufac-ture all those feel-good love hormones and if we've done it once, in time, we can do it again.

At the end of the day, you deserve someone who respects you as well as loves you. And you deserve to be able to love someone without losing your sense of self or your self-respect in the process.

I LOVE YOU, I HATE YOUR VIEWS!

We all know that relationships are about compromise. But certain conflicting views are impossible to ignore, especially in the long term.

The Black Lives Matter protests of 2020, the pandemic years, the #MeToo movement and climate change have sparked some big conversations about race, politics and personal freedom. If your beliefs are totally at odds with your partner's, it's become harder to ignore, because these important issues have been amplified in the public sphere (plus, some of us spent the whole of lockdown stuck inside together, which makes anything about your partner pretty much impossible to ignore!).

Try this simple exercise:

If your best friend kept saying these things, would you sweep it under the carpet?

If your best friend treated you like this, would you want to be around them?

We expect a certain level of respect in a friendship, so shouldn't we expect the same, if not more, in our romantic relationships?

When we love unconditionally, it's possible to get hung up on potential rather than facts. Instead of seeing the relationship for what it actually is, we can fixate on what we think it could be – or the person our partner could be if they would just stop doing X, Y, Z. The truth is, no amount of believing in someone's potential will make them do better. People only change if they want to. Values and attitudes are more deeply ingrained in people than we think.

WHAT IF YOUR FRIENDS UNCONDITIONALLY LOVE YOUR PARTNER?

It's not always the person in the relationship who is oblivious to the flaws of their partner. It can be hard to set higher standards in your relationship when your friends or your family think your partner is already 'perfect' – and push that opinion onto you.

This is a type of gaslighting – even if it's unintentional – in which the people around you convince you that your standards are just too high or that you're being overly sensitive about your partner's flaws. They may do this because they want the best for you and don't want to see you go through a break-up, however, it can also make you question your instincts.

Here's the thing: only you know how your relationship feels behind closed doors. Something I wish I'd been told in my early twenties is that feelings are not black and white, and a partner doesn't have to treat you badly to not be right for you. Sometimes it can feel like we need to have a 'valid' reason to walk away from a relationship. You can be with a great person, who is kind, loving and respectful, and still want more for yourself. More sparks. More laughter. More shared goals. More matching morals. Just more.

STANDARDS ARE SEXY AND CONDITIONS ARE COOL

I'm here for having hard conversations early about what you expect in a relationship – not when you get married or make another significant commitment to each other, but well before that. Get it all out on the table. Things like:

- ♥ What do you count as cheating and betrayal?
- ♥ How do you want to divide up household labour?
- ♥ How do you communicate?
- ♥ Do your words align with your actions?
- ♥ If you have kids, how will you share parenting responsibilities?
- ♥ How much alone time do you need?
- ♥ What are your other goals and priorities? For example, is staying healthy and fit something you both care about?

This isn't about forbidding your partner to gain five kilos, or making sure that they're doing the dishes exactly as often as you. It's about having shared hopes and standards, and also holding each other accountable for your actions and behaviour. You won't always get it right. Your needs can be fluid and change with different seasons of your relationship. It does, however, help to talk about what's important to you and the #couplesgoals to aim towards.

We can all get complacent in long-term relationships and start to take the people closest to us for granted – and the myth of unconditional love certainly makes this easier! But establishing and maintaining boundaries can keep you both accountable to each other.

I remember an Instagram post that professional funny man Hamish Blake posted last year. It was a tribute to his wife, writer and entrepreneur Zoë Foster Blake, on their wedding anniversary. In their wedding vows, they'd promised to love each other unconditionally, but, upon watching the wedding video back, they realised Zoë had accidentally said 'conditionally'.

'And THAT is why I love this woman,' wrote Hamish. 'She is a god-damn genius. It is my honour to spend the rest of my life learning those conditions and fulfilling them.'

Darn it, I just love these two! And I love love . . . conditionally, that is.

VISIBILITY

*The public self vs the private self: where
the hell do we draw the line?*

BRITT AND LAURA

SEE ALSO: PREGNANCY LOSS, TOXIC POSITIVITY

LAURA: To start our conversation, I wanted to hark back to an actual article that was published on 21 July 2021 by Nicole Douglas for the *Daily Mail* titled THE BACHELOR's LAURA BYRNE MAKES A TABOO SEX CONFESSION AS SHE OPENS UP ABOUT HER BEDROOM ANTICS WITH FIANCÉ MATTY JOHNSON, DURING A TELL-ALL PODCAST. Yikes!

The backstory of this is that a listener had written in asking whether Matt and I were into anal play.

'I like a finger in the bum sometimes, but no more. That's the pinkie in the stinky, long and short of it,' I'd said on the episode.

The listener had also added that they believed 'Brittany turns her nose up' at the thought of anal play – a comment you weren't too impressed by, Britt, haha!

BRITT: 'Brittany turns her nose up?' I'm sorry, I would never turn my nose up at anything. The only reason I don't talk about things like butt play is because I already share 99.9 per cent of my life on our podcast. There's got to be something, one tiny little sliver of our lives, that's kept sacred for our partners! And for me ... it's my body!

I still can't believe that you have an entire *Daily Mail* article written about how you like a finger in the bum. Deceased!

L: Look, I'm not going to frame it and pop it on the wall. But I didn't die of embarrassment either.

It's funny to think how much has changed in two and a half years, and how open we are now about the things we feel comfortable sharing. When we first started *Life Uncut*, I made a big point about how I was never going to speak openly about my private parts on a podcast that could be listened to worldwide. But fast-forward to the present day and if you're an avid listener of the pod, you've heard it all – intimate details of my sex life, my relationship fallouts, my pregnancy losses and how my vagina quadrupled in size when I was pregnant with Lola. It's a wild ride, but hey, IT'S LIFE!

Two things we often get asked are:

Why do you feel so comfortable sharing so much of your private life?

How do your partners feel about you sharing your personal stories on the podcast?

For me, these are two very different questions. Firstly, it wasn't an intentional shift; it pretty much happened naturally over time – there is something comforting and inclusive that comes from sharing the pitfalls and the embarrassing moments that we all experience as we stumble our way through life.

Looking back, I now understand that my reservations around talking openly came from my fear of being judged by the media. Being authentically real and unfiltered felt shameful at first, but the more we shared our vulnerable stories, the more our beautiful community of Lifers grew, because they (and hopefully anyone reading this) related to the content. It's always been our intention to have the sorts of conversations that you might have with your best girlfriends on a night out, or behind closed doors – gritty, real, vulnerable and often silly.

Most normal, level-headed people would think, *God, if the* Daily Mail *wrote an article about how I like a finger in the bum, well, the world might as well swallow me whole. I'll never leave the house again.* And if you had told me ten years ago that these were the sorts of articles that would be written about me, I'm sure I would have felt the same. But, as with anything in life, the more you are exposed to something (the article, not the finger!), the more you become used to it. What was once shocking is no longer all that alarming. It's what some people call the 'new normal'. And let's be real for a second: there is a good chance that you reading this have had a finger in your arse at some point, too. So, why are we so bloody *ashamed* of everything?!

In today's world of filters and Facetune and perfectly styled homes straight out of *Vogue Living*, I believe people no longer crave perfection. Instead we seek out relatability. Or, at least, I know I do. So, rather than becoming more filtered and more perfect over time, I feel like, for me, the opposite has happened.

B: I agree, we've definitely become more comfortable with taking off the filter as time has progressed, but if we are putting very personal stories out there it's because we are at a place where we feel comfortable to do so and have worked through any personal difficulties first. There are still a lot of things we haven't shared, and there are things we will never share.

Sometimes I do wonder, though, what does Matt think of it all?

L: Matt is the hype girl every woman needs! We have a saying in our house: if a joke is being made or a story is being told to get a laugh, or to help someone feel less alone, then 'win, lose or draw', shoot your shot – and if it doesn't go to plan, well, what's the worst that can happen? But, in all seriousness, Matt and I have had a lot of conversations over the years to ensure that we're acutely aware of where each other's boundaries lie in terms of what we share and what we keep private. It's an ongoing conversation and because of this we have a deep level of trust that the other person knows where to draw the line.

I would never share our personal experiences without making sure he's across it – for example, a moment that comes to mind is when you and I sat down to record my pregnancy loss story. Truthfully it wasn't just my story to tell, as it affected Matt equally. Before we made the decision to go ahead with that episode, Matt and I sat down and discussed it at length. I explained to him why I thought it was so important to speak about it openly: to give visibility to the topic. I remember how alone I felt the first time I suffered a miscarriage, and how it was hearing other women's stories that made me feel supported and less broken. I wanted to be able to give that to another woman experiencing the same thing. I wanted her to not feel as broken as I did.

I think the hardest thing about visibility isn't so much the sharing, it's being misquoted and misrepresented in the media. The media has real undertones of misogyny, and it can be difficult for women to feel empowered to be authentic and confident in themselves when there is so much judgement in the way it represents women.

B: It's funny you say that because just before I sat down to work on this chapter I was on Instagram and saw a post about that paparazzi shot of Lisa Wilkinson sitting in a restaurant drinking a margarita, with the *Daily Mail* headline EXCLUSIVE: LISA WILKINSON SIPS ON A MARGARITA AS SHE DINES ALONE AT A MELBOURNE RESTAURANT FOLLOWING *THE PROJECT*'S RECENT PANELIST SHAKE-UP. I felt like the headline and article were such a personal attack on Lisa's privacy, portraying her as lonely when it was just a photo of a woman enjoying a cocktail at a restaurant. What they were really saying was, 'How dare a woman enjoy her own company by herself?! She must be pathetic!'

I agree with you, Laura – this is the downside of being in the public eye: the constant misquoting and the clickbait headlines. Most are completely made up, yet people only need to read something somewhere once to believe it, whether it is actually real or not. You know the old saying 'Mud sticks'? This is why when I read any headline about anyone, I take it with a grain of salt. Besides the obvious misquoting to make us sound like absolute twats, something else that gets the blood boiling when it comes to the way the media portrays women is that everything I do and wear seems to be with the sole aim of 'showing an ex what they are missing', which suggests that everything I do is for someone else or with someone else in mind?! Like most women, I wear clothes for me! I do things that make me happy and make me feel good, not because I'm seeking validation from an ex.

When I think back to who I was before *The Bachelor*, I don't necessarily see a version of myself that is different, just one who has since been provided with the tools for growth. I have always been loud and outgoing. I have always been adventurous and up for travelling the world, wanting to entertain people and make them laugh. But when I was younger there was no social media – no one to impress besides the people physically in front of us! No one around the world to compare ourselves to. We just lived in the moment. It was a beautiful thing indeed to live in that world!

Even when social media started to become more popular, I didn't get it for years. It was only after my sister Sheri hounded me to. At the time I couldn't understand why anyone would want to share so much of their life (how ironic, considering the position I am in now and the fact that I am without doubt an oversharer!).

I remember Sheri messaging me before we went off overseas, saying, 'You should download this app. You put photos and stuff on there and other people can see. It's called Instagram.' To which I replied, 'Ha – why would anyone want to see *my* photos?' I thought it was ridiculous and could not figure out why anyone would care what I was up to. I look back now and think, 'Man, if only I'd been more on the ball – over three years of travelling and I've hardly got a decent photo to show for it!' But I really was living in the moment and loving it, and that's what counts.

There's a common misconception that if someone is in the public eye and they share their life across social media that they then forgo the right to any privacy. I strongly feel that is incorrect and unfair. Everyone has a right to a private life. It's true that some jobs and careers bring a level of public voyeurism with them, and of course that public interest has its perks, but it's not an all-access pass. It doesn't mean that the rest of our entire existence is fair game for scrutiny.

L: Yeah, and I think you have a really unique perspective on that, Britt. I know how much it affected you when people were speculating about your relationship with Jordan. Every day you were fielding messages from people demanding to know what your relationship status was. It's wild to think that there were people who were genuinely angry and felt as though you were keeping secrets from them, when you were really just finding your way through the heartbreak. I guess that's the double-edged sword: when you invite people into your life and share 80 per cent, some people are so invested that they feel entitled to the remaining 20 per cent, and it's hard to flick that private versus public switch when you've given people access to so much of your personal life.

B: Completely. That was probably the hardest thing I have ever had to navigate publicly.

Hardships and heartbreak are a part of life – but doing it in the public eye really adds an additional layer to how exposed and vulnerable you feel. Some people may want to share those moments and others need to deal with it on their own, and both are okay. For example, I have never really shared who I am dating on the podcast or on Instagram – we've always given them nicknames like 'Meat Raffle' or 'Sit-on-my-face Guy'. The only person I have ever been open about was Jordan because I knew we were going to be serious and I really believed he was my forever person. Of course, I shared photos of him and I always celebrated his career wins, but I also kept a lot of the details about our relationship private. There was the time he came on the podcast and we showed a side of ourselves that we hadn't ever shown. We waited a long time to do that and we had fun with it. It was okay for us to share that part of our life because we were in control, it was our narrative.

But Jordan is also a very private person. He hates being in the spotlight and he hates Instagram. So I was particularly careful with what I shared, because being in a relationship is about respecting each other's boundaries. In turn, that means the public should respect them too, which wasn't always the case. As you said, Laura, it was so hard when everyone started to bombard me with demands to tell them what was happening with us. Some people were actually so rude to me, I was shook. I would get daily DMs and tagged in Facebook threads about how I should be telling people what is going on and how I 'owe' it to them, when truth be told I was in a very dark place and navigating new terrain myself. I didn't even really know what was going on and I definitely wasn't ready to speak about it. This only added to the situation and made things so much harder for me.

L: This is definitely one thing that I think has defined the way we talk about personal topics on the podcast. We rarely do it when we are in the thick of it. Normally we like to give ourselves a bit of breathing space to work through our own junk and feelings before airing it out and sharing it across the platform. Nothing like a bit of hindsight and perspective! With you and your break-up with Jordan, you waited until you felt composed enough to talk about it. Same with me and my pregnancy journey.

It's an interesting thing to unpack the whole conversation around visibility and vulnerability – why in this day and age so many of us are comfortable broadcasting our lives on social media (or on a podcast). Every single one of us consciously and subconsciously chooses how much of our lives we feel comfortable sharing online.

I think this is where vulnerability links back in, and, although I believe vulnerability is an incredibly powerful tool, I also think we often see performative vulnerability on social media. We now see people publishing sensitive things before they might feel ready to because they think it is what they need to share on social media – or worse, because they're doing it for external validation, such as likes and comments.

I often wonder if there's some commodification of vulnerability going on when I see influencers in the middle of anxiety or a crisis making content and sharing images or videos of themselves crying. Personally, when I am in the thick of anxiety or when I am truly overwhelmed by what life is throwing at me, capturing content is the furthest thing from my mind! It can be hard to decipher true authentic vulnerability online from the instances that it's used to garner attention. For me, my personal lived trauma is *not* content, and I guess that is where I draw the line in terms of what I feel comfortable sharing on social media.

So, what is the alternative? Well, my friends, it is BEING REAL! Real in how you show up and share your thoughts, values and beliefs.

It could be witnessing other mums with a house as messy as yours, seeing women post images showing their unedited stretch marks and cellulite on social media, or hearing empowered survivors of sexual assault sharing their stories. All of it matters and all of it helps to destigmatise the feelings of shame we carry when we think we're the only ones experiencing a certain thing. Authenticity builds a sense of community, and reinforces to others that they aren't alone – but that doesn't mean you have to share everything.

Britt, how has the way you share stories changed?

B: At this point in time, like you, I'm disclosing more than ever about myself and my life. But I feel okay with that because I know our community is a safe space, and when we receive messages from people who've reached out to say specific episodes have helped them – that is what matters! If someone feels less alone, more understood or a little happier because of things we have shared, then I feel really good about that – keeping in mind there will always be parts of my life that I guard closely to my chest and no one will ever be able to touch. It is also easier because now, thanks to the podcast, we are in charge of our stories. We can tell the truth about an article that was written and we have more autonomy over what is said about us, which allows a level of comfort in telling more personal stories. That's a privilege in and of itself.

L: YES! There is real power and self-love in owning your life stories and not being held back by what people might think of you, but instead allowing yourself to be held up by an incredible sense of community that comes with knowing we are all in this together.

I guess ultimately by creating *Life Uncut* we've actually learned to approach life in a less filtered and edited way. It's been liberating, and I couldn't recommend it more.

WORTHINESS

You attract what you believe you're worth

LAURA

SEE ALSO: ATTACHMENT THEORY, BOUNDARIES,
BROKEN HEARTS, IMPOSTOR SYNDROME, JEALOUSY, MONEY

It's evident that one of the positives to come out of social media is the rise in conversations centring around self-love. Suddenly it's cool, not selfish, to be invested in taking care of yourself mentally, physically, spiritually and sexually (geddit, girl!) – and that's a great thing. #Selfcare is trending but what does it really mean beyond staying in on a Saturday night with a facemask and a tablespoon of Epsom salts? (Although that does sound pretty fab!)

To truly practise self-love, we need to talk about worthiness.

Worthiness: the quality of being good enough; suitability.

There have been times in my life when I've been overly critical of myself and haven't loved what I saw in the mirror – times where I punished myself with exercise because I thought I needed to be slimmer, or rushed out to the chemist and bought new makeup or skin creams because I hated the imperfections staring back at me. My twenties were peppered with these periods of self-doubt – usually following a bad break-up or rejection of some sort. I think a lot of us can identify with that feeling. When I was in my late twenties I had started to feel ever so slightly more comfortable in the sack of flesh I inhabited. That was until I did *The Bachelor*.

When you go on reality television, people assume that their comments won't reach you – or perhaps they simply don't care if they do. Either way, every evening after the latest episode had aired, I'd open my DMs on Instagram to a torrent of messages from strangers sharing their thoughts on how I looked and behaved. Some comments were, of course, positive, some were harmless and some were horrible: ranging from 'Girl, look at your abs' and 'Great teeth' to 'She looks like a prawn! Great body; throw away the head!' and 'Fuck, that Laura girl is fake.' Compared to so many other contestants I had it relatively easy, but the messages still came in thick and fast.

During season five of *The Bachelor* contestants had access to their own social media accounts while the episodes were airing and we were instructed to post during the season to help promote the show via our socials. We were the first season of the Australian version of *The Bachelor* to have these new social media rules, and there was no guide or support from production on how to navigate this. These days, contestants surrender their social media accounts so that they aren't exposed to the hateful messages and comments, but back in 2017 we contestants read every . . . single . . . one, and the onus was on us to delete them. But, as anyone who has been trolled on social media knows, deleting the comment doesn't erase the hurt.

Having complete strangers comment on my appearance both positively and negatively was death by a thousand paper cuts to my self-worth, especially because I was exhausted after trying so hard to be a polished, put-together version of myself, both on the show and then on social media after it had finished airing. I thought that in order to be liked I had to be perfect, and so I did my best to emulate the aesthetic of what I thought perfect was. The irony that my 'perfect' still wasn't good enough for a lot of people wasn't lost on me.

For about a year after *The Bachelor* wrapped, every time I looked in the mirror I'd think about how I didn't fit the mould of what a *Bachelor* 'winner' should be – my *Bachie* predecessors were the likes of Anna Heinrich, Sam Frost and Snezana Markoski – all classy bombshells. I couldn't even pinpoint what it was that I didn't like about myself, I just had this feeling that I needed to be better, to be prettier, to be . . . more.

As a result, I got filler in my lips and my cheeks, I got Botox, and I had a chemical peel so chaotic it blasted half the skin on my face off. I remember calling the doctor crying when I woke up the day after having the peel done and my skin was so hot and red-raw it looked like the inside of a labia – it was A LOT!

Despite being assured that I would love it so much and be back for more, from the moment I walked out the clinic door I fucking hated it, and so did Matt. Shortly after I'd had these 'tweaks' we took a trip to New Zealand. I sent a selfie to my sister, and she called me and said that my brother-in-law had seen the photo and said, 'What has she done to her face?!' Not what you want to hear when you're already feeling inadequate!

It was that phone call that made me realise that physical 'enhancements' were not going to make me feel better. What I really needed to work on was my sense of self-worth and getting to the bottom of who the hell I was now that my life was in the public eye.

Now, if you're partial to a nip, a jab or a tuck, all the power to you! This isn't about shaming anyone who embraces cosmetic enhancement – but it is about assessing the 'why' behind it. Are you doing it because you want to, or are you doing it because you feel you need to?

The moral to this story is this: if you've been thinking you'll like yourself more once you fit into that pair of jeans or once you get a new pair of tits, or buy that new dress you've been eyeing off online, I'm here to tell you that changing your external self isn't the golden bullet that will increase your self-worth. Being hotter on the outside won't make you love your insides any more. They're only temporary distractions. It's about knowing deep down at your core that, regardless of anything external, you are enough just as you are.

And if you know who you are and like who you are, but you still want a new nose? Go for it!

WTF IS SELF-WORTH, ANYWAY?

The terms 'self-worth' and 'self-esteem' are used interchangeably, but there is an important difference.

Self-esteem: how we evaluate ourselves, our internal assessment based on our achievements and characteristics.

Self-worth: the belief you are loveable and valuable regardless of how you evaluate your traits.

We're all familiar with that rush of happiness when our self-esteem is high, such as after we receive a compliment or a promotion at work. We tend to be less familiar with the comforting, warm, weighted blanket that is having a strong sense of self-worth. Knowing your worth means you know, and fundamentally believe, that you're loveable regardless of your relationship status, or your dress size. Your worth doesn't decrease because someone else doesn't see your value. Here are some signs your self-worth needs some work:

- ♥ You give your inner critic a lot of airtime.
- ♥ You're constantly comparing yourself to other people.
- ♥ You don't like what you see in the mirror.
- ♥ You feel too exposed presenting your natural state on social media, so always opt for filters or Facetune.
- ♥ You're co-dependent in relationships.

- ♥ You're a chronic people-pleaser.
- ♥ You blame yourself when anything goes wrong.
- ♥ You make jokes at your own expense.
- ♥ You don't think you deserve to be happy.

I spent a lot of my twenties monkey-branching from relationship to relationship. Looking back, it's clear I had a deep fear of being alone and therefore 'unlovable'. For years, I let two beliefs define my love life: the first was that I always needed to be in a relationship and the second was that being cheated on was a normal thing in relationships. I chased men who were emotionally unavailable and fobbed off nice guys who were stable and consistent as boring.

In retrospect I now can see that these TERRIBLE opinions stemmed from my low self-worth. I didn't want to be single, because I saw that as a failure (newsflash, it isn't!). I was addicted to the volatility and drama that came with toxic relationships and I didn't even pause between my relationships to learn any lessons or to question why I kept being attracted to men who were no good for me. Breakups suck, sure, but they can be an incredibly transformative time for healing and growth (see Broken Hearts).

Before Britt and I started the podcast and began unpacking the nuts and bolts of relationships, I hadn't fully realised how much my upbringing had affected my romantic choices. Our childhoods – and, more specifically, our relationships with our parents – can have an impact on the way we show up in the world, and, in turn, our self-worth.

There is no one-size-fits-all solution when it comes to increasing your feelings of worthiness. For me, things that have helped include understanding how my childhood (and particularly my relationship with my parents) and my attachment style have affected my relationships; forgiving myself for past mistakes and consciously refraining from seeking external validation and affirmation from people who don't have my best interests at heart. Working on these aspects of my life helped to rein in my inner critic.

THE INNER CRITIC

You know who I mean: the voice that tells you that you're 'not enough' in any given situation. Do any of these sound familiar?

- ♥ Everyone else on Instagram seems happier than me.
- ♥ All of my colleagues have better ideas than me.
- ♥ If I were smarter, prettier, funnier, better, my partner would love me more.
- ♥ I don't want to go for a swim because my thighs are too fat, or too dimply, or too hairy.
- ♥ Why would they want to be friends with me?

If so, then you've met your inner critic. Whenever you hear that derogatory voice in your head, you have to learn to flip the script. It might not feel genuine at first, but it's about resetting that habit of toxic self-talk. The good news is, the more you do it, the more you'll believe it. Ask yourself this: Would you let your friend speak to you in the way that your inner critic does? Would you speak to someone you love in the way you speak to yourself? No. So it's time to start showing yourself the same love, compassion and respect that you afford others in your life – because you deserve it.

Self-worth comes with not only loving the unique person that you are, but respecting yourself in the same way you would respect someone that you love – deeply.

AUTHENTICITY – AND WHY IT'S YOUR SELF-LOVE SUPERPOWER

It would be easy for me to sit here and say, 'Love yourself and don't worry about what people think', but you and I both know that's a pretty unhelpful way to approach self-love. It's like telling someone who's stressed to be less stressed! Ugh! Let's never be that person!

When we live handcuffed by a desire to be liked or to fit in, we spend so much of our energy trying to make other people happy that we turn our back on our authentic selves. When you betray yourself to fit in, you often wind up feeling even more isolated and alone.

Being authentic means having a deep understanding of who you are and what you stand for and expressing yourself honestly and consistently.

'YOU HAVE TO LOVE YOURSELF FIRST BEFORE ANYONE ELSE CAN LOVE YOU' – AND WHY THAT'S BULLSHIT

I'm sure you'll have heard this saying before; it's well-intentioned and meant to inspire self-love rhetoric. But I think as a concept it is pretty flawed and only works to reinforce feelings of unworthiness. Regardless of what you think of yourself, there are people around you who love you and see you for who you are.

Earlier in 2022, we had the absolute pleasure of interviewing Turia Pitt on *Life Uncut*.[44] If you're not familiar with Turia's story, in 2011 she suffered burns to 65 per cent of her body after she got caught in a grassfire while completing an ultramarathon in Western Australia's Kimberley region. She went on to become a force: a best-selling author, a two-time Ironman and a humanitarian, inspiring thousands of people around Australia.

When we spoke to Turia and she talked about her traumatic, life-altering experience and subsequent recovery, what struck me was the power of the unwavering love of her husband Michael. Michael was Turia's boyfriend at the time of the accident, and he stayed by her bedside throughout her recovery and beyond – even when that experience had impacted her self-worth. Turia told us:

'Michael is the most easygoing, humble bloke. He would just show up every day at the hospital at 7.30 in the morning. And some days I was like, 'What are you doing here? Go away, I don't want you here.' Because I felt so guilty, and because I felt like it would be easier to not have anyone who loves me.'

Turia's story goes to show that even if you don't love yourself – you are ALWAYS worthy of being loved.

Of course, it's important to love yourself, and yes, you will probably have healthier and better relationships with really great boundaries if you have a strong sense of self. But it's not true that if you don't fully love yourself, someone else can't love you. You are worthy of love – both romantic and platonic – even if you sometimes can't see that for yourself.

Our self-worth increases when we have strong loving connections around us. I'm not just talking about romantic relationships, but strong family connections, friends, colleagues and community. Surrounding yourself with people who build you up and support you during times of self-doubt is the warm embrace we all need when our inner critic comes knocking.

WE'RE ALL WORKS IN PROGRESS

In an ideal world, our self-worth would be unshakable. Loving yourself, no matter what is going on in your life, is the ultimate goal, right? But if you're not quite there yet, it's totally fine to acknowledge that. For most of us, the best we can do is to accept that self-worth ebbs and flows, and try not to tie our self-worth too closely to anything that we can lose (such as our jobs, our income, our relationship status).

For me, becoming a mum affected my self-worth in both positive and negative ways. My body changed and I don't have as much time for exercise these days. This was a bit of an adjustment for me, because I had previously pinned a lot of self-worth on looking and feeling good, and exercise was a huge part of that. But this hasn't actually impacted me as much as I thought it would. Plus, there are two incredible little humans who look to me as a role model for self-worth. How I talk to myself is how they will learn to talk to themselves. I want to teach them they are always enough.

I used to work pretty hard to ensure that my Instagram gave off a sort of effortless glamour, but now I no longer care about that – I love my life for what it is (and, let's be real, it can be total chaos at times!). These days, it's far more important to me to authentically show my world that I treasure so much.

THE SELF-WORTH CHECKLIST

Self-worth is less about evaluating yourself against external goals (e.g. *I got that raise!*) and more about valuing yourself as a person. Complete these sentences to give your self-love a nudge in the right direction.

Something that makes me unique is . . .
My favourite way to spend time alone is . . .
My favourite memory of being single is . . .
The special skill I bring to my relationship is . . .
My friends would describe me as . . .
I feel the most peaceful when . . .
I shine the most brightly when I . . .

XPECTATIONS

Should we lower our expectations, or does that mean we're satisfying ourselves with the bare minimum?

LAURA

SEE ALSO: HAPPINESS, OVERWHELM, QUITTING, SITUATIONSHIPS, TIMELINES, TOXIC POSITIVITY

As humans, expectations are an inevitable facet of our being. They help us kick goals and can be a motivating, productive force. However, somehow over time, we have evolved into thinking that high expectations are responsible for our feelings of unhappiness.

But I want to argue that high expectations aren't the culprit! They can be important! Imagine if parents had low expectations for their children – you could interpret this as parents thinking that their children simply aren't capable – or worse, that they aren't invested in their child's development. It's not so much having high expectations that is the problem, it's when we put pressure on ourselves (and others) to achieve *unrealistic* expectations. And sometimes figuring out the difference between 'high' and 'unrealis-tic' can be as tricky as sorting unripe lemons from limes.

I have always been passionately career-driven and competitive; my career has been at the forefront of what gave me purpose and made me feel successful. When I found out I was pregnant with Marlie-Mae I remember thinking, 'Nothing is going to change. I'll just be me, with a baby.' Already I was struggling to grapple with the identity shift from entrepreneur to mother, to the point where I was clinging tightly to how I thought things needed to be.

To me, success was linear. There wasn't room for setbacks or sidesteps. So when it came to having children, I had this overwhelming need to prove that I could do it all. The career, the business, the family. When people would say, 'GOD, how do you do so much?!' I'd wear it as a little badge of honour, a pat on the back that I was still climbing the ladder of success.

Marlie-Mae was (what I now know to be) an easy baby. She slotted relatively smoothly into our lives and gave me a false sense of security that juggling motherhood alongside running two businesses was manageable – so much so that we started trying for baby number two when Marlie was only ten months old.

Everything changed when I gave birth to Lola. I opted to have an epidural as early as possible, partly because I didn't want to feel any pain but also because I planned on using the eight hours or so of labour productively.

I brought my laptop to the maternity ward and lay there in bed, propped up by pillows, completely oblivious to the pain of Lola's head bearing down on my cervix. I had a catheter in my urethra, a needle in my spine and a laptop on my belly. Intermittently I'd watch the contractions go up and down on the monitor as I fired off emails for the podcast to our producer Keeshia, and sent off a marketing email for ToniMay.

I remember my obstetrician came in and told me I was ten centimetres dilated and that it was time to push. I felt a tinge of frustration that I hadn't gotten through everything on my to-do list. I was minutes away from holding my baby, and I was still thinking about work. I now know how toxic this mindset really was, not just for myself but also the standard that it implies for other women – but I learned those lessons the hard way.

When Lola was only four weeks old, I was functioning on four hours of broken sleep a night, and Britt and I had an important meeting for this very book. I strapped Lola to my body and met Izzy, our wonderful, ridiculously patient editor, for breakfast. It was in that meeting that we were offered this book deal. A BOOK DEAL! How could we possibly say no?! It was February and the deadline for the first draft was October. We had seven months to get all our thoughts onto paper.

I signed the contract, heaping more deadlines and expectations onto my already overwhelmed plate. I remember excitedly telling Matt about the book deal, and his reaction wasn't what I expected – it was concern. 'How are you going to do this?' he asked.

I felt irritated by his concern. I had no intention of slowing down! I thought, *I'll do it – because I have to do it. I'll do it while Lola sleeps and Marlie is at day care.*

Except Lola didn't sleep. Lola had colic and screamed blue murder for the first six months of her life. I wasn't kicking goals, I could barely string a sentence together, and I was utterly exhausted. October came and went and ... you guessed it, the book wasn't written. That's the thing about unrealistic expectations: you set yourself up for inevitable failure.

What was I trying to prove, and to who?

I still don't know the answer to that question. Maybe it was me desperately clinging to my past self, not wanting to surrender to this new identity, to motherhood. Maybe it was that my sense of self-worth was defined by my rigid ideas of success. The expectations I had set for myself were so wildly unrealistic. Of course I failed to meet deadlines – I was sleep-deprived, burned out, touched out and ultimately disappointed.

Even worse than feeling like I was doing a terrible job at everything were the feelings of guilt that ran alongside. I felt like I was letting Britt down, and constantly focusing on work meant I was letting my kids down.

What I learned from this period of life, my first year as a mother of two wild little people, is that it's still okay to set your expectations high, but you need to temper them with compassion for yourself and acceptance if things don't go to plan. When life gets derailed, it is okay to reset the bar – to slow down or take a sidestep. That does not mean that you have failed. Life is not a race, and no amount of accolades, money or success makes you a winner if you're burned the fuck out and unhappy at the finish line.

> *'My happiness grows in direct proportion to my acceptance, and in inverse proportions to my expectations.' – source unknown, but it's a bloody goodie.*

The older I get in life, the more I'm discovering that when it comes to expectations of ourselves, we often set them impossibly high. But when it comes to our expectations of people around us, we can set the bar low.

Recently, a DM slid in from a Lifer who had found herself in a friends-with-benefits situationship of over a year. They were seeing each other regularly, sleeping with each other every week, but he wanted to keep things casual because he wasn't ready for the commitment – and was 100 per cent stringing her along. She had just suffered a banged-up knee and had to have surgery when the guy refused to help her move some furniture that was being delivered to her apartment. His response was, 'We aren't in a relationship. That's what a boyfriend would do.'

Her question was: Am I expecting too much?

I wanted to climb through the computer screen and yank her by her good leg. Because, you see, the thing is we *should* have expectations of the people around us. Expectations equate to standards.

302

We should have expectations of our friends.

We should have expectations of the person that we have spent countless hours of extremely intimate time with.

The expectation should be that they treat us with respect! Our advice was of course to dump that boy like yesterday's kebab, but it did spark a pretty interesting conversation around why we tend to have these immeasurably high expectations of how we show up in life and how we want to appear to other people when we are often willing to accept far less from those around us.

COMPARISON CULTURE AND THE EXPECTATIONS TRAP

We spoke about comparison culture in the chapter about Happiness, but it's a recurring theme of the podcast, so it seems fitting to revisit it now that we're nearing the end of the book. The phrase 'the grass is always greener on the other side' is credited to a Roman poet named Ovid who was born in 43 BCE, which tells us that comparison culture has been a thing long before we had a trendy label for it.

Just like having expectations, comparison is part and parcel of human behaviour. We all do it to varying degrees in all different kinds of situations, from comparing yourself to a colleague who got a promotion you missed out on, to comparing yourself to your ex-partner's new girlfriend! But the reason comparison culture has become such a buzzword in recent years is because of the accessibility of social media and the vast expanse of comparisons we can now make. With a few clicks we can look in on the life of a total stranger on the other side of the world – and it's that accessibility to other people's successes that makes us wonder whether we measure up.

We all know that Instagram, Facebook and TikTok are often guilty of being a highlights reel of our 'best', most aesthetically pleasing or entertaining moments. We know it's curated. We know it's constructed. And for the most part we're all to blame.

It's unintentional the way so many of us contribute to 'highlights reel' culture. The truth is people don't really care about the mediocre moments of our lives; no one cares if you did three loads of laundry today, or if you found a limp cucumber turning into slime in the salad drawer in your fridge. Life's mundane boring bits get left behind.

We opt for sharing our big moments, whether it be a new job, a baby, a European holiday.

So while it may not always be deliberate, we're all small but integral cogs in the machine that is making us feel shit about ourselves.

As a lot of soon-to-be parents do when they are spiralling down the vortex of research and preparation for having a baby, I followed a whole host of mothers online. These women looked like they had their shit together – they were mummy bloggers who seemed to be successfully juggling careers, babies, media, fitness, happy rela-tionships with their partners. I would watch from the sidelines and think, *If she can do it, so can I.* But I couldn't do it all and I'm okay with that now.

Comparing myself to other mothers who made it all look so easy is what caused me to set such wildly unrealistic expectations for myself. The irony is that I was also adding to this. No doubt there was another mum out there who saw my Instagram and thought, 'Well, if she can do it, so can I', and if you're that mum, fuck I'm sorry, because you're enough.

Let's look at comparison culture through a science-y lens: our brains are built to look at things as though they are mathematical models and analyse the data. Instagram is data to our brain. So when we see someone on social media who's the same age as us, achieving things that we don't see ourselves achieving, our brain takes all of that in and we process it in a relative way; in that, relative to the data of the person who is 'killing it', we are doing shit.

The problem with this is that the data we are inputting from everyone's highlights reel is overwhelmingly based on assumptions. So if we are trying to build a metaphorical model in our brain of how well we are going in comparison to our peers, we would need to put in every single variable of the lives of the people that we are getting data from for it to be accurate. But we don't do that. Instead we home in on the 0.1 per cent of people our age that we think have found the pot at the end of the rainbow. When we compare ourselves to the 0.1 per cent we are doomed to set unrealistic expectations for ourselves, and we need to cut that shit out.

Sure, this book wasn't written in October 2021 – in fact we were a whole year behind our initial deadline – but as evidenced by these pages, encased in this flashy pink cover, it did get finished! Things may not have run to the original plan, but that is life and sometimes you have to hit the reset button in order to move forward. Not living up to your expectations doesn't have to be a failure. It's a sidestep, and sometimes in life it pays to take the scenic route.

YESTERDAY

Learning from the past (without getting stuck in it)

BRITT

SEE ALSO: BROKEN HEARTS, NARCISSISM, SOLITUDE

I once spent a month with a Buddhist monk. Not a month straight, one on one, all day – that would've been a lot! But I saw him probably five days a week for the month.

It's a funny story about how that came to be. During my round-the-world travels, I was going for a walk one day in London and decided to take a new route, for no particular reason. I always walked the same route every day because it was safe and I knew it well. But on this particular day I decided to wander aimlessly because, in typical Brittany fashion, I thought, *Why not? If I get lost I have Maps, and there's always transport to get home.* So I set off and let my feet lead me wherever.

After taking a few turns, I found myself in a beautiful old cobblestoned alleyway that had buildings below street level. The windows were at knee height, so if I bent down I could peer into the rooms within. As I was wandering and pondering (probably thinking about what I would have for dinner), I saw a flash of orange flit past one of the subterranean windows. It caught my eye and I stopped in my tracks, bending down to see what it was. I locked eyes with a man. He was quite pale and fairly thin but with a round face. He was bald and had the kindest eyes. We stared at each other

306

for a second, me on the outside looking down, him on the inside looking up. He smiled, I smiled. He waved, I waved.

Then he beckoned me over to the door around the corner and, as crazy as it sounds, I went. He met me at the door and I saw he was dressed in a long saffron-coloured robe. The building was an old church and I followed him in, because I was a) intrigued, and b) had this deep inner feeling that I was in the right place. We began to talk, and from there I decided to take classes with him. It really was as simple as that.

I was not, and am not, religious. But that day, for whatever reason, I was pulled in that direction. It was as if the universe was handing me what I needed at that time, without me trying or real-ising it. I think I was a little lost, and not just literally that day in the cobblestoned streets, but in life in general. I wasn't overly happy, but wasn't sad either, I was just living. I was confused, not sure of my direction or who I wanted to be and where I wanted to go. I really was waiting for someone to point me in the right direction. I believe that I was meant to get lost that day, to see that flash of orange, to meet this monk.

I learned many things from this wise and hilarious monk. Yes, he was hilarious – always cracking jokes and always in a good mood. This is their way of life. Happiness and calmness. I envied him for that, and it was something I really wanted to learn how to channel. We spent a lot of time just being. We meditated, emptied our minds, filled our bodies with light, calmed ourselves from the inside out. We spoke a lot about how life is what you make it and, while many things are out of our control, many things are within our control. One of those things is how we respond to a certain event and what we take away from it. In other words, we can learn from the past.

Bad things are going to happen to all of us at some stage. It is unavoidable. But life is defined not only by the events that happen to us but also by the way in which we respond to these events.

This is something that has stuck with me over the years. At some stage, we will all go through heartbreak and tragedy. We will all suffer from loss and disappointment. But we get to choose what we do with those feelings and how we let those experiences shape us. My monk explained it this way:

Say you go through a horrific break-up. There are two possible scenarios.

Scenario one: You've lost the love of your life; someone you thought you would be spending the rest of your life with. You can feel horribly sad, not get out of bed, not speak to anyone, not go to work, cry all day, refuse to date again, tell yourself you aren't good enough and stay in the depths of depression for a really long time.

Scenario two: You've lost the love of your life; someone you thought you would be spending the rest of your life with. You can feel horribly sad, but you can change your perspective on that sadness. You can still mourn your loss while making time for meeting new people and hanging out with friends. You can still feel withdrawn while going outside for a walk. You can still be confused while changing your internal monologue. Instead of telling yourself that you weren't good enough for the relationship, you tell yourself, 'It just wasn't right for me'. Then you think about what you learned from your relationship and what you can take forward into your future.

In both scenarios the catalyst event – the break-up – doesn't change. Either way you've still found yourself newly single. The only thing that changes is your quality of life moving forward. And of course, in scenario two you are still going to have moments where you feel shitty and sad, but they will be surrounded by moments of positivity and hope that will help to speed up the healing process.

Since my encounter with the monk, I have tried to shine a positive light on things that have happened to me, and I have made sure to take something away from every relationship or situation that I have encountered. For example, from my last relationship, I learned a little more about what I need in a romantic partnership to feel wanted and loved. I also learned just how deeply I could love someone, which was something I thought I wouldn't feel again. With every inch of my being, I loved so openly and deeply and purely. And while it doesn't look like that will be my happily ever after, I had a bloody amazing time. My heart hadn't known that kind of happiness for as long as I can remember. I can only hope I take that feeling forward. I know I will try.

So we've already established that it's important to learn from the past. The flip side to that is that we also have to let it go. But how do we do both? And how do we leave the past firmly behind us?

THE RUMINATION TRAP

Rumination is the act of obsessing about the past or overly fretting about something unfortunate that has happened; constantly replaying an event or situation you may wish had turned out differently. Rumination isn't just unpleasant, but, according to the *Harvard Business Review*, it's also closely linked to poor problem-solving, anxiety and depression.[45] It is not healthy so it's important to learn to let go and to forgive yourself.

When something goes wrong, we also tend to blame ourselves. We have a hard time accepting that making mistakes is part of life. Spoiler: you are human! Mistakes can be corrected. Mistakes are not a final destination. They are just speed bumps on the long road to the final destination – not that we even know where that is! So we need to try to get to a place where we aren't derailed by speed bumps. We need to learn from them and continue to move forward.

DON'T LET YOUR PROBLEMS AND HEARTBREAKS DEFINE YOU

When we find ourselves entangled in a problem, it can become hard to separate that problem from our self-worth. Eckhart Tolle, a world-famous spiritual teacher and self-help author, explains that we can also create and maintain problems because they give us a sense of identity. I think this is somewhat true. I'd say we all know someone who lets their past define their present and future; someone who holds on to past traumas and lets them dictate future decisions. As much as I hate to say it, we all know someone with the victim mentality.

Your stories shape you, of course – as they should. But don't let the negative ones define you or your identity. Don't let a toxic or unfortunate experience control who you are. Life is too damn short for that nonsense!

Another upside of letting go of past stories is that it frees up space for new experiences and new stories. When I broke up with Jordan, even though we both knew it was the right thing for us at that point in time, I had a hard time letting go for some pretty silly reasons. Of course, there was the fact that I loved him fiercely, but there were also the smaller things, like the idiosyncrasies we both had that no one else would understand or be able to recreate. And, for that matter, I didn't want to recreate them with anyone else. I had created so many beautiful memories with him, so many little personal jokes and moments that if anyone else saw them they would think we were ridiculous, and I didn't want to let those go. Those little things were my favourite parts, such as the tiny, stolen moments of playing hide and seek in our house and being filled with such uncontrollable laughter when we found each other that we'd run away and tackle each other on the bed.

Letting go of a relationship is really, truly, desperately hard – especially when nothing has really happened to cause the breach. It's incredibly challenging to stop wondering what you did wrong – but those are empty and useless thoughts. You can't change the past, but you *can* redirect your energy towards the future. It's in your power to focus on the here and now and find peace in the idea of tomorrow.

DISTRACTION, DISTRACTION, DISTRACTION

As soon as you notice yourself thinking of the past in a destructive way, change your train of thought. Try to change the voice in your head and how you speak to yourself about the situation. Being in control of your thoughts is key (something I learned courtesy of my monk). You need to try to distract yourself, even for a short time. Find something to do that's mentally absorbing but not that difficult. It could be a crossword, a jigsaw puzzle – heck, even if you're no master chef it could just be boiling some eggs! The activity you pick should be one that requires you to actively concentrate so that you are forced to let go of the train of thought you were following before. It might seem silly, but I promise you, even a momentary distraction can help to break the cycle of rumination before it completely takes over your brain. It really does make a difference!

Getting outdoors for a run, walk or swim or attending a gym class can also help with quieting negative thoughts. Exercise has been my long-time go-to in that respect, and I strongly recommend it.

Do not underestimate the power of making mistakes and what they can do for your future. We can gain so much knowledge from our past – whether that be work, relationships, health or family; the good, the bad and the ugly – and knowledge is what leads to growth. We learn what we want, what we don't want, what works for us and what doesn't. We develop strength, humility, passion and direction.

Yes, you lived through yesterday. Don't let it stop you fully living today and tomorrow, too.

Z

ZE END

A NOTE FROM BRITT AND LAURA

If you've made it here to the end – our souls laid bare, our stories told and our chequered morsels of wisdom bestowed – you, my friend, are a born-again Lifer. Let's all get matching tattoos!

When we started *Life Uncut* Laura was eight months pregnant and Britt was deep in long nights at the hospital. Neither of us knew a single thing about podcasting, but we knew at our core that we wanted to hold space for the conversations that women cared about. Because *we* cared about them. We hope the pages of this book have been left dog-eared with love, and that we are leaving you in a better place emotionally, mentally and physically than when we found you. (Hopefully you're poolside, drinking mojitos – definitely physically in a better place!)

It is a privilege and a joy to be in your ears each and every week, giving a platform to people with incredible stories and life lessons to share, while having a giggle along the way. We have learned so much from the people we have had the opportunity to speak with, and from each and every one of you through the discussion groups, DMs and emails.

As you have flicked through these pages of our lives we hope that our stories have brought you comfort, that you have laughed with us, cried with us, and ultimately felt a little less alone in this glorious mess that is life.

At the very beginning, *Life Uncut* started as a relationship podcast, where we talked about the peaks and pitfalls of navigating relationships and the universal pain of break-ups and breakdowns – but over the past few years, the podcast has evolved into so much more than that. We have found an incredible community of powerful humans, who raise each other up; we have found our voices and helped to amplify the voices of others. We have found a job that brings so much real meaning to our lives, and, above all else, we have found each other. A friendship that we will be forever grateful for.

As it now stands (and it will be many more by the time this bad boy is in your hands) we have recorded more than 300 episodes together. That is over 13,500 minutes of non-stop talking. Countless late nights, hundreds of hours of research (which is an eye-watering amount of study for two people who are still technically unqualified), enough laughter to have us institutionalised, a few lost voices and many, many mistakes! And, we wouldn't change a single thing.

Throwing ourselves into *Life Uncut* was one of the best decisions we have ever made. Thank you for being a part of the lollercoaster. (Laura will kill me for slipping that in but c'mon, is it even *Life Uncut* without the lollercoaster?!)

A recap on the past three years!

To wrap it up like a kebab on a Saturday night we wanted to answer some rapid-fire questions, because heck ... there isn't much left that you don't know about us.

FAVOURITE EPISODE

LAURA: 'Call it Daddy Issues: Attachment Theory' (Season 2, Episode 53). For me, learning about attachment theory was an 'aha' moment. It was like I'd been looking at my past relationships through a dirty camera lens and someone had just come along and wiped the smear off it. It also allowed me to be a little bit gentler with myself. Instead of thinking, 'What the hell is wrong with me? Why do I keep getting into these relationships with men who treat me badly?' I realised that a better question to ask myself was why was I attracted to men who didn't treat me well – and that's where attachment theory came in. It's a goodie.

BRITT: Ah, how is one to pick a favourite after 300+ episodes?! It's like trying to pick a favourite child (or dog). I have so many, for so many different reasons. Speaking with people like India Oxenburg from the NXIVM sex cult (Season 1, Episode 94) and Jess Buchanan (Season 3, Episode 52), who survived being kidnapped by rebels in the Somalian desert for three months, opened my eyes to a whole new world. The laughs with Rebel Wilson (Season 2, Episode 1) and Urzila Carlson (Season 2, Episode 34) are the pick-me-ups you need on a glum day.

FAVOURITE INTERVIEW

LAURA: I'm already breaking the rules, I have two!

'Kath Koshel: It's cool to be kind' (Season 2, Episode 186)

Kath was one of the most inspiring and grounded people we've ever interviewed. Life has knocked Kath down over and over again, and yet her incredible positivity in the face of adversity hits me at my core. Her story was a real reminder to get out of my own head and not ruminate on my own comparably insignificant issues. Speaking to her reminded me that I might not always be able to control what life serves up, but I *can* control my perspective and reaction. You can let it break you, or make you.

'Shonel Bryant: Leaving a legacy' (Season 1, Episode 200)

I will never forget speaking with Shonel. She was one of our incredible *Life Uncut* community members who was diagnosed with triple negative breast cancer. We had the absolute privilege of interviewing her at the end of 2021 before she passed away in early 2022. Hearing from Shonel about what it felt like to know her life was coming to an end, and that she would be leaving her two children behind, was a conversation that changed my life. It was a reminder not to ignore health concerns, to check my breasts on the first of every month, to keep my pap smears up to date and to get my skin checked. As Shonel said, 'No one else but you is going to advocate for your own health.' It was a reminder of how precious life is, and to never take it for granted. I remember rushing home after that interview with tears streaming down my face, and when I walked in the door, I scooped up Marlie and Lola and held them.

BRITT: I agree, Laura, with both of your choices. Both Kath and Shonel are absolutely incredible and the most inspirational and courageous women. Please, if you haven't listened, we can't recommend them enough. They will touch you in ways you didn't know possible.

FAVOURITE MOMENT

BRITT: Rebel Wilson being super famous and shitting in daylight on a stranger's lawn in Hollywood will forever hold a place in my heart. The fact that she is down to earth enough to share that story (because, let's be real, we all have a shit story) has done wonders for making us everyday folk feel better for our embarrassing shit story.

Also, finding out that Laura's ex-boyfriend used to have sex with the back of her knee. I will never get over that moment.

LAURA: Yep, if Rebel Wilson can come back from what was possibly the most embarrassing Accidentally Unfiltered story we have ever heard, there is hope for the rest of us.

I am glad my knee-sex story brings one of us so much joy, Britt.

MOST EMBARRASSING MOMENT

LAURA: The fact that everyone knows my ex-boyfriend used to have sex with the back of my knee.

BRITT: I guess it would make sense to take it back to where it all started and how Accidentally Unfiltered came to be, which is the time I sent literally the ugliest photo you could ever imagine to a guy I was crushing on and supposed to be going on a date with the next day. I thought I was sending the photo to my sister Sheri (sending horrible photos of ourselves is just what we used to do in response to the question 'what are you doing?' – normal, right?). Anyhow, completely out of nowhere this guy gets a photo of me looking like a prepubescent boy. As I am sure you can imagine, this was an accident and therefore it was unfiltered, and so Accidentally Unfiltered was born. RIP me.

MOST VALUABLE LESSON

BRITT: TOO MANY! I've learned so much about the world but mostly, so much about myself through the incredible people that we have interviewed on *Life Uncut*. One of the big life lessons that has really stuck with me is that failure is a necessary part of success. Stop worrying about what other people think – the truth is that they mostly don't think anything about your successes or failures. Most people are too busy thinking about themselves. It may seem depressing, but it's actually freeing. You are your biggest critic.

LAURA: One lesson that has stuck with me over the past few years is that vulnerability isn't a weakness, it is a superpower. Nobody wants perfect; what we all want is REAL.

FAVOURITE THING ABOUT EACH OTHER

BRITT: My favourite thing about Laura is her drive and her dedication to her work. She is a superwoman. She excels at everything she does, from business to research to being a mum. How annoying, haha. When she isn't grinding, she's a beautiful and caring friend. She's wiped snot from my nose with her sleeve more times than I care to admit.

LAURA: My favourite things about Britt are her loyalty, her humour and of course THAT LAUGH! It's infectious, and one of my favourite parts of every podcast.

LIFE MOTTO

LAURA: 'You create your own opportunities' and 'The grass is greenest where you water it'.

BRITT: 'Only those who go too far can possibly find out how far one can go.' AKA, you gotta try to know! If you don't try, it's an immediate fail. If you don't ask, it's an immediate no. Which brings me to my next fav motto: 'Risk it for the biscuit'.

Deep, I know. You're welcome.

We are so grateful for each and every one of you. For every episode, every page of this book. Every DM, email and comment, and every one of you that stops us on the street or yells at us from a moving vehicle. We feel like we have hundreds of thousands of best friends, and we hope you feel like we are yours, too. None of this would exist without you.

We love you all. Don't forget to tell your mum, tell your dad, tell your dog, tell your friends and share the love, because, well, WE LOVE LOVE!

B&L x

NOTES

1 Mark Manson, 'The quick & dirty to setting boundaries', Instagram, 7 March 2020.

2 'Broken heart syndrome', Mayo Clinic, 24 November 2021; mayoclinic. org/diseases-conditions/broken-heart-syndrome/symptoms-causes/ syc-20354617 (accessed 25 July 2022)

3 'Takotsubo cardiomyopathy (broken-heart syndrome)', Harvard Medical School, 19 May 2022; health.harvard.edu/heart-health/ takotsubo-cardiomyopathy-broken-heart-syndrome (accessed 25 July 2022)

4 'When to have sex with him', Matthew Hussey, 14 July 2019; howtogettheguy.com/blog/when-to-have-sex-with-him/comment- page-2/

5 Kato, T., 'Gender differences in response to infidelity types and rival attractiveness', *Sexual and Relationship Therapy*, 2019, pp. 1–17.

6 'Once a cheater, are they always a cheater? Uncut with Terri Cole', *Life Uncut* Season 3, Episode 58.

7 'EGGS ON ICE! Britt shares her egg-freezing story', *Life Uncut* Season 2, Episode 145.

8 'Think you're being gaslit? Here's how to respond', Healthline, 21 June 2022; healthline.com/health/how-to-deal-with-gaslighting; 'How to recognize gaslighting and get help', Healthline, 24 November 2021; healthline.com/health/gaslighting

9 'Think you're being gaslit? Here's how to respond', Healthline, 21 June 2022; healthline.com/health/how-to-deal-with-gaslighting

10 'Haunted: The trend toward ghosting', Cleveland Clinic, 1 June 2021; health.clevelandclinic.org/haunted-the-trend-toward-ghosting/

11 'Happiness', The Free Dictionary; thefreedictionary.com/happiness (accessed 25 July 2022)

12 'UNCUT with Shonel Bryant – A story of love, gratitude and leaving a legacy in the face of terminal cancer', *Life Uncut*, Season 2, Episode 200.

13 'From attitude to gratitude and resilience with Hugh van Cuylenburg', *Life Uncut*, Season 2, Episode 166.

14 'The Ick', Urban Dictionary; urbandictionary.com/define.
php?term=The%20Ick (accessed 25 July 2022)

15 Katsha, H., 'What is 'The Ick' and can we ever get over it?', Huffpost,
17 August 2021.

16 Peel, R., 'What is 'the ick'? A psychological scientist explains this
TikTok trend', *The Conversation*, 11 October 2021.

17 Weir, K., 'Feel like a fraud?', *gradPSYCH Magazine*, American
Psychological Association, November 2013, vol. 11, no. 4; apa.org/
gradpsych/2013/11/fraud

18 Mohr, T. S., 'Why women don't apply for jobs unless they're 100%
qualified', Harvard Business Review, 25 August 2014.

19 Clark, N. F., 'Act now to shrink the confidence gap', *Forbes*, 28 April
2014.

20 'Let's get kinky', *Life Uncut*, Season 2, Epsiode 202.

21 Brice, R., 'U up? How to bring up your kink to your partner',
Healthline; healthline.com/health/sexual-health/u-up-kinks#2
(accessed 25 July 2022)

22 'Marriages and divorces, Australia', Australian Bureau of Statistics,
released 24 November 2021; abs.gov.au/statistics/people/people-and-
communities/marriages-and-divorces-australia/latest-release

23 'Create the love – Uncut with Mark Groves', *Life Uncut*, Season 3,
Episode 31.

24 Lee, E., 'Here's the definitive data behind how Gen Z and millenials
meet and fall in love', The Knot, 17 December 2020; theknot.com/
content/gen-z-relationships-marriage; Ross, S., 'Millennials are way
more likely than other generations to delay marriage – here's why', The
Knot, 7 March 2019; theknot.com/content/millennials-delay-marriage

25 Hoffower, H., 'Millenials might lag behind their parents when it comes
to money, but there's something they do better: talk about it', *Business
Insider*, 1 November 2019.

26 'Money ruining marriages in America: A Ramsey Solutions study',
Ramsey, 6 February 2018; ramseysolutions.com/company/newsroom/
releases/money-ruining-marriages-in-america

27 'Uncut with She's on the Money', *Life Uncut*, Season 2, Episode 128.

28 Leonhardt, M., 'Half of millennials say social media drives them to
spend money they don't have', *Make It*, CNBC.com, 13 May 2019.

29 'Narcissistic personality disorder', Mayo Clinic; mayoclinic.org/diseases-
conditions/narcissistic-personality-disorder/symptoms-causes/syc-
20366662 (accessed 25 July 2022)

30 'Image-based abuse: National survey summary report', Office of the eSafety Commissioner, October 2017, p. 2; esafety.gov.au/sites/default/files/2019-07/Image-based-abuse-national-survey-summary-report-2017.pdf

31 'Our legislative functions', eSafety Commissioner; esafety.gov.au/about-us/who-we-are/our-legislative-functions (accessed 25 July 2022)

32 Regan, S., '13 red flags in a relationship you shouldn't ignore', mindbodygreen, 22 August 2021; mindbodygreen.com/articles/red-flags-in-relationships

33 Regan, S., '13 red flags in a relationship you shouldn't ignore', mindbodygreen, 22 August 2021; mindbodygreen.com/articles/red-flags-in-relationships

34 Marazziti, D. et al., 'Sex-related differences in plasma oxytocin levels in humans', *Clinical Practice & Epidemiology in Mental Health*, 2019, vol. 15, pp. 58–63.

35 'Talking loneliness report: Research into the state of loneliness in Australia in 2021', Telstra, 2021; exchange.telstra.com.au/wp-content/uploads/2021/10/Telstra-Talking-Loneliness-Report.pdf

36 Pennisi, E., 'How humans became social', *Wired*, 9 November 2011.

37 'Toxic positivity', Center for Spirituality and Healing, University of Minnesota; takingcharge.csh.umn.edu/survivorship/toxic-positivity (accessed 25 July 2022)

38 Chiu, A., 'Time to ditch "toxic positivity", experts say: "It's okay not to be okay"', *Washington Post*, 19 August 2020.

39 'When positivity turns toxic and 4 ways to combat it', Canadian Mental Health Association, 3 May 2021; cmha.ca/when-positivity-turns-toxic-and-4-ways-to-combat-it/

40 Raypole, C., 'Let it out: Dealing with repressed emotions', Healthline, 31 March 2020; healthline.com/health/repressed-emotions

41 'When anger's a plus', *Monitor on Psychology*, American Psychological Association, March 2003, vol. 34, no. 3; apa.org/monitor/mar03/whenanger (accessed 25 July 2022)

42 Forgas, J.P., 'Four ways sadness may be good for you', Greater Good Magazine, 4 June 2014; greatergood.berkeley.edu/article/item/four_ways_sadness_may_be_good_for_you

43 Mark Manson, Twitter, 30 January 2020.

44 'Bullying the bully? Talking resilience with Turia Pitt', *Life Uncut*, Season 3, Episode 55.

45 Boyes, A., 'How to stop obsessing over your mistakes', *Harvard Business Review*, 25 February 2019.

RESOURCES

Attachment styles

If you're keen to find out what your attachment style is, we recommend the following online quizzes:

attachmentproject.com/attachment-style-quiz/
psychologytoday.com/au/tests/relationships/relationship-attachment-style-test

Conflict resolution styles

To work out your conflict resolution style, try these quizzes:

oprah.com/relationships/whats-your-conflict-style-quiz-dealing-with-conflict/all
psycho-tests.com/test/conflict-mode

If anything in this book has raised any issues for you, please don't hesitate to contact the following organisations.

1800RESPECT
1800respect.org.au
1800 737 732
1800RESPECT provides confidential information, counselling and support service for people experiencing sexual, domestic and family violence.

Beyond Blue
beyondblue.org.au
1300 22 4636
Beyond Blue provides trusted resources and a support service for anxiety and depression.

Lifeline Australia
lifeline.org.au
13 11 14
Lifeline provides access to 24-hour crisis support and suicide prevention services for all Australians who are experiencing a personal crisis.

QLife
qlife.org.au
1800 184 527
QLife provides anonymous and free LGBTI+ peer support and referral for people in Australia wanting to talk about sexuality, identity, gender, bodies, feelings or relationships.

ACKNOWLEDGEMENTS

FROM LAURA

There are so many people who have contributed to this book in small and monumental ways. Firstly, to my biggest cheerleader, to the man who would happily bust out a leotard and some pom-poms if the occasion called for it, my number one – Matt. You are patience personified. Thank you for always being in my corner, for catching every ball I drop, for endlessly supporting me in my ambition, for your silliness, for your ten out of ten Dadding and for loving me so completely. You showed me that relationships can be exciting and still a safe harbour.

To my girls Marlie-Mae and Lola, you teach me every day what the meaning of love is. Being your Mama is the best thing that ever happened to me.

For my unofficial personal assistant, my sister, my best friend Alisha, thank you for always being the filing cabinet to my creativity, the paperweight to my paper, the yin to my yang. Without you I wouldn't know what day of the week it is.

To our producer Keeshia, my goodness woman, where would we be without you?! You are our lifeline and our lifesaver. We will never be able to thank you enough for everything you do for us, for all the prep, the 10 pm text messages, the hugs, the soft touch, the hard truths and the endless dedication that you have to *Life Uncut*.

Izzy Yates, our wonderful and patient publisher, thank you for always being cool as a cucumber, even when deadlines came . . . and flew by. Thank you for your vision, your revisions and your belief in seeing *We Love Love* in print.

To my mum, I will always cherish the night that we sat around my kitchen table drinking Penfolds and reading chapters together. My stories are also your stories, and although it wasn't always easy, thank you for always making me feel loved. I love you.

To Britt, there will never be words to express how meeting you has changed my life and what you mean to me. You are always the one to dream big, thank you for always believing in this little pod, for your hustle, your vulnerability and your friendship. We have shared everything over the past three years and sharing these pages with you is the biggest privilege of all.

FROM BRITT

I can't believe we made it! What a wild few years it has been since the inception of *Life Uncut*! And an even wilder ride getting this book out in the world! It is surreal to see our deepest, darkest and most embarrassing thoughts out there in the atmosphere. When we voice our thoughts on the podcast it is almost like it isn't real, but something about physically seeing it on the shelves makes it all the more real.

I have so many people to thank and so many people that I truly appreciate. To all my friends that have put up with me over the years. The tears, the stress, the 'Sorry I can't make it I am drowning in words and work please don't hate me' messages. I am so grateful for my very small but very big-hearted circle of people.

Our publisher Izzy Yates, wow you've had to put up with some tumultuous moments over the last 18 months! Thank you for believing in us, driving us and pushing us to create, when at moments we didn't think we could. Also thanks for all the publishing extensions; we literally wouldn't be here without that leniency!

To my family. Gosh you guys are my world. To mum and dad who gave me the best childhood I could ask for and equipped me with the tools to go out and navigate life, especially the moments when it wasn't in my favour. You taught me how to be my own woman and to depend on myself. The constant support for all my weird and wonderful ideas, which you often question, but support nonetheless. You always made me feel like I could do anything and I hope I have made you proud.

To my sister and best friend Sheri who has navigated life with me, every step of the way. Through the bad decisions (that, let's be real, you are usually involved in) and through the good. You do so much for me in every aspect of life and I am so lucky to have you by my side. You really are one of a kind.

To Mitch, my walking encyclopaedia. Your sensibility and knowledge has definitely made me smarter.

And Dane, for teaching me many things, mainly what not to do, but at the end of the day a lesson is a lesson! 😊 😂

Of course I couldn't forget all the guys that did me dirty – thanks for the content.

Every single Lifer, OG or new, we are here because of you. Because you laugh with us, cry with us and support us through it all. We love the community that YOU have all created. Seeing women thrive, grow and lift each other up is by far the best part.

And finally to Laura, co-host, business partner, wild, crazy, over-achieving friend – there's no one I'd rather be embarrassing myself daily with. 😂 There really isn't anyone else I would want to do this with. We have become more than the above and are now more like sisters. To have a podcast, national radio show, live show and a book together is truly something special. We spend more time together than I thought possible and you've let me wipe snot on your sleeve more times than I care to admit. Thank you for all that you do.

I love riding this lollercoaster called life.